WITHDRAWN
UTSA Libraries

IMITATION IN INTERNATIONAL RELATIONS

IMITATION IN INTERNATIONAL RELATIONS

OBSERVATIONAL LEARNING, ANALOGIES, AND FOREIGN POLICY IN RUSSIA AND UKRAINE

Benjamin E. Goldsmith

IMITATION IN INTERNATIONAL RELATIONS
© Benjamin E. Goldsmith, 2005.

First published in 2005 by
PALGRAVE MACMILLAN™
175 Fifth Avenue, New York, N.Y. 10010 and
Houndmills, Basingstoke, Hampshire, England RG21 6XS
Companies and representatives throughout the world.

PALGRAVE MACMILLAN is the global academic imprint of the Palgrave Macmillan division of St. Martin's Press, LLC and of Palgrave Macmillan Ltd. Macmillan® is a registered trademark in the United States, United Kingdom and other countries. Palgrave is a registered trademark in the European Union and other countries.

ISBN 1–4039–6780–6

Library of Congress Cataloging-in-Publication Data

Goldsmith, Benjamin E.
    Imitation in international relations : observational learning, analogies, and foreign policy in Russia and Ukraine / Benjamin E. Goldsmith.
        p.cm.
    Includes bibliographical references and index.
        ISBN 1–4039–6780–6
        1. Russia (Federation)—Foreign relations—1991– 2. Ukraine—Foreign relations—1991– 3. Russia (Federation)—Politics and government—1991– 4. Ukraine—Politics and Government—1991– 5. Imitation. 6. International relations. I. Title.

DK510.764.G65 2004
327.47′009′049—dc22   2004049007

A catalogue record for this book is available from the British Library.

Design by Newgen Imaging Systems (P) Ltd., Chennai, India.

First edition: February 2005

10 9 8 7 6 5 4 3 2 1

Printed in the United States of America.

This book is dedicated with love to my son, Max

CONTENTS

List of Tables

LIST OF FIGURES

PREFACE

This book is intended to serve two purposes. First and foremost, it seeks to show that imitation does occur in world politics. This is an empirical task on which I bring to bear both quantitative and qualitative analysis. The second purpose is to begin to create a general theoretical framework for the systematic study of foreign policy preferences. I argue that such a framework is essential for the study of foreign policy and international relations.

This book presents strong empirical evidence that states do indeed learn by observation, and shows when and how such learning is likely to occur. I also believe a compelling case is made in the pages to follow that the comparative study of foreign policy needs a single dependent variable if legitimate comparisons are to be made. Furthermore, foreign policy preferences are, implicitly or explicitly, a key independent variable in any theory of international relations. I make the argument that foreign policy preferences should be considered a state-level variable involving trade-offs between competing policy values, and I base those values on the logic of well-known theories of international relations.

My intention is to advance the comparative study of foreign policy, a promising area of inquiry that has received insufficient attention for decades, due, in my opinion, to the lack of a well-developed theoretical framework. I realize that to some the separation foreign policy and international relations may seem like a distinction without a difference. The theoretical and empirical work presented here, I hope, will demonstrate the usefulness of such an approach. It seems to me that failure to make this distinction has been the cause of a considerable amount of circular polemics and arguments over false dichotomies.

I also hope to make a specific contribution to the understanding of politics and foreign policy in Russia and Ukraine. In 1998, while flying home from a stint of field research in Moscow, I happened to sit next to a high-ranking official of the U.S. State Department. I recognized him and introduced myself. We had an interesting discussion about the differences between Russian and Ukrainian foreign policies. I asked why he thought that the Ukrainians had been relatively reluctant to open their economy to foreign trade and, especially, investment, and also why they had been reluctant to cooperate on issues of military security such as nuclear disarmament. He agreed that this was a fair characterization of Ukrainian policy, even in comparison to Russia, but the explanation he offered was to shake his head and say "stupid." Having just spent about a year living in Kyiv, meeting, interviewing, and otherwise observing Ukrainian foreign policy elites, I could not agree that they were any less intelligent than their Russian (or American) counterparts. Why do some foreign policy makers perceive their state's interests in one way, while others hold entirely contrary views of interests? This book will at least provide a better explanation of the differences between Russian and Ukrainian foreign policy preferences than that U.S. diplomat did.

Acknowledgments

Completing this project, which began as a doctoral dissertation, has been a humbling experience in a number of ways. One of the things I have come to understand in the process is just how much I am indebted to my teachers. I continue benefiting from their guidance long after leaving the safety of life as a graduate student. For his patience, insight, and honesty I thank especially my dissertation committee chair, Bill Zimmerman. His direct feedback has greatly improved the theoretical clarity and empirical quality of this book. But equally important is his role as an example for my own "observational learning" about what good social science is and how to combine rigorous analysis with contextual area knowledge, and a sense of humor and perspective. I also thank Paul Huth for the many, many hours he sacrificed reading my chapters, giving me feedback, and answering a lot of questions. The final product is much different, much more rigorous, and indeed very much improved for his efforts and guidance. Zvi Gitelman has been a critical but enthusiastic sounding board, and his questions led me to recognize, reconsider, and in some cases discard many of my implicit assumptions. He also helped me to understand nationalism and ethnicity as general phenomena. To David Winter I am grateful for sharing in a friendly and generous way his knowledge from the field of psychology. This is the area in which I perhaps most needed guidance, and David's guidance was always specific and relevant. If I had followed up on more of his advice, the work would undoubtedly be better. And I especially thank Harold Jacobson, who passed away before this book could be published, for introducing me to the analysis of international relations with balance, intellectual integrity, and wisdom. I consider myself one member of a large community of scholars who in various ways continue to benefit from his unique influence, and I feel extremely privileged to have known him. Although they each had considerable influence on the final product through their constructive criticism and suggested improvements, responsibility for the remaining shortcomings in the book of course rests only with me.

For their indirect but nevertheless "formative" influence on this work I thank Angela Stent for introducing me to the world of Russian and Soviet foreign policy, Bruce Parrott for first challenging me to think systematically about political analysis, and Gertrude Schroeder for sharing her knowledge and insight about the Soviet economy.

I also thank Leonid Gorizontov, Margaret Hermann, Patrick James, Markus Kemmelmeier, William Kincaid, Jack Levy, Larry Mohr, Sue

Peterson, Marek Steedman, Nick Winter, Nikolai Zlobin, and several anonymous reviewers who read or discussed various parts of this book at various stages and gave valuable feedback. The support and patience of David Pervin and Heather Van Dusen at Palgrave Macmillan made the complex process of publishing as smooth and simple as possible.

During my field research in 1997 and 1998, I benefited from the help of many people. I would especially like to mention Ihor Ostash of the International School of Ukrainian Studies, Polina Kozyreva of the Institute of Sociology, Russian Academy of Sciences, and Iuriy Marchenko, publisher of the *Who's Who in Ukraine* series. I thank Nataliia Nepeivoda for her many hours of patient instruction, which led to a vast improvement in my Ukrainian language skills, as well as some very enjoyable conversations. I was very lucky to have Christina Dikareva's excellent help coding many Ukrainian and Russian articles.

Funding from the following sources is gratefully acknowledged: the International Research and Exchanges Board (with funds provided by the National Endowment for the Humanities, the U.S. Department of State, and the IREX Scholar Support Fund), the Institute for International Education, and Rackham Graduate School at the University of Michigan.

I thank Heldref Publications and the editors of *Demokratizatsiya* for allowing me to reproduce most of my article "Economic Liberalism and Security Preferences: A Comparative Case Study of Russia and Ukraine in the 1990s," *Demokratizatsiya: The Journal of Post-Soviet Democratization* 9, 3 (2001): 399–433 in chapter 6. And I thank Taylor and Francis (www.tandf.co.uk) and the editors of *International Interactions* for allowing reproduction of the article "Imitation in International Relations: Analogies, Vicarious Learning, and Foreign Policy," *International Interactions* 29, 3 (2003): 237–267 in chapter 4.

I thank my parents for their love and support throughout this project. And finally, I thank Angie Ng for her patience and understanding as I spent hours away from her revising this manuscript, then spent much of our time together telling her about it. Knowing I have you to come home to makes all the difference.

CHAPTER 1

INTRODUCTION

A fool can learn from his own experience; the wise learn from the experience of others.

—Attributed to Democritus

Wise men profit more from fools than fools from wise men; for the wise shun the mistakes of fools, but fools do not imitate the successes of the wise.

—Marcus Cato in Plutarch, Lives: Marcus Cato

Experience keeps a dear school, but fools will learn in no other.

—Benjamin Franklin, Pennsylvania Almanac

What experience and history teach us is this—that people and governments never have learned anything from history, or acted on principles derived from it.

—Georg Hegel, Philosophy of History

Do states learn from other states' experiences in international relations? In the pages that follow I find that they do. But why ask this question? What will the answer reveal about foreign policy and international relations? In short, I argue that understanding patterns of imitation and other types of learning is important for understanding both the *goals* countries pursue and the *ways* in which they pursue them. This type of knowledge, in turn, is valuable for those who seek to explain and understand systems of international relations, and for those involved in analyzing or making foreign policy decisions.

Most studies of learning in international relations have focused on direct experience, or trial-and-error learning. This is somewhat surprising because one hypothesized source of learned interests and beliefs found in realist and liberal international relations theories is observational learning from other states' experiences, or imitation. There have been relatively few empirical tests of foreign policy learning models, especially those incorporating imitation.

Most formal or mathematical theories of learning also do not consider imitation. This book is based on the premise that imitation is important in international relations, just as it has been shown to be in domestic politics and in other areas of social science. In the book, I develop a theoretical model of imitation in foreign policy, and subject it to empirical testing. Perhaps most fundamentally, I think this book shows that understanding imitation in foreign policy can shed light on a basic question about states' goals, and the ways they are pursued, that still puzzles analysts and practitioners alike: what are the sources of states' "interests"?

LEARNING AND PREFERENCES

In recent research, the sources of states' interests, and the closely related concepts of foreign policy beliefs and preferences, and their variation, is increasingly taking center stage in areas including security studies and foreign policy (Fearon 1994; Gartzke 2000; Kimura and Welch 1998; Lepgold and Lamborn 2001; Moravcsik 1997; Pollins 1994; Wallander 1996), international institutions and law (Milner 1997; Roberts Clark 1998; Simmons 2000), and international political economy (Frieden 1999; Rosecrance 1986; Simmons 1994).[1] These studies have begun to fill a theoretical gap noted by Morrow (1988, 95): "Although structure has attracted much attention in theories of international relations, preference generally has not."

What shapes actors "preferences"? Given a constant external environment, one possible source of variation in state-level preferences is domestic regime type, as noted in the extensive literature connecting liberal market democracies to peaceful and open Kantian mutual relations (e.g., Cederman 2001; Mansfield, Milner, and Rosendorff 2000; Russett and Oneal 2001) and even characterizing democracies as more peaceful in general (Ray 2000, 300–302; Rousseau et al. 1996). Russett and Oneal (2001, 230) argue that "states' interests and preferences are not independent of the nature of their governments and their economic relations. Instead, they arise in large part from these very influences." This has also been applied to subnational institutions (Rogowski 1999). Another influence is size and resource factors, perhaps best elaborated in theories of international political economy such as the gravity theory of trade (Deardorff 1995).[2]

Although the importance of these influences seems clear, they do not account for variation in preferences within a particular regime type when institutions and resources don't change significantly. *But this is the situation of most states most of the time.* Theories of learning can address the issue of variation in interests without requiring variation in resources, regime type, institutions, or the environment.[3]

Learning is also an important area of new research in other fields of social science such as economics (e.g., Evans and Honkapohja 2001). I hope that the theoretical argument and empirical tests in this book will advance understanding of "social" learning processes (Bandura 1977) in other areas of politics and outside of the political realm as well.

IMITATION

Among prominent international relations theorists, neorealists like Waltz (1979, 118) expect that "if some [states] do relatively well, others will emulate them or fall by the wayside." Waltz identifies processes of competition, socialization, and selection that lead to a system populated by states that are sensitive to *relative* gains. Liberals like Rosecrance (1986, 212) expect that states will learn about the *absolute* benefits of cooperation through "social learning, which would accustom the members of the state system to behave in new ways." Russett and Oneal (2001, 192) suggest a similar process of learning "by example," tied to Gramscian hegemony. Kant ([1795] 1970, 104) argues that a liberal peace might spread through the international system even if only one major state initially became a republic. That state might serve as a "focal point" for other states.[4]

But these theoretical expectations might simply be wrong. The limited number of empirical studies tend not to support expectations of imitation[5] in international relations (Jervis 1976; Khong 1992; Reiter 1996; Reiter and Meek 1999).[6] Most of the evidence points to a learning process based on direct rather than observed experience. Reiter (1996, 204) concludes that "while states draw heavily on their own individual experiences, they pay little attention to those of other states. . . ."

Have the empiricists disproved the theorists' expectations? It is possible that the theorists are wrong. But vicarious learning seems to be both useful and common. It offers an efficient alternative to trial-and-error learning (Bandura 1986). It is widely recognized in human (and animal) behavior (Richerson and Boyd 2000; Wyrwicka 1996). There is evidence of imitative processes in *domestic* politics dating at least from Walker's (1969, 1973) pioneering diffusion studies, including demonstration effects that cross international borders (e.g., Berry and Berry 1999; Gitelman 1972; Jacoby 2000; Kopstein and Reilly 2000; Midlarsky 1978; Rogers 1995; Siverson and Starr 1990; Strang 1991). Imitation appears to be common in the behavior of businesses and other organizations (e.g., Boxwell 1994, chapter 1; Rogers 1995). The concept of "copying" is also prominent in general evolutionary and complexity theories (Axelrod and Cohen 1999). Why should it be present in so many contexts but absent from international politics?

I suggest that we have not known how to evaluate this proposition empirically because the theory has been underdeveloped. In the chapters that follow I develop a theoretical framework and subject it to empirical testing. The framework hinges on the concept of "formative events"—widely used in psychology and studies of political learning (Jervis 1976; Khong 1992; Levy 1994; Reiter 1996). I test my expectations about the sources of learning on two states that have experienced major formative events recently—Russia and Ukraine—which were literally formed in their current international borders with the traumatic collapse of the USSR in 1991. The results suggest that, when it operates, imitation is a major factor determining states' fundamental foreign policy preferences.

THEORETICAL GOALS OF THE STUDY

Beyond developing a framework for identifying and understanding imitation in international relations, one goal of this study is to improve our general understanding of states' behavior in the international arena, both in terms of individual states' foreign policies and in terms of the functioning of the international system as a whole. In the concluding chapter, I sketch a model of the international system that includes imitation, and suggest how such a model could account for major systemic change. Another is to suggest ways in which decision makers can modify their decision processes and heuristics in order to consider more relevant types of information and therefore make better decisions. It hardly need be mentioned that poorly informed foreign policy can lead to costly mistakes.

One common example of a costly foreign policy mistake helps to illustrate the potential importance of imitation. In a study of the U.S. decision in 1965 to become seriously involved in the Vietnam War, Yuen Foong Khong (1992) points out that Under Secretary of State George Ball was keenly aware of France's difficulties with insurgency in colonial Indochina. He strongly advised President Johnson against U.S. intervention in a way that, in hindsight, seems little short of prophetic. Ball was certainly correct in his main cautions about the dangers of the decision, and these were based on his knowledge of the *French* experience. However, the Vietnam decision group was not swayed by Ball's insistence that the analogy to the French defeat at Dien Bien Phu was applicable (Khong 1992, 170). Johnson and key advisors such as Robert McNamara chose to discount his arguments. Thomas Thayer cites one U.S. General as declaring: "The French haven't won a war since Napoleon. What can we learn from them[?]" (quoted in Khong 1992, 148).

Why would such arguments carry the day? Why was Ball's strong protest dismissed? Khong presents evidence that U.S. success in the Korean conflict predisposed members of Johnson's decision team to expect that—by analogy—the United States was likely to succeed in Indochina.

The implicit suggestion of Khong's study is that one heuristic employed by foreign policy decision makers to distill a large amount of information is to discount evidence originating from foreign experience. In some sense, this might be a reasonable shortcut. Evidence from observation is likely to be less complete than that from direct experience. The individuals involved, all of the concerns voiced, and the documentary records of how the decisions were made are likely to be less accessible. Also, the capabilities and interests of states vary, so the result of any particular foreign policy of one state may not be a reliable indicator of how another state will fare with a similar policy. These unknowns may increase the perceived risk of relying on evidence derived from foreign experience (I tie this to prospect theory in chapter 3). Nevertheless, Khong's study strongly suggests that observed experience can indeed be relevant, and if considered seriously, valuable.

THE EXAMPLE OF JAPAN

Perhaps the obvious choice for a study of imitation in politics would be Japan. Although Japan is a major state with a reputation as an imitator, this does not necessarily mean that it would have been an appropriate case to examine in a study of *whether* observational learning really is a factor in foreign policy making in general. Choosing Japan would amount to selecting on the dependent variable (Geddes 1990), stacking the deck in favor of my hypothesis. It would be difficult to determine whether the conclusions reached were valid and could be generalized to other cases.

Nevertheless, it seems appropriate to briefly examine the case of Japan in order to introduce some ideas about state-level imitation. I return to the Japanese example in the conclusion, to assess how well the theory I develop, and the results of the analysis of Ukraine and Russia, "travel" to this important case.

Reischauer's (1974) classic survey of Japanese history persuasively argues that the Japanese have been "borrowing" from foreign societies, in deliberate attempts to emulate their successes, intermittently since the sixth century A.D. There was, Reischauer writes, "an abrupt acceleration in the rate of learning from [China] . . . when the Japanese suddenly became conscious of the advantages of the superior continental civilization and the desirability of learning more about it" (18).

Since this time, Japan has had a history of alternating periods of imitation and isolation. In the thirteenth century, Mongol invasions certain to devastate the island nation were twice thwarted by typhoons. Social psychologists would not be surprised to learn that the Japanese leadership attributed this great "victory" not to the accidents of history, but to Japan's superiority among nations. Japan, they reasoned, must be truly exceptional in order to have received such gracious intervention by "kamikaze," or divine wind.

This success against the Mongols was followed by a turn toward isolationism in Japanese foreign policy. Japan stopped looking to foreign models, and developed its own ethic of the "warrior-trader" in foreign policy. By the sixteenth century, Japan had achieved a level of development and national power easily rivaling European states, and probably China as well. Then, as western European states began to gain in power and reach, the Japanese became aware of their colonial expansion in Asia. In response to what was perceived as a growing threat, the early-seventeenth-century Tokugawa regime undertook a policy of extreme isolation. Only the port city of Nagasaki was allowed to continue trade relations with the outside world, and only the Dutch were allowed to trade directly with Japan.

This policy led to the relative decline of Japan among world powers. In Japan, however, it was seen as a considerable success. The foreign threat was apparently eliminated, and the primary goal of domestic political stability was achieved and maintained for centuries. It was only the national trauma caused by the appearance of the famous "black ships" of U.S. Commodore Matthew Perry in Edo (Tokyo) Bay in 1853 that caused Japan to again turn outward.

Thus began another period of extensive and deliberate imitation in foreign and domestic policies. The model the Japanese chose to emulate this time was not the Chinese, but the dominant western powers, especially Britain, France, and the United States. In domestic policy, the Japanese undertook liberal reforms, moving toward parliamentary democracy. In foreign policy, they abandoned isolationism for imperialism. During the Meiji restoration, Japan experienced considerable success with these new policies deliberately modeled on the successes of western liberal empires.

Reischauer (1974, 123) writes that, unlike the Chinese, the "Japanese, because of their old pattern of borrowing from China and their continuing awareness that things could usefully be learned from abroad, had no difficulty in realizing that the strong nations of the West offered valuable economic and political models. They quickly seized on the idea that the best way to make their country secure from the West was to modernize it along Western lines . . ."

The 1930s saw a period of increasingly authoritarian rule in Japan. The same tendency of course occurred in Germany and Italy in this period, but there is no evidence in Reischauer's account that the Japanese were borrowing their authoritarian leanings. Japanese imperial foreign policy suffered a catastrophic defeat in World War II. This failure again opened Japan to the influence of the United States during the post-war occupation. Reischauer concludes that the Japanese were not just passive recipients of the political principles the United States tried to transfer during the occupation. If they had not been open to different political ideas, it is unlikely that the occupation would have had such a profound impact.

> The American occupation brought a massive flood of new attitudes and new institutions comparable only to the Western impact in the nineteenth century, but much more sudden and pervasive. The effects were greatly heightened by the changes war and defeat had brought within Japan and in her relationship with the outside world. The disastrous failure of the foreign policy of the military and the terrible suffering of the war years produced a revulsion against military leadership and any form of militarism. . . . Even for more hard-headed Japanese, the military solution for Japan's great economic problem stood entirely discredited. . . . Clearly, Japan could not conquer and hold her own economic empire. If the destitute, overcrowded country was ever to reestablish a viable economy, it would have to be through trade and in an internationally open and peaceful world. Even former military expansionists turned rapidly into sincere internationalists.
>
> . . . If the militarism and authoritarianism of the past had proved so wrong, then the democracy the Americans extolled or the socialism or communism of other Western lands, all of which Japan's recent leaders had condemned, must be right. . . . Japan lay entirely open to new influences. (Reischauer 1974, 220–221)

The fact of centuries of Japanese imitation in domestic politics and foreign policy seems well established. But, how does one account for such imitation? What patterns can be observed? Reischauer considers Japan the most geographically isolated civilizational center in history, and implies that such physical isolation makes Japan more sensitive to foreign influences.

He discusses the apparent contradiction: "[o]ne popular concept is that the Japanese have never been anything more than borrowers and imitators. The truth is quite the contrary. *Although geographic isolation has made them conscious of learning from abroad*, it has also allowed them to develop one of the most distinctive cultures to be found in any civilized area of comparable size" (Reischauer 1974, 7, emphasis added).

But does isolation lead to imitation? The evidence is not clear. Reischauer (1974, 8, 17–30) draws several parallels between early Japanese borrowings from China and the process of Europeans' imitation of the more advanced Mediterranean civilizations of Greece and Rome. Another major historical instance of foreign policy emulation came after the Pelopennesian War. Psychological historian Daniel Robinson notes that much of the great thought from the ancient Greek world grew out of the defeat handed to Athens by the Spartan war machine in that conflict. In the *Republic*, Plato describes Athenian foreign policy as a failure, while Sparta's was clearly successful. He draws lessons for reshaping Athenian foreign relations based on Spartan principles. According to Robinson (1976, 56), the "Spartans— strong, self-denying, regimented, orderly, traditional have become, by the time of the *Republic*, the model. . . . Plato is unequivocal in his respect for the political order and military achievements of fifth-century Sparta. What the *Republic* struggles to achieve is a reconciliation of the opposing elements of the Athens of Pericles and the Sparta of Pausanias."

While Reischauer looks to Japan's geographical isolation as part of the cause of the tendency to imitate, this cannot apply to either Europe or Athens. This brief survey of some major cases of apparent foreign policy imitation suggests a more generalizable explanation. It appears that polities tend to maintain or abandon basic policy preferences in reaction to major perceived successes and failures. Major successes such as the *kamikaze* destruction of the Mongols, which saved thirteenth-century Japan, or major failures such as the defeat of Athens by Sparta, seem to reinforce or reorder fundamental foreign policy preferences. The new orientation then appears to persist until another major event occurs. The process suggested is simple, but the effect appears to be profound.

But evidence from a few prominent historical cases can only be suggestive. Alternative interpretations are certainly possible, and the cases themselves may be unusual. Much more in terms of theory and evidence is needed to allow any claims about the general relevance of imitation. In the next two chapters I develop in detail a theory of foreign policy imitation. I employ insights from social psychology, organizational behavior, and political science. My starting point is the expectation that "formative events," success and failure, analogical reasoning, and state-level organizational dynamics play important roles.

UKRAINE AND RUSSIA AS CASE STUDIES

The cases I have chosen for this study are Ukraine and Russia, 1990–1999. Because doubt is cast on the existence of observational learning in foreign policy in the excellent works of Jervis, Khong, and Reiter, and because it is simply ignored by many others, I place central emphasis on attempting to demonstrate empirically whether Russia and Ukraine have indeed learned from foreign experiences in important ways. It is essential to show, first, that lessons of foreign states are recognized as relevant by Russian and Ukrainian foreign policy elites, and second, that these lessons are used as more than simply rhetorical tools.

Ukraine and Russia are chosen for this study for several reasons. First, they are similar in many ways, including their concurrent emergence from the former USSR in 1990–1992, which I categorize as a formative event for each state. But with the important exception that their historical perspectives are quite different. Second, they both are significant countries in world politics. Russia is still considered a major power and Ukraine is often considered a key factor in issues of European security (e.g., Garnett 1997). And third, the Russian Empire/USSR has been considered by many analysts an archetypal "realist," "autarkic" state (e.g., Lairson and Skidmore 1993; Rosecrance 1986), historically immune to learning or basic change. Today's Russia—still run from the same Kremlin offices—can therefore serve as a least likely case for learning (Eckstein 1975), providing a challenging test for learning hypotheses.

But the primary reason for choosing Ukraine and Russia is the first listed above: their comparability. This will be important not only in the comparative case studies, but also in the quantitative analysis. One of the important advantages of comparative analysis is the control it gives the researcher over independent variables held constant (King, Keohane, and Verba 1994, 199–206). Both because my topic and theory are relatively unexplored, and because I conduct comparative case studies, it is important to control for as many variables as possible.

Russia and Ukraine have many economic, political, and cultural similarities. With these cases it is possible to control in a general way for many domestic factors that might influence foreign policy. Ukraine and Russia are similar in levels of socioeconomic development, elite and mass characteristics, education, political system, bureaucratic structure, and industry (see table 1.1).

This broad domestic comparability is largely due to the shared Soviet and pre-1917 Russian imperial legacies. For example, Beissinger (1992) discusses how Soviet nationalities and cadre policies during the 1970s and 1980s led to increasing similarities in outlook and background between Russian and Ukrainian elites. The few remaining domestic differences, notably energy resources and ethnic identity (see table 1.2), can then be treated as possible factors causing variation between Russian and Ukrainian foreign policy preferences. It should also be noted that Russia and Ukraine differ to some degree in terms of their strategic positions in the world. Both are important states in world politics, but Russia is of course much larger in terms of population and resources than Ukraine, and its military, including a superpower's nuclear arsenal, is far more powerful. These factors are important for foreign policy preferences, but they can be accounted for in the analysis.

Table 1.1   Comparisons of Russia and Ukraine at independence: Socio-Economic Indicators

Social indicators	Population (in millions)	Higher education (Students/1 million population)		Life expectancy
Russia	147.4	16.3		69.6
Ukraine	51.7	15.3		70.9
USSR Republics				
high/low	1.6/147.4	16.3/8.2		72.1/65.2
Soviet Union	286.7	15.2		69.5
Economic Indicators	Percent urban population	Workforce		Corruption rating[b]
		Industry[a]	Agriculture[a]	
Russia	74	29.4	14.1	2.4
Ukraine	67	29.0	21.3	2.7
USSR Republics				
high/low	32/74	29.4/9.0	40.2/14.1	3.8/1.7
Soviet average	66	21.5	26.5	2.6[c]
Standard of living	Average personal savings (rubles)	Square meters of living space (per person)		
		Urban		Rural
Russia	1146	9.9		13.3
Ukraine	1270	10.2		14.3
USSR Republics				
high/low	1347/28	12.7/7.5		17.1/6.0
Soviet average	1034	9.8		12.2

Notes
[a] International Monetary Fund, et al. 1991. *A Study of the Soviet Economy. Volume 2.* Paris: [OECD], 198. Includes Collective Farms, State Farms, and Private Agriculture.
[b] Average of Transparency International *Corruption Perception Index* score for 1998 and 1999. A score of 0 indicates "entirely penetrated by corruption" and a score of 10 indicates "a perfectly clean country." Accessed at Transparency International Homepage, www.gwdg.de/~uwvw/histor.htm, 5 March 2000.
[c] Includes 1999 scores for Lithuania, Moldova, Armenia, Georgia, Kazakhstan, Kyrgyzstan, Uzbekistan, and Azerbaijan, and mean of 1998 and 1999 scores for Belarus, Ukraine, Latvia, and Russia.

Source: Goskomstat 1991. *Sotsial'noe razvitie SSSR 1989. Statisticheskii sbornik* [Social Development of the USSR 1989. Statistical Collection]. Moscow: "Finansy i statistika."

Perhaps the only other major difference is in the type of historical experience each state has had recently and over the past several centuries. This relates closely to learning and perception in each state, and is discussed in chapters 5 and 6 in detail. In brief Russia has been the dominant metropole, while Ukraine has been a colonial holding or administrative province of the Russian/Soviet empire (parts of western Ukraine have also been held by the Austro-Hungarian and Polish-Lithuanian empires). I expect that different experience has taught Russians and Ukrainians (elites and masses) different lessons, given them different perceptions of successes and failures, and therefore shaped their preferences in different ways.

These conditions of control of many domestic factors and exposure to formative events give my study characteristics approaching a natural experiment. I expect that the differences in the particular "lessons" of each state's formative period explains the variation in their foreign policy preferences.

Table 1.2 Comparisons of Russia and Ukraine at independence: industrial indicators and ethnic groups

A. Russian percentage share of proven world oil and gas reserves, 1998

Russia	Crude oil	Natural gas
	4.8	33.4

Source: Congressional Quarterly 2000. *The Middle East.* Washington, DC: CQ Press, 157.

B. Percentage share of Soviet energy-sector and other industrial production, 1990

	Russia	Ukraine
Petroleum industry equipment	**80.5**	**17.8**
Chemical industry equipment and parts	63.5	28.4
Electricity	**62.7**	**17.3**
Steel pipe	61.1	33.3
Cement	60.5	16.6
Agricultural equipment	59.6	26.3
Refrigerators and freezers	58.1	13.9
Steel	58.0	34.1
Furniture	57.4	18.0
Coal	**56.2**	**23.5**
Cast iron	53.9	40.8
Canned goods	39.9	23.5
Color televisions	37.0	37.1
Electric motors (AC)	22.7	36.9
Average share (unweighted)	55.1	26.3
Share of agricultural production	46.7	22.4
Share of USSR population (1989)*	51.5	18.0

Note: Bold type indicates energy sector.

Source: Goskomstat 1991. *Narodnoe khoziaistvo SSSR v 1990 g. Statisticheskii ezhegodnik.* [Economy of the USSR in 1990. Statistical Yearbook.] Moscow: "Finansy i statistika."; *Goskomstat 1991. *Sotsial'noe razvitie SSSR 1989. Statisticheskii sbornik* [Social Development of the USSR 1989. Statistical Collection]. Moscow: "Finansy i statistika."

C. Ethnic Russians and Ukrainians, percentage of population, 1989

	Russia	Ukraine
Russians	81.5	22.1
Ukrainians	3.0	72.7

Source: Ministerstvo Statystyky Ukrainy 1993. *Naselennia Ukrainy 1992. Demohrafichnyy shchorichnyk.* Kyiv: "Tekhnika."; Goskomstat Rossii 1997. *Rossiiskii statisticheskii ezhegodnik. Statisticheskii sbornik.* Moscow: [Goskomstat Rossii].

    The period 1990–1999 (1990–1997 for the quantitative analyses in chapters 4 and 5) is chosen because it includes both a "formative event" for each state and a subsequent period of adjustment to new conditions. This allows for the examination of hypotheses about the effects of specific cognitive patterns or schemata (to be discussed in chapters 2 and 3) in each state resulting from the formative event.

What is a "Formative" Event?

A central proposition of a learning approach to foreign policy is that states' preferences are strongly affected by formative events, and that such effects have staying power due to cognitive and organizational inertia. The question of operationalization of the concept of formative events is somewhat difficult, especially because of the possibility of *ad hoc* theorizing. However, it is difficult to deny that certain classes of events are highly likely to be formative. Major wars are one such type of event. In fact, most studies of learning have looked to major wars as formative sources of enduring lessons (e.g., Jervis 1976; Khong 1992; Reiter 1996). Periods of economic disaster such as the Great Depression can also be expected to serve as formative events. Periods of great prosperity or international dominance may also qualify (e.g., the 1950s or the 1990s in the United States). Another class of event, which is very likely to be—quite literally—formative of basic foreign policy preferences is the creation of the state itself. The particular circumstances associated with the appearance of a new independent actor on the world stage are likely to make a lasting impression on the state organization and its leaders. For example, the reluctance of many states achieving independence from imperial powers in the middle decades of the twentieth century to engage in economic or security cooperation with great powers (e.g., the Non-Aligned movement) may be a policy preference resulting from the lessons of emergence from colonial domination.

Russia and Ukraine experienced a significant formative event in 1990–1992, when the Soviet Union ceased to exist and both states were "created" within their current international boundaries. Although Russia and Ukraine were incorporated into the same state until the end of 1991, their formative experiences and general histories are markedly different. In particular, the creation of the Russian Federation involved the deliberate dissolution of a larger state with a long history. The creation of modern Ukraine involved the consolidation of a nation-state in a region with a long history as a territory of provincial administration. Both formative events involved successful state creation, but the important details vary and can be expected to have a lasting impact on foreign policies. This is examined more fully in chapters 5 and 6.

Quixotic Westernizer?

As mentioned, there is another reason that the Russian case is especially interesting. Russia can be considered a crucial "least likely" case for the study of learning in international relations. The concept of a "crucial" case is developed by Harry Eckstein (1975). "Most likely" cases can be used to cast doubt on a theory if expectations are not fulfilled; "least likely" cases can lend it support if expectations are fulfilled.[7]

Russia has for centuries been trying to "catch up" with the West. The argument can be made that Russia never learns, and especially not from others' examples. Peter the Great's late-seventeenth-century visit to western Europe is an early and poignant example. He went to learn how Western states and societies functioned in order to emulate them. He returned to Russia and undertook reforms of unprecedented scale and impact to westernize Russia. But it can easily be argued that his reforms were brutal, and illiberal (e.g., Cracraft 1988). They did not, one could say, set Russia on a path toward European-style political or economic development. Russia's continued authoritarian, illiberal, and economically backward nature can be contrasted with the tremendous social, economic, and political changes in western Europe over the past several centuries.

Neither Peter's deliberate attempts to imitate western Europe, nor more limited reforms under Catherine II or Alexander II, seemed to transform Russia into a "modern" state. The same can be said for Lenin and his successors' reliance on an imported ideology. In spite of several attempts to imitate or emulate foreign experience, Russia seems to have maintained its own approach, problems, and preferences. These may be determined by geographical, strategic, cultural, or other immutable factors that frustrate observational learning at the state level even if the leadership wants change. In spite of these factors, if in the post-Soviet period learning seems to cause change in Russian foreign policy, this will lend support to the learning approach.[8]

WHY FOCUS ON ANALOGIES?

There is a great deal of anecdotal evidence that has led me to believe that Russian and Ukrainian elites are indeed attentive to foreign experiences. The use of analogies from other states' experiences by political elites is fairly widespread. For example, the Commonwealth of Independent States (CIS) has regularly been compared to the European Union; Russia's policy in the "near abroad" was compared to the Monroe Doctrine; former Russian General Alexander Lebed was compared to General Pinochet and the "Chilean model" has often been referred to in Ukrainian and Russian political polemics. The late-twentieth-century economies of both states were compared to the late-nineteenth-century or Depression-era economy of the United States, Ukrainians, and Russians wonder whether to use the Chinese or the Polish model of economic development. Both Ukrainians and Russians have studied the structure of the U.S. Security Council as a model for their own institutions.[9] Russia's declaration of a policy of "first use" of nuclear weapons was compared to the same policy in U.S. strategic doctrine.[10] The situation in the Caucasus has been compared to that in the former Yugoslavia—the list could go on.

Russian and Ukrainian elites, apparently, consider foreign states' experiences relevant to their own policies, and in some cases have studied them closely.[11] However, talk may be cheap. Politicians and policy makers have been known to stray from the truth in their public statements. And analogies may just be used as rhetorical devices even if leaders claim that they have some substantive influence. But there is reason to believe it is unlikely that this borrowed knowledge is used only instrumentally to support previously held positions. As Jervis (1976, 215–219) and Khong point out, lessons and analogies can shape the way policy is made even if they are not initially used as analytical tools. "Even when analogies are used for advocacy and justification, it does not follow that they will have no impact on the decision outcome" (Khong 1992, 15n44). Khong points out that cognitive psychology gives analogical reasoning a central position in human thinking—analogies contribute to, or even function as, cognitive "schemata" (25–26). He also finds a significant similarity between the public and private uses of analogies (60–61). Thus, there is empirical evidence to support the claim that foreign analogies have wide currency in Russia and Ukraine, and there are theoretical arguments claiming that analogies are likely to have an impact on policy. This establishes the plausibility of the potential impact of analogies; in chapters 2 and 3 analogy use and schema theory are integrated into my theoretical framework and I defend their validity in more detail.

POLICY RELEVANCE

One way in which this study ought to be of use to foreign policy decision makers is that it should give clear indications of when decision makers are likely to ignore relevant foreign information. The policy process can be corrected to consider relevant foreign experiences (e.g., the French in Indochina) and give them proper weight. The results should also indicate when the decision process might be biased against direct experience. Also important is the insight to be gained about these types of bias in other states' behavior. Neither type of bias has been addressed in any detail in previous studies of foreign policy or other decision processes, as far as I know. But, as social scientists are well aware, selection bias can have a tremendous influence on outcomes and conclusions.

Another policy-relevant area to which I hope the results of this study will be applied is technical aid, or the transfer of knowledge (rather than money or material goods) from one state or group of states to another. Russia and Ukraine have both received a considerable amount of technical aid since 1991. Why has some of this "good advice" been used well, while some has been ignored (Wedel 1998)? One technical aid program I learned of during my field research was created by the Canadian Ministry of Foreign Affairs at the request of Ukraine: the Managing Asymmetrical Relationships (MAR) program. The object was to help Ukraine better deal with its large and often difficult neighbor, Russia, especially by institutionalizing and compartmentalizing various aspects of the relationship (Markevych interview, 11/13/97; Waschuk interview, 11/10/97).[12]

The initial request came from Ukrainian Foreign Minister Hennadii Udovenko in 1996 (Waschuk interview, 11/10/97). The Ukrainians chose Canada because of what they saw as its more or less analogical situation as a neighbor of the United States. One internal Canadian MAR document drew the following parallels. "The population of the USA is approximately ten times that of Canada. The population of Russia exceeds that of Ukraine by a factor of six. The American economy dwarfs that of Canada's [*sic*] while Russia's is significantly larger than Ukraine's. There is a heavy economic and trade interdependence in both situations. Canada is awash in American culture and the same situation prevails with respect to Russian cultural inroads into Ukraine" (Canadian Embassy in Ukraine. [n.d.] Document A).

The Canadians running this program saw much in their state's experience that seemed applicable to Ukraine's relations with Russia. The first phase of the program was conducted by an important Canadian diplomat, Jeremy Kinsman, former ambassador to Moscow and at the time the Deputy Head of Mission at the Canadian embassy in Washington. The program involved a range of activities including meetings at the highest levels, and consultations and seminars for practicing diplomats and those in training. It involved not only the Ukrainian Ministry of Foreign Affairs and the foreign minister himself, but also the Ministry of Information, the Presidential Administration (which has its own department of foreign affairs), the Ministry of Culture, and the Diplomatic Academy.

But, according to my interviews with Canadian officials directing the program in Kyiv, the Ukrainians appeared to discard all of the advice that they themselves had requested. The advice might have actually been irrelevant. Perhaps the Ukrainians were never really interested in the Canadians' experience. These are possibilities, but it is also possible that the Canadian advice was inconsistent with dominant cognitive patterns in the thinking of Ukrainian foreign policy elites and therefore simply discounted and ignored by them. I return to the topic of MAR and technical aid in the conclusion, to assess what the implications of the findings of my research might be for technical aid in Russia and Ukraine, and for the design of such programs in general.

OUTLINE OF THE BOOK

The remainder of the book is organized as follows. Chapter 2 discusses the central concepts of foreign policy choice, learning, and preferences. Chapter 3 then develops my theory of learning and imitation in foreign policy. I intend this theory to be applicable to any instance of the formation of foreign policy preferences. I hope, ambitiously, that it provides a new and useful general theoretical framework for the comparative study of foreign policy. Seven falsifiable hypotheses about foreign policy learning are developed. General issues of research design for both the quantitative and qualitative analyses to follow are also discussed.

Chapter 4 uses pooled data for Ukrainian and Russian elites to test seven basic hypotheses. Chapter 5 elaborates on the Ukrainian and Russian "schemata" and presents quantitative analyses involving comparisons of elites in each state. This provides a test of my expectations for the effects of Ukrainian and Russian formative experiences. Chapter 6 uses comparative case study method to assess the effect of imitation and "schematic" learning more generally on actual state behavior. This is another test of my expectations about the effects of formative events, and of my general theory. Privatization of, and foreign investment in, major "strategic" enterprises, including the defense industry, in Russia and Ukraine are examined. A concluding chapter then summarizes the results, assesses the evidence supporting imitation in foreign policy, discusses policy-relevant conclusions, and explores the implications of my findings for the study of both foreign policy and international relations.

CHAPTER 2

CHOICE, LEARNING, AND
FOREIGN POLICY

In 1936, Harold Lasswell published an influential book titled *Who Gets What, When, How?* In the study of politics, at least in the study of international politics, I believe there is an even more fundamental question analysts should ask: Who *wants* what, when, and why? In chapter 1 this question was stated as "what shapes actors' preferences?" The hypothesis driving this book is that preferences are shaped in systematic ways by experience and observation. In much of the international relations literature, preferences are assumed to be either constant and immutable, or idiosyncratic and unpredictable. This convention severely limits our understanding of world politics. As noted, there is increasing interest in what influences preferences in international relations. But, as illustrated with the example of Japan, we still do not have a general framework that explains when and why states "learn," either directly or vicariously.[1]

Recent research in both security studies and international political economy has emphasized the lack of systematic understanding of foreign policy preferences. Brian Pollins (1994, 49–50) writes that "We are left . . . with a claim that decision makers will make rational choices when motivated to act but no underlying theory of motivations or the perceptions that frame that rationality. . . . Realism is impressive for both its power and its limitations." Beth Simmons (1994, 6) also notes the importance of having "some information about the preferences of the dominant economic power and the other states in the system" in order to understand hegemonic or other systemic theories. These statements imply that preferences vary independently of systemic structure or states' relative capabilities. How can experience and observation be expected to influence this variation in preferences? In order to answer this question, it is necessary to establish clear definitions of three concepts: choice, learning, and foreign policy. The concept of "learning" has proven particularly difficult for political scientists to deal with. It is also important to discuss briefly the comparative study of foreign policy, the connection between foreign policy and international relations, and how states can be considered entities that learn in coherent ways. These are the tasks of this chapter. The concepts discussed are used as building blocks in chapter 3 to develop my theory of imitation in foreign policy.

CHOICE, LEARNING, AND FOREIGN POLICY
Choice

There are many terms commonly used by analysts of foreign policy to represent what states want and how decision makers believe they should pursue these ends. Some of the most common are interests, goals, beliefs, priorities, tactics, and strategies. There are no unambiguous, widely accepted definitions of these terms beyond what can be found in a standard dictionary. In spite of the lack of precise definitions, taken together, these terms describe what is commonly understood as "foreign policy." Most important for my purposes, they all denote a *choice among options*. I take the term preferences to be a better-elaborated expression of the concept of choice than these other more vaguely defined concepts (Lake and Powell 1999, 8–20; Frieden 1999, 41–47). The idea of preferences can be used to generalize about the choices among options that comprise foreign policy. The concept of making a *tradeoff between competing values* is inherent in the idea of preferences because the values over which preferences are distributed must be mutually exclusive (Morrow 1994, 17).

An inquiry into the origins of foreign policy preferences must necessarily deal with the question of perception of interests. Unlike much of the literature dealing with this (e.g., Goldstein and Keohane 1993; Jervis, Lebow, and Stein 1985; Stein 1996), this work accepts, or at least does not claim to contradict, the assumptions of the rational choice analytical framework. I believe that many claims of contradictions between perception-based approaches and those accepting rationality are based on a false dichotomy. For example, Morrow writes: "[p]sychologists may interpret utility theory as requiring that all facets of an outcome and all available information must be used in a decision, but this is a non sequitur. *Nothing in the assumptions of utility theory supports this interpretation*" (1997, 15 emphasis in original).

Borrowing the concept of preferences from rational choice encourages analysts to think rigorously about what we mean when we discuss "foreign policy;" and it allows for integration of foreign policy studies into the broader study of domestic and international politics by using common terms and concepts (e.g., Milner 1997). I believe that the interesting question to ask is not whether people or states usually have goals and pursue them—an assumption which any critic of rational choice must undermine, particularly on its analytical merits (Clark 1998, 249; Riker and Ordeshook 1973, 10). Rather, a fundamental question in world politics, political science, and other social sciences which has yet to be satisfactorily addressed is: What causes any given set of preferences?

One author who has recognized the importance of "considerable variations in perceptions from actor to actor" while working within a rational choice (expected utility)[2] framework is Bruce Bueno de Mesquita (1994, 89, also see 92n11). He recognizes variations in salience of particular policy issues among states (92). However, he does not address the origins of these variations. They remain assumed inputs for his models. A prominent scholar of international affairs working outside of a rational choice perspective, Alexander Wendt, also fails to provide a systematic framework for understanding preferences. While he asserts that "Anarchy is What States Make of It," he does not provide a systematic explanation for why which states make what of anarchy. His "systematic communitarian ontology in which intersubjective knowledge constitutes identities and interests" (1992, 425) is at best vague.

Morrow (1994) provides a clear description of the rational choice approach to political science. He writes (1994, 16–19) "Utility is a measure of an actor's preferences over the outcomes that reflects his or her willingness to take risks to achieve desired outcomes and avoid undesirable outcomes." Preferences are assumed to be "complete," meaning that they are relevant to all possible outcomes, and "transitive," meaning that they are not cyclical. If an actor prefers A to B, and B to C, he must then prefer A to C in order to be considered rational. Morrow continues

> Preferences over outcomes are assumed to be fixed. They do not change during the course of the decision being examined. . . . The assumption of fixed preferences restricts the situations we can model. But it is not as restrictive as it seems because we can select the outcomes to suit our purposes. We distinguish between preferences over outcomes and preferences over actions (or strategies). . . . Preferences over outcomes are assumed to be fixed. Preferences over actions can change as the actors gain new information about the efficacy of different actions. By choosing outcomes carefully, "shifts in preferences" are shifts in preferences among actions, rather than outcomes.

Thus preferences can denote the principles that guide choice between any options, rather of a fundamental nature such as a basic "goal" (e.g., survival of the state) or of a strategic (e.g., with whom to form an alliance) or even tactical nature (e.g., whether to hold negotiations this week or next). In this book I take such distinctions to be ones of degree, not of kind. But how are preferences formed?

Kimura and Welch (1998, 216, 239–240) claim that any theoretical understanding of preferences is a hopeless task. I think there is more to be said about foreign policy preferences than that they are "inescapably idiosyncratic" and tied to the "historical, political, or cultural context."[3] Other studies suggest not only that preferences may vary, but indicate factors that may cause them to do so. Moravcsik (1997) is interested in the effects of subnational political actors and institutions, as well as ideas, on preferences. Jervis (1999) focuses on the effects of institutions. Ruggie (1997) explores the close connections between identity and interests. Hemmer (1999) points to the effect of analogies. Like Hemmer, my focus is on analogies and cognition—the way the mind processes information.

Within any particular rational choice model of strategic interactions, preferences are assumed to be fixed. However, the rational choice framework does allow for preferences over strategies to change, even within a particular modeled interaction, in reaction to new information. Bayesian updating is one such procedure, allowing for subjective probabilities to be updated in response to new information (Morrow 1994, chapter 6). My approach differs from Bayesian updating in that it includes cognitive processes rather than incremental probability updating (for a study of state learning using Bayesian updating, see Farkas 1998).

Dan Reiter (1996, 17n3, 20–21) discusses both practical and theoretical problems inherent in using Bayes's theorem to model learning. Jack Levy (1994, 285) makes the point that Bayesian updating is "rational" in that it uses all available information, while cognition does not. It is correct that cognition can introduce bias, as demonstrated by prospect theory (Kahneman and Tversky 1979; Farnham, ed. 1994). I would argue that cognitive heuristics may weight different pieces of information differently than Bayesian updating, but the definition of preferences is flexible enough to incorporate some concepts of cognitive bias (see Riker and Ordeshook 1973, 21).

The phenomena of people being "willing to pay excessively to obtain a certain outcome" or of their changes in risk aversion due to reference points are considered by Morrow (1994, 44–49). His rationale for relying on utility theory is not stated in terms of theoretical consistency, but rather in terms of analytical simplicity. Prospect theory introduces complexity into the calculations and requires more information. My justification for using cognitive factors to analyze foreign policy is that this sacrifice in simplicity is outweighed by the explanatory power I expect it to add. I do not abandon the rationality assumption of goal-oriented behavior, nor that of complete, transitive, and fixed preferences over outcomes within a given interaction or decision. In any event, research into areas such as incomplete information, cognitive bias, signaling, and updating is a promising and growing area of inquiry (e.g., Fearon 1994; Gerber and Green 1999). This approach is sometimes called "bounded rationality" but I think it is not necessarily inconsistent with "pure" rationality (e.g., Morrow 1997, 16–17, 25).

Particular preferences are the product of perceptions of the available information about which goals or outcomes are desirable, or dangerous, and about relative costs, benefits, and risks. Consideration of perceptions is an accepted part of both "qualitative" and "quantitative" approaches to political science, although there is of course debate over their role and importance (e.g., Fearon 1994; Jervis 1976; Jervis, Lebow, and Stein 1985; Kim and Bueno de Mesquita 1995). Perceptions are the understanding of the environment by the actor or actors involved in decision making.

Since preferences are shaped by perceptions, they can be thought of as a product of cognition. An appropriate term for a cognitive function that revises preferences based on new knowledge is learning.

Learning

But what is learning, exactly? I have not found a consensual definition of learning in the psychological literature.[4] Psychologists associate it with memory and the creation of knowledge (e.g., Gleitman 1991, 123–124, 141–143; Hilgard and Bower 1975, 2). In one sense, learning is simply everything we remember. In another sense, however, learning is associated with insight and understanding. In either case, learning does not necessarily imply accuracy or better or "correct" understanding. This is true because memories and perceptions can be "inaccurate, distorted, and subjectively biased" (Hilgard and Bower 1975, 3).

Several previous studies of learning in foreign policy have employed the concept of "correct" learning, with predictable results. When policy makers' behavior is in line with the beliefs and values of the researcher, the conclusion is that learning has occurred. When the researcher disagrees with a policy, he finds that learning is absent, or the phenomena of "unlearning" or "failed learning" are observed.[5] I take issue with Philip Tetlock (1991, 51) when he suggests that it is not necessary for analysts "to use the term learning in a completely value-neutral way." That is exactly what social scientists should strive to do if we seek to understand the phenomenon, regardless of any value-laden everyday usage of "learning." It is much more interesting and useful to understand why decision makers have the preferences or beliefs they do, than it is to discover why they don't have the preferences or beliefs of social scientists.

In the present context, the association of learning with insight and understanding is relevant, but not in the sense that I intend to judge which specific policies are more or less insightful. Rather, I am interested in understanding the origins of whatever particular subjective "insight" or "understanding" might inform foreign policy preferences. There is broad consensus among both behavioral and cognitive psychologists that temporal contiguity of events is an important, necessary part of this type of learning. If one event follows another, humans will tend to "learn" that there is a causal link between them. The first event, it is assumed, caused the second. This type of reasoning can lead to mistaken inferences, but it is also probably the most basic tool of scientific method.

Behavioral psychologists focus exclusively on this type of association. Cognitive psychologists supplement this approach with theories about the mind's interpretation of experience. They argue that interpretation is necessary for humans to make any sense of the information they receive, and that interpretation is guided by preexisting or acquired principles about what is important information. These principles can be contained in the mental constructs called "schemata" which provide patterns to which new information can be compared. Schemata are often based on simplified narratives of a memorable past experience, its context and consequences. For example, a person whose car was hit by another car running a red light might develop a schema for intersections causing him to slow down and look right and left even when he has a green light. His new or updated schema is learned from experience. The schema of a driver who did not have such an experience might simply tell him that green means "go."

Schemata can give rise to biased perceptions because people tend to try to reduce the amount of "cognitive dissonance" caused by contradictions between existing expectations and new information. For example, our driver might put himself in greater danger if he always slows down for green lights. Suggestions that this practice is actually counterproductive might be ignored or carry little weight with him because of the power of the extant schema based on a traumatic event. This tendency toward "cognitive consistency" can be expected to make human learning somewhat inertial. Information that challenges existing schemata is more likely to be ignored than information that is consistent with expectations (Gleitman 1991, 457–469).

For cognitive psychologists, therefore, learning can be associated with the often inertial acquisition of schemata to process new information. For convenience I use the term "schematic learning" to refer to this process. But how can learning be identified and operationalized in international relations?[6] It should not simply be equated with a change in behavior because this may not always be the product of learning. And of course if the goal is to explain behavioral change, any definition of learning involving change in behavior would be a tautology. One distinction which can be made is that learning occurs before a resulting change in behavior.[7] But, a change in behavior may never even be observed if there is no relevant future event to trigger the appropriate schema.

Clearly, it is important to have a theoretical conception of learning in international politics that does not rely on observed behavior. Because learning itself, like preference, is not directly observable, it will not be possible to conclusively demonstrate that learning has occurred without evidence of changed behavior. But this does not justify the theoretical tautology of equating learning with changed behavior. And there is no reason to associate all behavioral change with learning.

One criterion developed by psychologists is that learning entails more complex thinking (cited in Jervis 1976, 235). In the international relations literature, John Steinbruner (1974, 40–44) has used this definition of what he calls "causal learning," involving the ever-increasing "lateral" and "upward expansion" of analysis to include more information.[8] Ernst Haas (1990, 3, 36–38,192–193)[9] has usually adopted a similar definition of learning, and it has influenced many others (e.g., see contributions to the project on foreign policy learning during the Cold War: Tetlock 1991, 32–35; Spiegel 1991; Griffiths 1991; Breslauer 1991; Legvold 1991; Anderson 1991, 101; Dallin 1991, 421; and Blacker 1991, 444). Etheridge (1985, 66) also associates increased intelligence, part of his definition of learning, with increased complexity of understanding and therefore policy.

However, defining complexity is itself problematic. What exactly is a more complex policy? Further, this approach works on the assumption that complex understanding is more accurate. But just how much complexity is enough?

Are all policy questions highly nuanced, or can policy be oversubtle? Tetlock (1991, 35) himself writes "Increasing evaluative complexity . . . can . . . be dangerous. In part, this is so because reality is sometimes simple. Chamberlain would probably enjoy higher historical esteem today if he had had a less evaluatively complex view of Hitler's intentions in 1938."

Empirically, associating complexity with learning is also unsatisfactory because it does not account for the mechanistic nature of some learning. Reiter (1996), for example, demonstrates that states learn to make dichotomous choices between alliance and neutrality based on previous experience of success or failure with either policy. He posits that, if alliance leads to negative consequences in a conflict, a state is not likely to ally in the next conflict, and vice versa. Learning in international relations in this case is not a question of greater cognitive complexity; rather, it is a question of policy success or failure. It facilitates a choice between options based on past experience, not necessarily on more complex thought patterns.

I do not wish to exclude by definition this type of learning, so I don't see increasing complexity as a necessary component of learning. Rather, any rearranging or reinforcing of preferences (fundamental, strategic, or tactical) based on lessons of success or failure can be called learning. States can learn to prefer, for example, alliance to neutrality, trade to protection, isolation to interaction, appeasement to war, guns to butter, or vice versa. I therefore define foreign policy learning as *the effect of previous experiences and observations on a state's subsequent foreign policy beliefs and preferences.* This provides a nonbehavioral criterion which both recognizes the essential ingredient of choice or trade-offs, and is agnostic on the issue of complexity.

Foreign Policy

How can "foreign policy" be defined in a way consistent with my definition of learning? A closer look at what exactly is meant by learning in foreign policy is instructive. Levy's (1994) survey of the literature on foreign policy learning highlights several areas of scholarly disagreement. Since I have already addressed two of these issues, cognitive complexity and "correct" learning, I now turn to a final major point of disagreement. What sort of impact on beliefs or preferences is appropriate to justify use of the term "foreign policy learning?" This question has led scholars to inquire whether there are important distinctions between more and less far-reaching forms of learning, as well as to ask whether the content of the lesson matters. Levy notes distinctions between "causal learning," "diagnostic learning," "normative learning," "[l]earning to learn," and "adaptation or structural adjustment" (285–286, 296). These distinction to some degree hinge on how "foreign policy" itself is defined, and how foreign policy change is measured.

Levy defines "causal learning" as "changing beliefs about the laws (hypotheses) of cause and effect, the consequences of actions, and the optimal strategies under various conditions," while he characterizes "diagnostic learning" as "changes in beliefs about the definition of the situation or the preferences, intentions, or relative capabilities of others" (285). However, these two types of learning can describe the same thing. For example, assume that the United States learned a "causal" lesson suggesting that deterrent threats which are not credible will not be effective, such as the Eisenhower administration's threat of "massive retaliation" to local aggression (e.g., Divine 1985, 53, 62–63, 64, 105; George and Smoke 1974, 29–32). In essence, the causal lesson is that a lack of credibility causes deterrence failure. This lesson was also "learned" by the Kennedy administration (George and Smoke 1974, 31).

Now suppose that the United States learned a "diagnostic" lesson that its potential adversary, for example, North Vietnam, did not intend to withdraw its territorial claim based simply on the United States's deterrent rhetoric about "massive retaliation." Or, with regard to the USSR, suppose the United States recognized that "the Soviets would be less and less likely to believe that the United States would risk its cities by launching nuclear war in response to some relatively modest Soviet probe" (George and Smoke 1974, 30). Are these instances of "causal" learning about the relationship between deterrence and credibility, or of "diagnostic" learning about the definition of the situation based on the intentions and preferences of the adversary? It seems that both descriptions are accurate, and describe the same process. The causal lesson has its basis in the process that is diagnosed, while the diagnostic lesson is only important because of its causal consequences. More important, is there any improvement in our understanding of foreign policy learning even if we are able to make such distinctions? It does not seem to me that this distinction is a very useful one.

There are certainly many imaginable ways to subdivide the concept of foreign policy learning, including the others suggested by Levy. However, I believe that most such categorizations are of degree or emphasis, rather than of kind. Defining learning as I have, in terms of the impact of past events on present preferences, it is essential only that the phenomenon under examination be describable in terms of a choice between options, and that the source of the preferences guiding that choice be found, to some degree, in a past event, either directly experienced, or observed. "Foreign policy" therefore need only be thought of as *a state's choices among options in its relations with other actors*. This concept has both parsimony and, I hope to show, analytical and explanatory power. In the next section I discuss why this simple definition has advantages over others, especially because it facilitates comparative analysis of foreign policy choice.

THE COMPARATIVE STUDY OF FOREIGN POLICY

Most students of international politics would agree that there is variation in important aspects of foreign policy, both among different states, and within any given state over time. Since the 1960s, students of foreign policy have developed several approaches to their topic, which, although often contradictory and inconclusive, have nevertheless resulted in a certain degree of understanding of "foreign policy" (for a useful review see White 1989).

Kenneth Waltz, who is not often associated with the study of such variations in foreign policy, has written: "[t]he foreign policy of a country is
formed by its political institutions, tempered by its experiences and
traditions, and shaped by the pressure of other states upon it" (1967, 1).
James Rosenau (1966, 36, 43), also recognizing the role of both "external
and internal stimuli," developed a more detailed scheme for categorizing
forces presumed to affect foreign policy into "idiosyncratic, role, governmental, societal, and systemic variables." Jacobson and Zimmerman (1969, 7)
develop a similar categorization scheme, and cite others. Rosenau also introduced concepts for characterizing the degree of international influence or
penetration within a society, and the variation in processes associated with
different issue areas (53, 65).

Rosenau noted that "foreign policy analysis is devoid of general theory . . .
[it] lacks comprehensive systems of testable generalizations that treat societies
as actors subject to stimuli which produce external responses" (1966, 32).
He also noted the existence of "partial" theories designed to explain narrowly
defined phenomena such as alliance behavior or international integration
(33–34). "Not being able to draw on general theories, work in the foreign
policy field has been largely historical and single-country oriented" (35). Both
published research and university course offerings have followed this trend.
Rosenau lamented the lack of progress in foreign policy theory in contrast to
the relative success of studies of domestic politics (38–39), and found the
cause in a lack of even a "pre-theory" (40) which would allow for comparable analysis, presumably through a standardized system for categorization of
variables. Therefore, he developed an elaborate categorization scheme (48,
90–91), responding to "the need to develop an explicit conception of where
causation is located in international affairs" (41).

The lack of significant progress since these earlier attempts is noted by
Steve Smith (1986, 20–22). Smith writes that "[b]y the mid-1970s it was
evident that, despite the hopes and despite the claims, a general theory of
foreign policy was simply not going to emerge . . . All in all, there has been
a massive retreat from [comparative foreign policy]-type analysis in the
United States and a resurgence of interest in an analytical focus on one
country. . . . [I]n this regard [foreign policy analysis] has not come very far
in the last thirty years."

Smith's excellent overview of the literature cites five central reasons for
this state of affairs. These are: the inductive approach to theory building
through pattern hunting in data; the focus on quantitative description of
correlations rather than causal explanation; the lack of theory testing
which would allow for cumulative knowledge to emerge; the reliance on the
notoriously vague concept of "national interest;" and "the inability to agree
on what a state is and what foreign, as opposed to domestic, policy consists
of" (23–24).

As Smith (19) recognizes, there has been some progress in what he terms
"middle-range theories" of foreign policy, focusing on decision-making
processes. He cites the work of Janis, Jervis, Steinbruner, and Allison. In the

years since his article was published, a fairly large body of work has emerged focusing on the relationship between mass publics and foreign policy, as well (e.g., Gaubatz 1991; Holsti 1992; Russett 1993; Shapiro and Page 1988; Zimmerman 1994). There has also been considerable additional progress in our understanding of factors affecting decision making (e.g., Farnham 1994; t'Hart 1990; Herek, Janis, and Huth 1987; and Khong 1992).

Nevertheless, Smith's original point remains valid; a general theory of foreign policy has yet to emerge. I propose that the basic reason why there has been such limited progress in our theoretical understanding of foreign policy is that the dependent variable itself has remained ill-defined. This is implicit in Smith's criticism of the overreliance on the vague concept of "national interest," and in his recognition that there is no consensual under-standing of the distinction between domestic and foreign policy. Rosenau's pre-theory develops a complex categorization scheme for the independent variables assumed to affect foreign policy, but the dependent variable itself is defined only as "external behavior" (43). White (1989, 1–10) and Clarke (1989, 189) use a similar approach. Rosenau seems to be satisfied with defining foreign policy as "external behavior," but what he focuses on in practice is specific decisions, such as the U.S. decision to invade Cuba in 1961 (45), on a case-by-case basis.

Why has it been so difficult to generalize about "foreign policy" as a dependent variable? Certainly there is a wide range of phenomena students of foreign policy include under the heading, ranging from decisions regard-ing war, peace, commerce, and morality, to complex sets of interdependent issues regarding one state's relations with another over a period of time, to a state's strategic approach to relations with all other states to accomplish certain goals. What is needed is a theoretical concept that captures the *essential* characteristics of all these types of "external behavior." This would allow students of foreign policy to generalize across space and time and across various issues, about the outcome of interest, "foreign policy."

One such framework, using categories including "militant international-ism," "cooperative internationalism," and isolationism, has been proposed by Wittkopf (1990), and employed with considerable analytical success in studies by Hiaddy (1992), Holsti (1998), Holsti and Rosenau (1993), and Wittkopf (1996). This "MI–CI classification scheme" (Holsti 1998) con-ceives of foreign policy as a multidimensional variable based on preferences for cooperative or militant policies and for isolationist or internationalist policies. Holsti (1998) has proposed a third axis, as well, based on prefer-ences for unilateral or multilateral action.

There is no doubt that this framework provides one method for under-standing fundamental aspects of foreign policy. Its usefulness has been demonstrated by the empirical results of the studies cited above. Nevertheless, I believe that an alternative approach is possible, and may lead to better understanding. Because the MI–CI framework is multidimensional, it is really a combination of variables, rather than a single dependent variable. If it were possible to develop a more abstract concept that could capture the essential choices implied by MI–CI along a single continuum, this could add both parsimony and theoretical clarity.

I propose that the concept of choice between competing values introduced above is such an abstract construct. Such a definition allows us to speak of foreign policy preferences in a clear-cut way. It requires that "foreign policy" be represented as a single variable, with trade-offs characterized in a single dimension. Helen Milner has adopted a similar approach to characterizing the "structure of preferences" of international actors at the substate level (1997, 37). My approach focused on trade-offs guided by preferences also ties the study of foreign policy closely to the study of decision making, allowing for some distinction to be made between a given state's policy and its actual behavior resulting from interactions between two or more players, which often include unanticipated constraints, unforeseen events, or unintended consequences. These are elements of interaction which are best considered the dependent variable for a theory of international relations.

Further, it forces students of foreign policy to explicitly define their *a priori* assumptions about the content of foreign policy. Any study of foreign policy should explicitly state what type of choice it seeks to understand and why that choice is important. Just as, for instance, the study of international relations has largely focused on the dependent variable of systemic "stability," or the occurrence or absence of major war, so the study of foreign policy should have a consensus on a dependent variable or set of variables of ultimate interest.

The question of whose choices between which values is obviously key. Students of world politics have provided a general consensus that states address foreign policies to at least two basic types of issues economic, and military (e.g., Waltz 1979; Rosecrance 1986). Some authors consider political issues separately as well (e.g., Carr 1939). Moravcsik (1997, 519) uses basically the same formulation, remarking that states "pursue particular interpretations and combinations of security, welfare, and sovereignty" which I understand as corresponding to military, economic, and political issues, respectively. I assume that policy on these issues is designed to serve the ultimate goal of state survival (although it is really a question of semantics whether we speak of "military/political/economic strategy" or "military/political/economic goals"—see above).

What is essential, is that there are basic ways in which these values can be considered to conflict. Briefly, following Rosecrance (161), I am interested in the relative importance of security concerns and openness and efficiency. I am also interested in the relationship between each of these and the degree to which political cooperation and political agreements are preferred to guarantee or structure interactions. I assume that these relationships can be represented by a continuum with poles representing the extremes of wholly force-based (realist) preferences and wholly interdependence-based (liberal) preferences. Purely force-based preferences arise when a state perceives its interests as entirely incompatible with those of other states. This corresponds to Helen

Milner's definition of "hawkish" preferences (1997, 37). This is a self-help system in the extreme. Purely interdependence-based preferences correspond to a world in which a state perceives complete community or compatibility exists between its interests and those of other states. This corresponds to Milner's definition of "dovish" preferences (1997, 37). On the continuum between these two extremes, a preference for negotiated relationships, or political interaction, defines the midpoint. This continuum will be operationalized in chapter 3 based on absolute- and relative-gains concerns.

Clearly, on such a continuum, real-world foreign policies will tend to fall between the polar extremes. Such a conception of "foreign policy" is desirable for several reasons. First, it provides a well-defined dependent variable, allowing scholars to generalize about foreign policy outcomes regardless of the issue or state under analysis. Second, it is based on well-accepted and long-standing policy areas in world politics. Third, it allows for the analytical identification of the state as the unit of analysis for the dependent variable, which is important because "foreign policy" is usually implicitly associated with states, not with subnational actors. Finally, it improves our ability to consider foreign policy itself as an independent variable in the study of international relations by identifying essential characteristics which can be held constant or varied.

FOREIGN POLICY AND INTERNATIONAL RELATIONS

Developing a comparative tool for characterizing foreign policy and its variation cross-nationally would seem to be important for our understanding of international relations in general. What is the place of assumptions about foreign policy preferences in international relations theory? Most authors have accorded them a central role. "Theories of foreign policy are . . . intrinsic to theories of international relations" (Smith, 1986, 12; see also White 1989, 2). But in what way do such concepts contribute? Wolfers (1962, 67) writes:

> It might seem that the mere existence of a multitude of nation-states, each capable of independent decision and action, would suffice to explain the peaceless state of the world and the power struggles that fill the international arena. Undoubtedly, the anarchical condition inherent in any system of multiple sovereignty constitutes one of the prerequisites of international conflict; without it, there could be no international relations, peaceful or nonpeaceful. Yet, in the last analysis, it is the goals pursued by the actors and the way they go about pursuing them that determine whether and to what extent the potentialities for power struggle and war are realized. This can be seen by imagining two extreme sets of conditions, both theoretically compatible with a multistate system, in which, as a consequence of the wide differences in the objectives pursued by the states in question as well as in the means they are willing to employ, the chances of peace would stand at opposite poles.

Wolfers's view allows for variation in foreign policy preferences.[10] Realist thinkers, however, have usually based their theories on assumptions about the lack of variation in preferences. Morgenthau and Thompson (1985, 5) see the unchanging character of human nature as the constant motivating force behind international politics. "All history shows that nations active in international politics are continuously preparing for, actively involved in, or recovering from . . . war" (Morgenthau and Thompson 1985, 52). The assumption of the primacy of "power" as a motivating force relieves the student of world politics from need for further consideration of "two popular fallacies the concern with motives and the concern with ideological preferences." Although they distinguish between status quo and imperialist powers, Morgenthau and Thompson (1985, 67–69) trace these variations in behavior to a state's power position relative to other states, not to variation in basic preferences.

Kenneth Waltz's conception of foreign policy preferences is only marginally different.[11] He assumes that some variation may occur, but that change in preferences based on experience and observation (in my terminology, foreign policy learning) will be unidirectional. According to Waltz (1979), while "strong states . . . can afford not to learn . . . because only a few threats, if carried through, can damage them gravely" (195), "middle powers . . . are in the . . . position of imitating the more advanced weaponry of their wealthier competitors" (181). Structure dominates, allowing foreign policy preferences to tend only toward one equilibrium situation, the pole of power or primacy of force *realpolitik* outcome. "In international affairs, force remains the final arbiter" (180).

Clearly, Wolfers presents us with a different picture of international politics based on his assumption of bidirectional variation in foreign policy preferences. Deutsch's (1968 [1957]; see also Adler and Barnett 1998) concept of "security community" can also be seen in this light. Certain groups of states, at least when interacting with each other, no longer order their preferences according to the *realpolitik* dictum of the "primacy of force." Indeed, this claim seems to be supported, since the end of the Cold War, for relations between several of the worlds' premier powers in terms of material capabilities, the United States, Germany, and Japan.

More recently, Rosecrance (1986, 212) has pursued a similar line of inquiry. Focusing on the tension between military and economic values, he writes "the comparative cost and benefit of force and trade will influence the balance between systems." One factor Rosecrance identifies as influencing the respective costs and benefits is the "degree of social learning, internationally."

Keohane and Nye (1989) develop similar ideas. They write "we identified 'political realism' with acceptance of the view that state behavior is 'dominated by the constant danger of military conflict,' and we argued that 'during the 1960s, many otherwise keen observers who accepted realist approaches were slow to perceive the development of new issues that did not center on military-security concerns' " (245–246). "*State choices reflect elites' perceptions of interests, which may change in several ways*" (264, emphasis added). One of the sources of change in "national interest" which they identify is "learning . . . to alter one's beliefs as a result of new information" (264).

The concept of preferences is a fundamental part of understanding international relations. Alan Lamborn writes that "a theory of preferences is crucial to our understanding of politics" (1997, 203). Greater understanding of foreign policy preferences can provide answers not only to long-standing questions in the comparative study of foreign policy, but also to central issues of international relations theory. When realist and liberal authors have discussed issues of change in international relations, there is a surprising similarity in their approaches, if not their conclusions. Variation, or the lack thereof, in foreign policy preferences over military and economic values is a central theme, with political values sometimes included as well. The idea of foreign policy learning is more prevalent than one might expect from recent work in the field, as well. Some authors have even touched on the role of observational learning or imitation. However, progress has been hindered by the lack of a clear theoretical framework for understanding foreign policy preferences as a general phenomenon.

Building on previous contributions, and noting some of the extant shortcomings, I have developed concepts of choice, learning, and foreign policy that are designed to facilitate comparative foreign policy analysis. I believe that this is a significant contribution to a general theory of foreign policy, the possibility of which has long been recognized by Rosenau, Smith, and others. In particular, I provide a way for students of foreign policy to define the dependent variable with accuracy and precision (validity) as well as generalizability (reliability) (Campbell and Stanley 1966 [1963], 5–6; King, Keohane, and Verba 1994, 25).

ORGANIZATIONS AND DECISIONS: THE STATE AS AN ACTOR

But my approach to foreign policy learning begs the question of the unit of analysis. Building on work by Leites (1951), George (1969), and Allison (1969), Levy assumes that learning is an elite-level, individual decision-making phenomenon. The focus is on the particular ways in which *individual elites* learn. Given the high degree of influence that psychological theories of learning have had on the study of foreign policy learning, this seems a logical focus. Larson (1985) relies heavily on such an operationalization, and it is central to Khong's (1992) study as well.

However, given that state-level choices, not those of particular individuals, are the ultimate dependent variables of interest to the study of foreign policy, it is important to consider ways in which state-level learning might be theoretically and empirically distinct from learning by individual elites. Farkas (1998) points out that "states are, by definition, collectives not individuals" and develops a formal model for the aggregation of the preferences of foreign policy elites. Reiter (1996) introduces idea of mass public learning, and defines learning as a phenomenon at the state level. Jervis (1976) and Rosecrance (1986) identify psychological theories of generational learning, implying that shared experiences can have systematic effects on large groups of elites or even the mass public. The existence of generational effects influencing which events people consider important and how they are interpreted is widely accepted (Schuman and Scott 1989; Stewart and Healy 1989). Regarding foreign policy in particular, Holsti (1996, 162–66) raises questions about the empirical support for generational learning hypotheses among mass publics and among elite opinion leaders, but recognizes that the evidence is not conclusive.

A rational actor has coherent preferences, pursues goals, and responds to new information (Morrow 1988, 80–81). Is it possible to think of the state as such an actor? Organizational theory provides a rich and appropriate body of literature on which to base analysis of states (e.g., Allison 1969; Cyert and March 1963; Hampton et al. 1987; and, on organizational learning in particular Argyris 1992; Argyris and Schon 1978; Cohen and Sproull 1996). Reiter (1996, 30–31) makes use of three basic assumptions from the organizational behavior literature: organizations are goal-oriented, their behavior is shaped by routines or standard operating procedures designed to achieve goals, and these goals and routines are based on information gained from experience. In particular, experiences of success and failure provide organizations with important information about goals and routines. He thus assumes organizational rationality.

Clearly, such theoretical insights have the potential to help students of foreign policy think in terms of dependent variables at the state level, rather than in terms of the preferences of particular decision makers. Although it is well-known that issues of interest aggregation are somewhat problematic, such state-level analysis is necessary if we are to try to understand foreign policy as more than an idiosyncratic phenomenon. Cognitive factors must be considered within the context of an organization if we are to understand subjects such as "U.S. foreign policy" as opposed to "Jimmy Carter's foreign policy." Without some conception of the state as the unit of analysis, there can be no generalizations about foreign policy, and no comparative study of foreign policy, as opposed to the study of foreign policy makers.

Cognitive learning, of course, can only take place in individual humans. However, if there is a systematic way in which this individual learning interacts with outcomes at the organizational level, then we can logically speak of state-level learning. Jervis (1976, 238) writes "when an event affects the perceptual predispositions of many members of an organization we can speak of organizational learning. The lessons can become institutionalized."

Learning among individuals in the state "organization" can occur at both the mass and the elite levels. When the "lessons" of experience and observation are shared unanimously among and between masses and elites, the state can be seen as learning almost as an individual would. The individual's and the state's preferences are identical. "When actors within an organization have sufficiently homogeneous preferences . . . the organization can be treated as an actor" (Clark 1998, 248). This seems unproblematic. It also seems unlikely.

When there is disagreement between masses and elites on the meaning of "lessons," or when there is not unanimity within either group, or when both

conditions hold, then either one set of preferences will prevail, or a compromise position will emerge. In such non-consensual instances, certainly the
norm, there are organizational dynamics that influence which preferences
prevail, how and when. Herbert Simon (1996 [1991], 177) has noted
the importance of focusing on the "organizational level" rather than just the
"social psychology of people living in an organizational environment" in
order to understand organizational outcomes.

If the state is considered as a single large organization, including both
elites and masses in their respective roles, several aspects of organizational
theory can help identify how experience and observation may be translated
into state-level foreign policy preferences (Farkas [1998] provides an
alternative approach for aggregating elite preferences to model incremental
state learning). Levitt and March (1996 [1988], 521) note that "features of
individual inference and judgment" contribute to the interpretation of
experience by organizations. However, organizational learning differs from
individual-level learning in several respects. Organizations "devote considerable energy to developing collective understandings of history" (521).
The "interpretive frames" through which history is viewed in an organization add another layer to individual interpretations. These interpretative
frames can be expected to be more difficult for an organization to discard for
several reasons.

Organizations are more likely than individuals to ignore new information
that contradicts existing beliefs. In order to react to such discrepant information, the various subdivisions of an organization must work out an
agreement about how to interpret the new data. There may be varying interpretations among individuals or departments within the organization. Even
if there is a consensus on the logical implications of the new information,
there may be reasons of self-interest which cause important actors to resist
change.

Military procurement in the United States is well known for such resistance to change. For example, although the Pentagon declared its preference
to build a new generation U.S. jet fighter in response to technological
advances—the Joint Strike Fighter—Congress moved to cut large portions of
the new jet's $856.7 million budget in 2000. The source of these cuts was
not doubted regarding the Pentagon's need for the plane, but rather the self
interest of legislators, workers, and corporations. "While Lockheed
Martin . . . builds the F-22 at big factories in Georgia and Texas, and
Boeing . . . builds the Super Hornet in Missouri and part of the F-22 in
Washington, there is no huge work force yet that is dependent upon the Joint
Strike Fighter." Similarly, although the Pentagon did not declare any desire
or need for them, "[t]he same House panel that recommended a cut in funding for the Joint Strike Fighter . . . added three new F-15s to the military
budget" in order to shore up the fortunes of Boeing's production facility in
St. Louis (*Washington Post* 5/13/2000). Entrenched financial and political
interests within the state "organization" can inhibit change in reaction to new
information, such as the need for a new jet fighter, although few congressmen

would probably deny in private that the Pentagon's requests better suited the state's needs. This contributes to organizational inertia.

Also, actors who were key proponents of the old set of beliefs may fear a loss of influence due to admitting they were wrong. Departments which played important roles directly related to the old beliefs may fear marginalization if these beliefs are abandoned. Clearly, various bureaucratic interests within the state can influence policy (Allison 1969). Although cognitive factors themselves contribute to individuals' resistance to discrepant information (Jervis 1976, 161–202), these additional organizational factors can be expected to make large organizations such as states especially subject to inertial forces (Scott 1993 [1961]; Gardner 1993 [1965]; Hampton et al. 1987).

The large proportion of organizational memory which is routine-based or impersonal also contributes to this inertial effect. "Routine-based conceptions of learning presume that the lessons of experience are maintained and accumulated within routines despite the turnover of personnel and the passage of time. Rules, procedures, technologies, beliefs, and cultures are conserved through systems of socialization and control. . . . Written rules, oral transitions [e.g., when jobs change hands], and systems of formal and informal apprenticeships implicitly instruct new individuals in the lessons of history" (Levitt and March 1988, 524).

Thus routines can have a life of their own, outlasting individuals within departments and organizations, and little affected by personnel turnover. If an individual policy maker's preferences change due to experience or observation, she may attempt to change the state's preferences, but she also may suppress her new beliefs, or she may simply leave her job. This again makes organizations, and especially large and complex ones such as states, more resistant in general than individuals to changing preferences based on observation or experience.[12]

With these strong inertial tendencies, why might organizations nevertheless alter their preferences? Jervis (1976, 56) notes that "shocks and unpleasant choices" are usually necessary to alter individuals' "basic beliefs." This should be even more the case for organizations comprised of many individuals and subject to the influences of inertia. I expect that states tend to respond only to major events because of the many factors contributing to organizational inertia. If individual elites act on narrowly perceived "lessons" which are contrary to these forces, they tend to be removed from power (or prevailed upon to conform). Following Reiter (1996, 35–37), I believe that the most important types of events for state-level learning are "formative events." I expect that masses and elites are affected in similar, but not identical, ways by such events, causing the state to "learn" from experience and observation. I assume that mass publics, which are rarely involved directly in consideration of policy options, are less likely to consider observed lessons. Elites, because they must make concrete choices, are more likely to search for additional information by examining foreign experience.

I have suggested that foreign policy learning is best thought of as a state-level phenomenon involving choice or trade-offs based on schematic learning from experience and observation. Organizational theory leads to the expectation that states have a high level of resistance to rearranging their foreign policy preferences due to organizational inertia. They tend to respond only to major events which have clear, cognitively attractive "lessons" or implications. With these assumptions in mind, we address the role of imitation in this process. That is the topic of chapter 3, which builds a theoretical framework for understanding imitation in foreign policy.

CHAPTER 3

A THEORY OF IMITATION IN
FOREIGN POLICY

*But why do we pay attention to some things, and not to others? We ought to
analyse everything. . . .*

—*President Leonid Kravchuk addressing the Ukrainian Rada,*
September 1, 1993

So far I have discussed the potential importance of imitation and learning
in international relations, and explored the general context of foreign policy
decision-making within which foreign policy imitation could be rigorously
explored. This chapter builds on the general discussions so far by presenting
the specific theoretical and analytical frameworks of the book. Here
I develop a theory of imitation in foreign policy, derive the hypotheses to be
tested empirically in subsequent chapters, and deal with key issues of research
design.

The discussion of examples of imitation in chapter 1 and of the concepts
related to state-level foreign policy choice and learning in chapter 2 provide
the foundation on which I here attempt to build a coherent theory of imitation
in foreign policy. Three basic distinctions can be derived from the previous
chapters and are necessary components of my approach. Most obvious is the
need to distinguish between direct and vicarious experience. How might
each type of experience influence foreign policy preferences? It also seems
clear that the impact of experiences of policy success versus those of policy
failure must be considered. Success is likely to be followed by policy continuity, while failure would make a change in preferences more likely. Prospect
theory (Farnham 1994; Khaneman and Tversky 1979) would also predict
that an experience of failure or the anticipation of failure would put decision
makers in the domain of losses, and therefore make them more risk acceptant. If learning from vicarious experience is more risky than learning from
direct experience, as suggested in chapter 1, then observational learning
would more likely follow failure.

And the complexity of the choice involved can affect the learning process. Simple dichotomous choices should be distinguished from more complex polytomous choices. In a dichotomous choice situation, if one of two possible options has failed and we assume that the failed option will not be chosen again, then a decision maker requires no additional information to choose the only remaining option. But in a polytomous situation, information in addition to knowledge of one failed option is a logical necessity in order for a choice to be made between the two or more options that remain viable. *I expect that this additional information will be supplied by observation of others' experiences.* Note that the same logic would apply to a truly unprecedented situation, no matter the complexity of the choice. With no precedent for decision, by definition there can be no relevant direct experience.

These three basic distinctions can be combined to form expectations for the shaping of foreign policy preferences. Observation, which is more likely following failure and supplies additional information, is likely under complex choice conditions in the wake of policy failure (figure 3.1). And because this observational or vicarious learning is in response to failure, I expect that in particular *imitation* or *emulation* of others' success will be likely. This is the core logic of my theory, but it requires further elaboration.

One important point to note is that, within this framework, there is no situation in which learning, the effect of experience and observation on beliefs and preferences, is absent. I expect that states are always "learning" something. What is crucial and what varies, however, are the type of effect (continuity or change) and the likely source of resulting preferences (direct experience only or observed and direct experience). A response of policy continuity in either a dichotomous or complex decision setting in the wake of success can be considered learning because new information based on experience is still acquired; the "lesson" of most experience consistent with prior preferences is probably to reinforce those preferences.

The role of choice complexity also deserves further discussion. Although Reiter does not find evidence of observational learning, he recognizes that the particular type of foreign policy decision he examines is a dichotomous one between alliance and neutrality (1996, 53, 59, 91, 121, 129, 137, 145, 165). His results are therefore *consistent* with my framework for vicarious learning.[1] He suggests that learning theory may be "less applicable or at least more difficult to apply to decisions that are more complicated" (121).

But my framework allows us to disagree that learning is less applicable here. In fact, complexity might increase the role of the type of cognitive patterns

Event	Choice	
	Dichotomous	*Polytomous*
Success	Continuity	Continuity
Failure	Invert preference	Choice guided by experience and observation

Figure 3.1   Interaction of experience and choice complexity

that are the focus of learning theory. If Reiter had studied a more complex choice, such as the one he portrays twentieth-century Japan repeatedly facing between no alliance, a defensive alliance, or an imperialistic alliance, my approach would expect vicarious learning to play a greater role. Japan does not eschew alliances after a disastrous defeat in 1945, as his framework would predict. Reiter (1996, 116) notes that "Japan would have been unlikely to look to either its World War I or World War II experiences for guidance." I agree, and believe this is a situation in which imitation would be likely, and the discussion in the first chapter provides some support for this.

If imitation is more common when a state responds to failure in a polytomous choice setting, this still does not indicate *which* foreign experiences will be imitated. Organizational and social psychological theories suggest that there are at least three contributing factors: the degree of perceived *success* of the model state's particular policy, the *prestige* or status of the model state, and the perceived *similarity* of the model state or its situation to the state in question (Bandura 1986; March et al. 1996 [1991]). Two studies of cross-border lesson-drawing with regard to domestic policies (Bennett 1991, 51–52; Hoberg 1991, 107) have noted the power of a prestigious model to attract imitators, rather than those that might be more empirically relevant (a particular policy) or practically applicable (a similar state).

Finally, as noted in chapter 1, cognitive theories suggest a mechanism by which states' experiences of success and failure are likely to be understood and communicated. Analogical reasoning is widely accepted as a fundamental part of human cognition. Analogical reasoning can be seen as either a deliberate process employed in problem solving when no "learned deductive rule" is found to deal with a situation, or as an "extremely basic" characteristic of human inference which is "all-purpose, ubiquitous, unconscious . . . [and] used in perception and categorization" (Beike and Sherman 1994, 236–239). In either case, what is important is "perceived similarity" not "objectively verifiable" similarity of the analog. The case for the ubiquity and unconsciousness of analogical reasoning is supported by studies, which show that "completely irrelevant similarity" can be sufficient to trigger analogical inferences. Some researchers in social cognition even assert that all human reasoning, whether deductive or inductive, is based on analogical inferences (Beike and Sherman 1994, 273–274). It is reasonable to expect that "lessons" of success and failure, both direct and observed, will be expressed as analogies by political elites and mass publics. These analogies thus should be consistent with and representative of underlying schemata.

Therefore, the process of imitation outlined here has five sequential components (figure 3.2).

These fundamental premises lead to clear expectations about when states are likely to learn from observation and which models they are likely to choose.

Imitation in foreign policy
Failure → complex choice → observed models of success → analogies → preferences

Figure 3.2 The process of imitation

These expectations can now be developed into a number of falsifiable hypotheses.

PROPOSITIONS ABOUT FOREIGN POLICY LEARNING

In this section I draw heavily on the work of Dan Reiter because his approach to foreign policy learning, like mine, focuses on state-level learning from formative events. Reiter (1996, 39) summarizes his approach to learning in the following propositions.

Proposition 1. Beliefs are used in international politics to inform decisions in the face of uncertainty. Beliefs are derived from interpretations of past events. . . .

Proposition 2. Learning in the international arena occurs infrequently and is driven by formative events. Events that have great impact, such as great successes or great failures, are more likely to be formative than are events of lesser impact.

Proposition 3. Events experienced directly are more likely to be formative than are events experienced vicariously.

Proposition 4. Successes encourage continuance of policy, and failures encourage innovation.

My approach is consistent with Reiter's in many important respects, and I see this book as adding to the results of his study, supporting rather than questioning them in most respects. But I also attempt to refine his framework in important ways, making it both more clearly specified and more generalizable. In particular, the concept of preferences operationalized as trade-offs between values, is more specific than that of beliefs.[2] Also, although uncertainty is common in foreign policy decision making, the level of uncertainty probably varies greatly. Reiter implies that beliefs are important when uncertainty is great. Uncertainty is not a necessary condition for the influence of preferences to be felt. Rather, preferences are more likely to *change* given uncertainty resulting from perceived failure. In addition, the frequency of learning is an empirical question, and one which can be expected to correspond to the frequency of formative events. Assumptions about the rarity of such events are not necessary to the theory. Finally, and most important, I expect that imitation will be likely to impact foreign policy in certain situations; Reiter does not. My approach is based on the following revised propositions.

Proposition 1. Preferences guide choices between competing values. Preferences are at least partly derived from interpretations of the consequences of past events.

Proposition 2. Preferences are likely to be affected in the international arena by formative events. Events that have great impact, such as those perceived as great successes or great failures, are more likely to be formative than are events of lesser impact.

Proposition 3. Successes reinforce existing preferences, while failures encourage change in the preferences, strategic or fundamental, which are perceived to have led to the failure.

Proposition 4. If more than one option remains after a failed preference ordering is abandoned, a state will likely be influenced by vicarious experience.

Proposition 5. When facing a choice recognized as unprecedented in its own organizational memory, a state will likely be influenced by vicarious experience.

The preference expectations based on the interaction between experience of success/failure and dichotomous/polytomous choices are represented in figure 3.1.

HYPOTHESES TO BE TESTED

The five propositions I have outlined, combined with the cognitive and organizational dynamics already discussed, lead to the following hypotheses. Hypotheses 1, 2, 3, and 7 make predictions about when observational learning is or is not likely. Hypotheses 4, 5, and 6 produce competing claims about which models are attractive.

H1. Foreign policy preferences are not likely to change if they meet with subjective success, regardless of whether the policy choice context is dichotomous or polytomous.

H2. Foreign policy preferences are likely to change if they meet with subjective failure. In a dichotomous choice situation, preferences will be inverted (i.e., if policy A was preferred to policy B, policy B will now be preferred to policy A). Imitation is unlikely.

H3. Foreign policy preferences are likely to change if they meet with subjective failure. In a polytomous choice situation, preference orderings other than the failed policy will be considered. Imitation is likely.

H4. In a polytomous choice following a policy failure, or in an unprecedented situation, a state will tend to imitate other states which it perceives as generally successful or prestigious.

H5. In a polytomous choice following a policy failure, or in an unprecedented situation, a state will tend to imitate other states which it perceives as successful in the particular policy area in question.

H6. In a polytomous choice following a policy failure, or in an unprecedented situation, a state will tend to imitate other states which it perceives as similar to itself.

H7. Due to organizational and cognitive inertia, states tend not to change their preferences in reaction to other states' failures.

These hypotheses are tested in chapters 4–6. Now I turn to questions of the design of these empirical tests.

RESEARCH DESIGN

It is now common practice in social science to use more than one method of analysis to provide a more robust test of hypotheses. Here I use both statistical analysis and a comparative case study. The former is appropriate for assessing the hypothesized general regularities of experience and preferences, while the latter can provide evidence of specific examples of the process of imitation in actual foreign policies—if such evidence exists. The details of the analytical methods are discussed in the corresponding chapters, and further details are found in the appendix. In this section, I address some basic issues relevant to the design of both types of analysis. In particular, good operational indicators for the dependent and independent variables are needed. These measures are used for the coding of preferences and analogies in the quantitative analysis and as an interpretive guide in the cases to be compared. It is also important to guard against confounding factors and spurious inferences using control variables, which are discussed here in general terms.

The dependent variable of this study is foreign policy "preferences." A construct for inferring preferences is necessary because, as Morrow (1994, 19) notes, "[p]references are unobservable." They cannot be directly observed, only inferred. And inference of preferences from behavior is untenable if they are also expected to explain behavior. Making informed assumptions about them is not a straightforward task. It is my intention to develop a framework for understanding the origins of preferences which are more rigorous than current practices, which include unquestioning acceptance of prevailing views or conventional wisdom, or simple inference from past behavior (Morrow 1988, 95–96 and 1994, 17; Riker and Ordeshook 1973, 14), which is open to the charge of tautology. Riker and Ordeshook's concept of "revealed preference" fits this description. My approach is along the lines of the "posited preference" approach of Riker and Ordeshook (1973, 14), or what Frieden (1991, 61) calls "deduced" preferences, based on prior theory.

Standard assumptions that states seek "survival," "maximize national security," or "maximize power" seem insufficient except as constant, basic assumed preferences that have few if any meaningful implications for policy choices.[3] But it would be useful if basic foreign policy preferences could be represented along a single continuum, as discussed in the previous chapter. Such a framework would be more parsimonious than typical classifications, and more amenable to statistical analysis.[4]

Preferences are distributed over outcomes. In international relations theories, one common general characterization of outcomes is in terms of relative and absolute gains. Traditionally the preference for relative or absolute gains (or aversion to relative or absolute losses) has been accepted as an important difference between realist and liberal theories.[5] I think this traditional approach is logically valid and analytically useful, but below I discuss some important criticisms of this approach as well.

I have also noted that preferences imply trade-offs that guide choices. The logic of value trade-offs has been considered in some detail by Keeney,

Raiffa, and Meyer (1975, ix, 1, 4–5, 66). They recognize that utility can be an overall measure of many parameters combined into one. "In essence, the decision maker is faced with a problem of trading off the achievement of one objective against another objective." I propose that foreign policy can be usefully considered as such a "multiattribute value function" in which various states have various (and varying) marginal rates of substitution for important policy trade-offs. It is the *degree* of concern for relative and absolute gains that guides these trade-offs. I propose that this framework can usefully be applied to *any* foreign policy decision or issue. If there is no trade-off to be made, then I argue there is no nontrivial decision or issue at stake.

Although I find the absolute/relative gains distinction useful, it is somewhat controversial. I note that the results presented here regarding imitation do not depend wholly on this characterization. Some of the key hypotheses are *tested without reference to their coding in terms of concern for absolute or relative gains*, but only as examples of analogies to observed/direct success/failure (see tables 4.3–4.5). In addition, I suspect other coding schemes would produce similar results.[6]

I recognize that recent work, including formal models, has taken a close look at the logic of absolute and relative gains, and raised important questions.[7] Powell has demonstrated that relative gains "concerns" can arise out of the strategic environment even if only long-term absolute gains are assumed as initial preferences (Powell 1991, 1993; Grieco, Powell, and Snidal 1993). Snidal has shown that a degree of preference for relative gains does not always lead logically to the noncooperative outcomes realists expect, especially if there is a large number of important actors (Snidal 1991a and b; Greico, Powell, and Snidal 1993).

However, these useful criticisms are far from claiming that relative gains concerns are irrelevant. Powell writes "We must make some assumptions about preferences. Should we assume that states solely maximize absolute gains or that their utility is at least partly a function of relative gains? The logic underlying [his 1991 and 1993 models] does not answer this question." Rather, it (convincingly) refutes the realist claim that "there is an *a priori* answer to the question of what to study about state preferences" (Grieco, Powell, and Snidal 1993, 737). I think this points to the importance of frameworks such as the one presented here that develop a systematic way to understand the origins of preferences and the sources of change in preferences.

The poles of the continuum in figure 3.3 represent preferences for wholly absolute-gains based outcomes, at one extreme, and wholly relative-gains based outcomes at the other extreme. The midpoint represents a preference for balanced "mixed-gains" outcomes that recognize both the advantages of interdependence and the vulnerability of states that is inherent in the security dilemma. The continuum corresponds to a measure of the proportionate value, or trade-off, accorded to relative and absolute gains. This is conceptually equivalent to Snidal's "r" term (Snidal 1991a; Grieco, Powell, and Snidal 1993). This continuum will be used as a guide to data coding for the

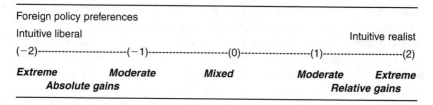

Figure 3.3 Scale of foreign policy preferences (coding scheme)

quantitative analysis and to interpretation for the case studies. For coding purposes, I treat the continuum as an ordinal scale with five values ranging from an extreme preference for relative gains (realist) to an extreme preference for absolute gains (liberal). Because decision makers are not expected to literally use academic international relations theories as guides to foreign policy thinking, I use the terms "intuitive realist" to "intuitive liberal" to characterize them.

It is important to note that preferences in this scheme should not depend on the issue at stake. Whether economic, political, or security issues are involved, preferences can take any value along the continuum. This stems from the concept of value trade-offs, and can be illustrated with examples from theories of international relations.[8]

Preferences for Absolute or Relative Gains across Issue Areas

Regarding economic policy, the distinctions between *laissez-faire*, mercantilist, and autarkic policies are key, representing various degrees of protection or openness. An emphasis on pure absolute gains (*laissez-faire*) would "promote the benefits of markets and their capacity to solve virtually all problems in the most efficient manner." A proponent of pure relative gains (autarky) would prefer an "economic policy designed to promote an extreme version of economic self-sufficiency. . . . Such a policy is frequently designed to defend the nation against political and ideological imports that accompany trade along with the organization of the economy for war." And a mixed-gains approach (mercantilist) would balance preferences for protection and preferences for efficiency and "call on governments to manipulate markets so as to capture special benefits for their nation" (Lairson and Skidmore 1993, 8, 333).

In terms of international organizations and law, which often address issues related to basic political values at an international level, an exclusive concern for absolute gains would allow a state to relinquish a high degree of sovereignty and autonomy to a supra-national authority in pursuit of cooperation. For example, states would be "willing to live with unanticipated outcomes" that arise from an organization pursuing its goals (Martin and Simmons 1998, 751). An exclusive concern for relative gains would mean that a state would only be willing to use international law or organization to pursue its own positional goals, but would not be bound in any way by a supra-national authority, especially in the face of new, unanticipated demands that conflicted with its positional goals. The European Union perhaps comes closest to exemplifying a lack of relative-gains concerns among its members (e.g., Russett, Starr, and Kinsella 2000, 62), while the United Nations often appears to be used instrumentally by great powers when convenient, and otherwise ignored (e.g., Morgenthau 1967, chapter 28). As a state's preferences move from either endpoint toward the midpoint, the balance between supranational authority and positional guarantees evens out. The mixed preferences found in arrangements such as the Association of Southeast Asian Nations (ASEAN) or the Organization of American States (OAS) are located in this middle area.

In terms of military security, a focus on absolute gains would imply the absence of a security dilemma. "Military force is not used by governments toward other governments . . . when complex interdependence prevails." It could be "irrelevant" for certain relationships or certain issues (Keohane and Nye 1989, 25). Relative gains concerns, on the other hand, would rely on the dictum that "[i]n international politics force serves not only as the *ultima ratio*, but indeed as the first and constant one" (Waltz 1979, 113). Absolute gains concerns also make "collective security" arrangements preferable, while loose balancing alliances would be preferred by those interested in relative gains (e.g., Mingst 1999, 167–175; Waltz 1979). The midpoint of the continuum is defined by a mixture of these two extremes. As preferences approach the midpoint, negotiated policies are preferred which trade the value of pursuing mutual interests off against the danger of failing to guard against military aggression. A foreign policy based on political "guarantees" and assurances of "equal rights" among states, often in the context of an international treaty, is preferred. I would argue that arms control agreements among adversaries (such as the ABM, SALT, INF, CFE, and START agreements between the United States and the U.S.S.R./Russia) and multilateral alliances that provide relatively solid commitments (such as NATO or the Concert of Europe) represent such a mixture of absolute and relative gains concerns. Gains from cooperation are achieved, but only with some degree of negotiated assurances of security to ameliorate positional concerns.

In addition to including military, political, and economic issue areas in the analysis, I do not exclude preferences or statements that mention domestic factors as relevant considerations for foreign policy. The concept of value trade-offs is one tool that can be used to incorporate both domestic and international dynamics and military, political, and economic issue areas into the study of foreign policy. Crossing these borders defined for analytical convenience has been suggested by many authors and has proven useful in recent studies.[9]

The ordinal scale of foreign policy preferences presented above (figure 3.3) is used in the empirical analysis to measure the dependent variable, foreign policy preferences. *It is also used to code analogies*, which are the key independent variables of my study. This is discussed in more detail in the relevant chapters.

Control Variables

As noted in chapter 1, although Ukraine and Russia are quite similar in many respects, there are still important differences which necessitate the inclusion of some control variables in the study. In addition, there may be some factors influencing foreign policy preferences in both states that compete with my learning hypotheses and also need to be controlled in the analysis as much as possible. In chapter 1, I noted that Ukraine and Russia differ in terms of energy resources and ethnic identity (table 1.2), as well as strategic position in the world. These factors are dealt with in a general way by including a dummy variable in the quantitative analysis controlling for which state a particular observation belongs to. In the comparative cases, I discuss in some detail the role of the difference in energy resources in particular, as well.

The other major difference I noted in chapter 1 was in the historical experience of each state. However, this difference relates directly to my hypotheses and to expected differences in preferences and perceptions in Russia and Ukraine. I develop this idea in chapter 5 with a discussion of the differing Russian and Ukrainian foreign policy schemata at the time of independence.

While noting these differences, I want to emphasize the considerable similarities between the two states, as discussed in chapter 1, including socioeconomic development, elite and mass characteristics, education, political system, bureaucratic structure, and industry (see table 1.1). There is little variation in these factors across the two states and therefore their effect is largely controlled in the analysis.

But some factors also need to be considered because they compete with my hypotheses independent of differences between the two states. One of these factors is change in the international environment that affects both states similarly. If there are changes in the international system that have a similar effect on Russian and Ukrainian foreign policy over the time of the study, then these external changes, rather than the specific learning dynamics I propose, might explain change in foreign policy preferences. I account for such change by including a counter variable in the quantitative analysis. This is a measure of the passage of time (monthly), and it controls for unidirectional change in preferences over time in both states.

Another possible confounding factor is generational differences among elites. Although Russian and Ukrainian political elites are similar, elites from, for example, the generation that came of age in the decades after World War II might have systematically different foreign policy preferences than those that came of age during the Brezhnev or Gorbachev eras. This type of generation difference is related to theories of learning, but offers a different explanation of foreign policy preferences than my framework does. I control this generational effect by including a measure of age (Year of Birth) in the quantitative analysis. I also discuss it as it relates to some individual elites in the cases. Finally, in the case-study section, I also discuss a number of competing factors related to the particular issue addressed, economic security, including the *process* of large-enterprise privatization, state-level related economic and security interests, and constitutional power-sharing provisions.

This chapter has developed a theory and derived a set of hypotheses about imitation in foreign policy, and discussed some basic issues of research design. Now I turn to testing my hypotheses in the next three chapters. These progress from elite-level to state-level analysis by first examining Russian and Ukrainian elites overall (chapter 4), then examining elites from each state as a distinct group (chapter 5), and finally using case study method to examine state-level behavior in a particular area of foreign economic policy (chapter 6).

CHAPTER 4

ARE ELITES INFLUENCED BY
FOREIGN ANALOGIES?

Why should what has happened to the decision maker and his state be so much more relevant than the fates of others?

—*Robert Jervis* (1976, 281)

This chapter employs statistical analysis of individual-level data to begin to assess the seven hypotheses developed in chapter 3. The intention is to present an initial evaluation of my theory of imitation in foreign policy using pooled data from Ukrainian and Russian elites. I do find preliminary support for most of the hypotheses. In particular, the analysis here shows that subjective failure is strongly associated with attention to foreign success, and that lessons from vicariously observed experience are strongly related to foreign policy preferences. I also take a close look at a few of the individuals, analogies, and issues behind the data. First, evidence directly testing hypotheses H1–H7 is examined. Second, further investigation of the evidence relating to imitation is presented. And finally, I discuss possible alternative explanations for the results and summarize the findings.

The unit of analysis for this chapter is the individual decision maker, at any given time. The dependent variable is foreign policy preferences, measured along the ordinal scale discussed in chapter 3, ranging from −2 through +2. There are four independent variables measuring usage of different types of analogies, and three control variables, all discussed in detail below.

THE DATA

The target population here is the foreign policy elite of Ukraine and Russia. I have collected data on their foreign policy preferences and use of different types of analogies from three sources: articles authored by elites and published in the journals of their respective foreign ministries, published speeches or other policy statements, and in several cases interviews conducted with a consistent questionnaire designed for this study.[1]

There are many possible ways to identify foreign policy elites (Lasswell, Lerner, and Rothwell 1952, 6–13; Zimmerman 1994, 105). I am interested in individuals at the highest possible decision level because I assume they perform agenda-setting functions and aggregate preferences of lower-level elites and the population within the state "organization." I am also interested in a range of issues including military security, political issues, and foreign economic relations. Therefore, I capture a wide but exclusive sample of the elite: those holding high offices or wielding considerable influence, and involved in security, political, or economic issues of relations with other states.

I defined this group by formal and informal roles, including: presidents; prime ministers; deputy prime ministers; ministers of foreign relations, trade, defense, or economy; security council members; directors of intelligence agencies, ambassadors to the united states and Russia/Ukraine, central bank heads, parliamentary speakers/chairs, chairs of the parliamentary foreign relations committee, a foreign policy intellectual closely connected to the state, a top presidential adviser, and a national opposition leader.

For the period 1990–1997, all articles and speeches (and interviews) of these high-level foreign policy decision makers and advisers were used. There are a total of 148 observations (79 Ukrainian, 69 Russian) in the data set, representing 49 individuals (26 Ukrainian, 23 Russian). Twenty-seven individuals are represented more than once (the observations can be considered independent, however, with no significant effect of the lagged dependent variable, see the appendix). Nine individuals are counted five or more times. Among these are four Ukrainians (Foreign Minister Henadii Udovenko [14], President Leonid Kuchma [10], Foreign Minister Anatolii Zlenko [8], President Leonid Kravchuk [7]) and five Russians (Foreign Minister Andrei Kozyrev [19], Foreign Minister Evgenii Primakov [8], President Boris Yeltsin [5], Prime Minister Viktor Chernomyrdin [5], Foreign Policy Adviser Sergei Karaganov [5]). Theoretically the overrepresentation (81 observations, or 55 percent of the data) of these individuals at the highest levels is justified because my sample is designed to reflect the foreign policy decision-making elite of both countries.

The publications chosen are assumed to play a sampling role in that when top decision makers and advisers write articles or publish statements in them, this indicates an active interest in influencing the state's foreign policy. I do not claim that all relevant decision makers are included, but I believe most are, and that they represent the range and types of approaches to foreign policy of the top decision-making elite. For this reason, and because some individuals move regularly in and out of power, 24 instances of articles by high-level *former* officials are not excluded. But removing these observations gives very similar results to those presented in tables 4.1 and 4.2 (there are no changes in significance or sign for the analogy variables, and very few changes in significance for the control variables).

The five-point scale (− 2 through 2) of foreign policy preferences in chapter 3 was used to code the data. The policies advocated are coded along this scale for each observation. Then, analogies are coded along the *same* scale, based on the analogy's meaning as expressed by the foreign policy elite.[2] The coding scheme is discussed in detail in the next section. Coding was done by myself and a hired coder unaware of the theme under study other than the coding instructions. Analogies are also categorized according to whether they refer to success or failure and to vicarious or direct experience, resulting in four *analogy types:* Direct Success, Direct Failure, Observed Success, and Observed Failure.

These four analogy types are then treated as independent variables expected to affect foreign policy preferences. As discussed in the previous chapter, some control variables are added to capture unidirectional effects of events or changes in the international environment occurring over the time of the study (Time), generational differences (Year of Birth), and whether the individual is a foreign policy elite of Russia or Ukraine, thus controlling for the states' differing assets and strategic positions (State).

It would be surprising if analogies and foreign policy preferences were not related in these data because each comes from the same source for any observation. Elites can be expected to try to present internally consistent positions in their writing and other statements. What is more interesting, and can be tested here, is the consistency and magnitude of the relationship of any given analogy type to foreign policy preferences, while controlling for other analogy types and the three control variables. Do these relationships vary as predicted by the hypotheses? If analogies are mainly rhetorical and utilitarian (the null hypothesis, see chapter 1), the type of analogy used should not matter, and correlations will be comparable across independent variables. In addition, I expect certain patterns to prevail for the interaction among analogy types, most importantly between Direct Failure and Observed Success (H3).

Due to the nature of the data set, it is not feasible to make distinctions between dichotomous and polytomous choices. Rather, I assume that all choices are polytomous—a reasonable assumption given the complexity of international politics. This actually provides a conservative test of the observational learning hypotheses because imitation is assumed to be likely only in polytomous choices. If some dichotomous choices are included in the data, this will make it more difficult for the effects of observational learning to emerge as substantively or statistically significant in the analysis.

DO ELITES IMITATE?: ANALOGIES AND POLICY CHOICE

Testing the Seven Hypotheses

The primary statistical method used to analyze the data is ordered probit, a form of maximum likelihood estimation. Ordered probit is appropriate for these data because the dependent variable is represented by ordinal categorical rather than continuous data (Aldrich and Nelson 1984, 11–12; Long 1997, 114–115, 119). Although I use a number of different specifications, the general equation to be estimated can be stated as follows.

$$\text{FOREIGN POLICY PREFERENCE} = \beta_1(\text{STATE}) + \beta_2(\text{YOB})$$
$$+ \beta_3(\text{TIME}) + \beta_4(\text{DS})$$
$$+ \beta_5(\text{DF}) + \beta_6(\text{OS}) + \beta_7(\text{OF})$$

STATE = Russia (0) or Ukraine (1)
YOB = Year of birth (19–63, for years ranging between 1919 and 1963)
TIME = Month of observation (1–96 for the period January 1990–December 1997)
DS = analogy to Direct Success
DF = analogy to Direct Failure
OS = analogy to Observed Success
OF = analogy to Observed Failure

However, the estimation is done with two alternative configurations of the data. One version involves leaving the four analogy variables (Direct Failure, Observed Success, etc.) coded as described above. This amounts to treating them as survey data often are, ranging along a scale of possible responses (e.g., agree strongly, agree somewhat, indifferent, disagree somewhat, disagree strongly), with the scale in this case ranging from extreme "intuitive liberal" to extreme "intuitive realist" preferences. This treatment of the data is consistent with theoretical expectations of the role of analogies: they are, literally, analogues for foreign policy. It also treats the absence of a particular analogy type for a particular observation as missing data, just as a "no answer" or "don't know" might be recorded in survey data. This treatment is conservative in that it makes no assumptions about the "meaning" of not using a particular analogy type, and simply drops that observation from the relevant equation.

The problem here is that most foreign policy elites do not use all analogy types in any given article, interview, or policy statement. This severely reduces the number of observations that can be included if the entire equation is estimated due to listwise deletion of observations,[3] and so does not allow for meaningful assessment of the impact of one analogy type while controlling for the use of other analogy types. I use two strategies to compensate for this. First, I estimate five separate equations, each including the control variables and one (or two) of the analogy variables (table 4.1). Then, I estimate the general equation above using an alternative coding of the analogy variables, as dummy variables to record each possible value assigned to each analogy type (table 4.2). Therefore, when an analogy type is not used at all for a given observation, it is simply coded as "0" for each possible value. In order to reduce the number of variables in this specification, the five-point scale is reduced to a three-point scale by combining values of −2 and −1 into a "Liberal" dummy variable, combining values of 2 and 1 into a "Realist" dummy variable, and leaving values of 0 to be coded as a "Mixed" dummy variable. This gives three variables for each analogy type (e.g., Direct Failure: Realist, Mixed, Liberal).[4]

This allows for all observations to be included in equation 6 (table 4.2). The advantage is that the effect of each of the analogy types can be

Table 4.1 Ordered probit estimation of effects on foreign policy preferences

Variable[a]	Equations				
	(1)	*(2)*	*(3)*	*(4)*	*(5)*
Control variables					
Time	0.001	−0.003	0.008	0.007	0.008
	(0.005)	(0.005)	(0.006)	(0.011)	(0.007)
Year of	0.027*	0.005	0.006	0.018	0.045*
Birth	(0.014)	(0.013)	(0.016)	(0.027)	(0.024)
State[b]	0.426*	0.117	0.447	0.627	0.662*
	(0.239)	(0.251)	(0.293)	(0.479)	(0.365)
Direct					
Success	0.890****				1.148***
	(0.319)				(0.485)
Failure		0.764*****			
		(0.183)			
Observed					
Success			1.134*****		0.960****
			(0.268)		(0.331)
Failure				(0.749)**	
				(0.386)	
N	*102*	*92*	*76*	*30*	*57*
Correctly predicted[c]	63.1%	58.1%	69.7%	30.0%	63.2%

* $p < 0.10$; ** $p < 0.05$; *** $p < 0.01$; **** $p < 0.005$; ***** $p < 0.001$. Table shows coefficient and standard error.

Notes
[a] One-tailed tests for "analogy" variables.
[b] Russia = 0, Ukraine = 1.
[c] Correct prediction based on probability > 0.5 for the given value of the dependent variable. Overall $N = 148$.

controlled. The disadvantage is the insertion of "0"s in dummy variables where "no answer" seems more appropriate. But this would only serve to dilute the impact of the analogy variables, so it does not exaggerate the effect of analogies. The best option is to accord greater weight to the effects that are robust in both analyses.

> *H1. Foreign policy preferences are not likely to change if they meet with subjective success, regardless of whether the policy choice context is dichotomous or polytomous.*

This hypothesis implies that experiences of Direct Success will be strongly related to policy preferences. Relative to the control variables, analogy to Direct Success does have a strong effect (equation 1, table 4.1). It's coefficient is positive and statistically significant. This equation correctly predicts 63.1 percent of foreign policy preferences. Direct Success is also the most common analogy type, recorded in 107 observations, or about 72 percent of the total.[5]

Table 4.2   Ordered probit estimation of effects on foreign policy preferences: alternative coding (equation 6)

Variable[a]	Coefficient[b]	Standard error	Z	Significance
Control variables				
Time	0.002	0.005	0.50	$p = 0.62$
Year of birth	0.021	0.013	1.63	$p = 0.10$
State[c]	**0.418**	0.225	1.83	$p < 0.10$
Direct Success				
Realist	0.496	0.584	0.85	$p = 0.20$[d]
Mixed	−0.079	0.286	−0.28	$p = 0.78$
Liberal	−0.310	0.516	−0.60	$p = 0.27$[d]
Direct Failure				
Realist	0.166	0.333	0.50	$p = 0.31$[d]
Mixed	0.157	0.270	0.58	$p = 0.56$
Liberal	**−0.979**	0.391	−2.50	$p < 0.01$[d]
Observed Success				
Realist	**1.150**	0.587	1.96	$p < 0.05$[d]
Mixed	0.012	0.240	0.05	$p = 0.96$
Liberal	**−1.128**	0.370	−3.05	$p < 0.005$[d]
Observed Failure				
Realist	**0.827**	0.334	2.47	$p < 0.01$[d]
Mixed	**1.064**	0.414	1.57	$p < 0.05$
Correctly predicted[e] = 65.2%				

Notes:
[a] Independent variables coded as dummy variables with 1 indicating analogy usage, 0 no usage.
[b] Bold type indicates statistically significant coefficient.
[c] Russia = 0, Ukraine = 1.
[d] One-tailed test.
[e] Correct predictors based on probability > 0.5 for the given value of the dependent variable.
$N = 132$.

Equation 6 (table 4.2) indicates that the variables for realist and liberal lessons embodied in analogies to Direct Success produce coefficients of the predicted sign (because these are dummy variables, the coefficient for "Liberal" analogies should be negative), but neither is statistically significant. We see below that the relationship to foreign policy here is not as robust as that of Direct Failure or Observed Success. *Elites appear to make more gratuitous or rhetorical references to their own states' successes than to other states' successes or their own states' failures.*[6] But these results do establish that references to Direct Success are moderately well correlated with foreign policy preferences. Direct Success retains statistical significance and a positive coefficient when control for Observed Success is introduced in equation 5.

A closer look at one example involving analogy to Direct Success from the data may help determine whether such correlations represent a causal relationship. Iurii Dubinin, a senior Russian diplomat and ambassador to Ukraine (1996–2001), used two analogies in an article in support of his preference for strengthening the Organization for Security and Cooperation in Europe (OSCE). This addressed an important issue for Russia at the time, how to counter or even block anticipated NATO expansion. The first analogy is to Charles de Gaulle's "Greater Europe" policy. The second analogy is to Soviet participation as a founding member of the Council on Security and Cooperation in Europe (CSCE, predecessor to the OSCE). Dubinin believes that "the Helsinki Agreements gave a powerful stimulus to the general European process" (Dubinin 1995, 87–88).

The first analogy is coded as moderately intuitive realist (1), because of the heavy emphasis in Gaullist foreign policy on sovereignty and independence, explicitly excluding any surrender of national prerogative to international rules or organizations. It is categorized as Observed Success because it is a positive reference to French experience.[7] The reference to Soviet participation in the CSCE is also positive, so it is coded as Direct Success.[8] The creation of the CSCE is best seen as an instance of political compromise based on a negotiated agreement, trading Western recognition of the status quo in Europe for Soviet concessions on international norms, especially relating to human rights. It also was part of a Soviet strategy to loosen the trans-Atlantic bonds of NATO.[9] Thus the analogy is to negotiated, limited cooperation—a trade-off that balances competing values of security and interdependence. It shows an even mixture of primacy-of-force concerns and recognition of the constraints of interdependence, and is therefore coded as an analogy for "mixed" preferences (0).

Dubinin's stated foreign policy choice is "for increasing the effectiveness of the OSCE, transforming it into a full-fledged international organization. We are in favor of the formation of the OSCE's own legal base, for the improvement of its institutions and mechanisms. The major new direction in the activity of the OSCE should be the development of a model for genuine all-encompassing European security." He also mentions shared principles such as "democracy," "principles of market economics," and "a single approach to humanitarian issues (Dubinin 1995, 87–88)." This indicates a preference for a broad negotiated agreement for organized international cooperation in Europe which includes the United States, an OSCE member, but will lessen the importance of NATO and its expansion, and is coded as a preference for "mixed" policy (0). The desire for gains from cooperation is tempered by the concern for position and threats implied in the need for an explicit security arrangement. As was the case 20 years previously, Russia seeks a place in the European status quo, but is concerned that it might lack legitimacy or be marginalized if its position is not formally recognized.

There are four things to note about this combination of analogies and policy choice. First, in this example the analogy to Direct Success is better correlated with policy choice than is the analogy to Observed Success. There is no analogy to Direct Failure, so this is *consistent* with my expectations. As the statistical results for H1 show, there are many such correlations in the data—but equation 6 also indicates that not all references to Direct Success correspond so well with the preferred foreign policy.

Second, a key question is whether the analogies are used *only* as rhetorical tools to promote a preexisting policy orientation, in which case there is no causal effect of analogies on preferences. It is not possible to "show" what happens in a person's mind, but in this case it is clear that the CSCE analogy should have substantive significance to Dubinin because he was one of the Soviet diplomats involved in negotiating the Helsinki Accords in 1973–1975, and in subsequent CSCE meetings (Dubinin 1995, 87). The analogy to de Gaulle should also be meaningful to Dubinin because he was directly involved in Soviet relations with France and other European states for much of his career, beginning with his first diplomatic posting to Paris in 1956–1959 (de Gaulle established the Fifth Republic in 1958) through his time as Soviet Ambassador to France in 1990–1991 (Dubinin 1997). Neither analogy seems chosen at random, and each seems significant and *instructive* to the decision maker. Indeed, each is accorded an entire chapter in his 1997 memoirs.

Third, it is neither advisable nor necessary to take the decision maker's words at face value in order to argue for the importance of analogies. As noted, analogies can represent underlying thought-association patterns, or cognitive schemata. It is enough to note that Dubinin is positively inclined toward the USSR's experience in the CSCE and toward Gaullist foreign policy. It is not necessary to believe, as implied by his rhetoric, that he is actually a liberal–democratic activist for international humanitarian norms and free markets. This was not the content of the CSCE experience for the USSR. Moscow's acceptance as a legitimate "European" state is likely to be much more salient. Analogies can provide clues to underlying schemata that are distinct from more self-conscious, deliberate explanation, and rationalization.

Fourth, it is not the environment or circumstances *alone* that determine or dictate Dubinin's choice. The objection could be raised that Dubinin and any other Russian strategist would prefer a policy of "political independence" and the exclusion of the United States from Europe along Gaullist lines, but this is simply beyond Russia's capabilities, so Russia must settle for some influence through the OSCE. This objection misses the point. Foreign policy choices by definition represent trade-offs. If there were no significant trade-offs involved, any leader would prefer to maximize all values. But these values compete. Rather, the non-vacuous question is how much Dubinin is willing to pay to pursue these goals. His advocacy of expanding the role of the OSCE provides enough evidence to judge his preferences relative to those of the other elites in the data set. *Given Russia's situation*, Dubinin prefers security cooperation within a strengthened OSCE. *In the same situation*, other Russian elites advocate different policies for the same issue. The environment is held constant, but elite choices and analogy usage vary.

For example, in the same number of the foreign ministry journal with Dubinin's article, Iurii Skokov (secretary of the Russian security council, 1992–1993) advocated a "strong foreign policy based primarily on national interests" to resist NATO's expansion. He placed priority on integration within the former Soviet region. Relations with the United States and

Western Europe should be based on "equal rights," but he does not advocate institutionalized security cooperation for Russia outside of the space of the former USSR. This policy orientation is coded as moderately "intuitive realist" (1). The analogies used also reflect moderate realist preferences. He saw allowing the USSR to collapse as a negative experience that left the world without a "strategic balance, burdening the world with the chaos of local conflicts that threaten humanity not less than does nuclear catastrophe." And he saw post-Soviet Russia needlessly sacrificing "strategic position" through an inconsistent policy toward the West that "completely ignores Russian national interests" (Skokov 1995, 12–13). These analogies to Direct Failure reveal a schema concerned with strategic position in a dangerous world, but not inclination toward institutionalized cooperation if Russia will not be the dominant player, and are coded as (1). Skokov's preferences vary significantly from Dubinin's even though each writes from the Russian perspective, at the same time, and addresses the same general issue.

H2. Foreign policy preferences are likely to change if they meet with subjective failure. In a dichotomous choice situation, preferences will be inverted (i.e., if policy A was preferred to policy B, policy B will now be preferred to policy A). Imitation is unlikely.

H3. Foreign policy preferences are likely to change if they meet with subjective failure. In a polytomous choice situation, preference orderings other than the failed policy will be considered. Imitation is likely.

H2 and H3 imply that elites who use analogies to their own state's failure are likely to search for alternative foreign policies. The effect of Direct Failure on policy choice should therefore be significant, but it should not predict policies as well as does Observed Success. It is clear that Direct Failure is related to policy preferences (equation 2, table 4.1). The effect is statistically significant, but the prediction rate is only 58.1 percent. As expected, analogies to Direct Failure do not correspond to policy choice as well as do analogies to Observed Success, which predict 69.7 percent of foreign policy preferences correctly (equation 3). Direct Failure is the second most common analogy type in the data set, used in 102 observations or about 69 percent of the total. It seems that direct experience *in general* (of either success or failure) is more likely to be used rhetorically by elites than observed experience. Analogies to direct experience are more common but are less related to foreign policy, while analogies to other states' experiences are less common but more strongly related.

H3 also predicts that *decision makers who use analogies of Direct Failure will be more likely to recognize foreign states' successes*. A bivariate table shows that there is a significant, positive relationship (table 4.3). As noted, this connection does not rely on coding along the intuitive liberal/realist scale, only on the less demanding categorization of observed/direct experience and success/failure (for these categories, there was 100 percent agreement among coders, see appendix).

Table 4.3   Analogies: Direct Failure and Observed Success

Observed Success	Direct Failure		Total[a]
	Not used	Used	
Not used	26(56.5%)	40(39.2%)	66(44.6%)
Used	20(43.5%)	62(60.8%)	82(55.4%)
Total	46(100%)	102(100%)	148(100%)
	Value	P	
Chi-square	3.843	0.05	
Phi	0.161		

[a] Percentage totals vary due to rounding.

Table 4.4   Analogies: Direct Success and Observed Success

Direct Success	Observed Success		Total[a]
	Not used	Used	
Not used	17(25.8%)	24(29.3%)	41(27.7%)
Used	49(74.25%)	58(70.7%)	107(72.3%)
Total (column percentages)	66(100%)	82(100%)	148(100%)
	Value	P	
Chi-square	0.225	0.635	
Phi	−0.039		

[a] Percentage totals vary due to rounding.

However, it could still be that foreign policy elites are simply prone to analogize, for rhetorical purposes as Snyder argues, or just as a habit of expression. If this were so, then the relationship between any two types of analogies ought to be similar. But for three of four other possible analogy-type pairings, there is no discernable relationship. Table 4.4 shows this for Direct Success and Observed Success, and similar results are obtained for Direct Failure and Observed Failure (chi-square = 0.438, $p = 0.508$) and Direct Failure and Direct Success (chi-square = 0.479, $p = 0.489$). This pattern corresponds well to my expectations, and otherwise would seem quite puzzling.

However, there is a strong correspondence between Direct Success and Observed Failure (chi-square = 5.598, $p = 0.018$), although instances of analogy to Observed Failure are relatively rare, used in less than a quarter of the observations. Note that this is the complementary pattern to the connection between Direct Failure and Observed Success. It was not anticipated by my hypotheses, but is perhaps more evidence that cognitive patterns, not just rhetoric or habit, are operative in analogy use.

An example from the data which demonstrates the pattern connecting Direct Failure, Direct Success, and policy choice is that of Oleksandr Razumkov, Ukrainian presidential adviser (1994–1995) and first-deputy secretary of the Ukrainian security council (1997–2001) (author's interview with Razumkov, April 15, 1997, Kyiv). Note that in this statement, as in many others, military, political, and economic issues are considered simultaneously, and in terms of trade-offs. He argues for involving Ukraine in international organizations and for "maximum economic cooperation with all countries." He plays down issues of military security because "military threat for Ukraine is far from the primary form of threat today. . . . [A] much greater danger is presented by economic problems. . . . Authority in international relations comes from economic performance." He argues for "the superiority of international law over national law . . . the sovereignty of every state, if on equal-rights conditions, in agreement with international law can be partially relinquished." These preferences are coded as moderately "intuitive liberal" (-1). His concern for efficient cooperation is primary, but is tempered by concern with guarantees of equal rights and the goal of international authority, positional concepts.

This is consistent with the analogies he uses. His first analogy is to Ukraine's failure to liberalize domestic and foreign economic policy. "Why has the market developed so poorly in Ukraine? We have not been able to create the conditions within our country for normal commercial relations." He specifically mentions the failure to create private "trans-national corporations" with U.S., German, and Russian firms. This analogy implies moderate liberal preferences (-1). The second analogy is to Observed Success. "Any form of international cooperation . . . involves a willing delegation of functions to some international structure. If this is a willful choice, then this is normal. The European Union involves a partial transfer of sovereignty by states." This is also coded as an analogy supporting a moderate liberal policy (-1). As expected, Observed Success corresponds well with policy choice when the decision maker also refers to Direct Failure.

Another example comes from Russian Foreign Minister Andrei Kozyrev (1991–1995). In a 1992 speech at the Foreign Ministry he discussed the lessons of Soviet foreign policy: "our country has been hostage to messianic ideas for which we sacrificed the national interest . . . the attempt at expansion and ill-considered confrontation . . . led to the exhaustion of our own economy." While Gorbachev's "new thinking" in foreign policy implied some positive change, "we failed to abandon the socialist choice." These statements are coded as analogies to Direct Failure, with moderate "intuitive-liberal" content (-1).

Kozyrev's analogies to Observed Success follow logically as correctives to past failures. In contrast to the USSR, he uses the United States as an example of a democratic state which has declared its basic foreign policy interests, and their limitations, in a "normal" way. He also argues that Germany, Japan, Italy, and the United States all experienced difficulties during their development but did not abandon their basic democratic and open economic principles. "Italy and Japan . . . were helped by more developed countries . . . but this did not transform them into colonies of, say, American imperialism . . . and now they have achieved successes in economic, political, and other spheres. I think, we can go bravely along this route" (Kozyrev 1992, 91–92). These references are also coded as moderate intuitive liberal (−1).

Kozyrev's foreign policy preferences are coded moderate intuitive liberal (−1) as well. He believes that "The goal [of Russian foreign policy] is a broad one: the thorough economization of our policy and diplomacy. . . . The most important criterion here is achievement of an organic commonality with the world economy, speedy entry into the IMF and other institutions" (Kozyrev 1992, 97). Kozyrev's thought pattern seems clear: it is the failure of Soviet foreign policy that turns his attention to Western models, and he adopts—probably in an overly simplistic way—what he sees as their basic liberal values and nonthreatening concepts of "national interest."

H4. In a polytomous choice following a policy failure, or in an unprecedented situation, a state will tend to imitate other states which it perceives as generally successful or prestigious.

The prediction of H4 is that among observed-success analogies, prestigious states will be overrepresented. I assume that states with the greatest capabilities and wealth are the most prestigious, such as the United States, Germany, Japan, France, and the United Kingdom. The results support the case for imitation based on prestige. Fifty-three out of 101 analogies to Observed Success referred to western Europe or the United States (table 4.5). The paucity of references to Japan may indicate the need for

Table 4.5 Content and region of analogies to Observed Success

Region	International relations in general	Military issues	International political cooperation organizations	International political economy	Total
Global	4	2	12	10	28
Western Europe	5	4	20	5	34
USA, "the West," NATO	9	4	4	2	19
Post-Soviet Central and Eastern Europe	3	0	0	5	8
Asia	1	0	0	3	4
Middle East	0	1	0	3	4
Soviet Bloc	0	3	0	0	3
Canada	0	0	1	0	1
Latin America	0	0	0	0	0
Africa	0	0	0	0	0
Total	22	14	37	28	101

some cultural similarity or geographic proximity in order for prestige to translate into imitation (i.e., H6 below).

H5. In a polytomous choice following a policy failure, or in an unprecedented situation, a state will tend to imitate other states which it perceives as successful in the particular policy area in question.

There is some support for this hypothesis, although it pales in comparison to what appears to be the strong prestige factor. States in Asia and Central and Eastern Europe did gain attention for their success in attracting foreign aid and investment, and exporting (5). Western Europe was used as an analogy for successful cooperation within an international organization (20).[10]

H6. In a polytomous choice following a policy failure, or in an unprecedented situation, a state will tend to imitate other states which it perceives as similar to itself.

There seems to be a limited amount of support for this hypothesis as well. Eleven references were made to successes in Central and Eastern Europe (8) and the former Soviet Bloc (3). Cultural and historical ties, as well as geographic proximity, make it likely that states such as Poland, the Czech Republic, and Yugoslavia are considered similar in many ways to Russia and Ukraine.

H7. Due to organizational and cognitive inertia, states tend not to change their preferences in reaction to other states' failures.

The finding here is not the weak relationship that was expected. In equation 4 (table 4.1) the effect of Observed Failure is statistically significant and positive. In equation 6, the coefficients for "Realist" and "Mixed" lessons of Observed Failure are significant. But, as discussed, few instances of reference to Observed Failure occur in the data—only 34 observations, or 23 percent of the total. The implication here is that, while it may be a potent factor when recognized, Observed Failure is simply not on the radar screens of most foreign policy elites. This is partially consistent with my expectations. Given the strong coincidence of analogies to Direct Success and Observed Failure noted above, the apparently rare but potentially powerful phenomenon of learning from vicarious failure may merit further investigation.

THE POWER OF IMITATION

The central issue of imitation of foreign success remains to be examined in detail, but the analysis so far tends to support hypotheses 1–4.

Analogies to vicarious success are less common than those to either type of direct experience, with 82 observations using them, about 55 percent. In equation 3 (table 4.1), there is little doubt ($p < 0.001$) that the relationship

Table 4.6 Average absolute value of marginal probabilities from equation 6*

Variable	Prob.	Percentage of observations
Time	0.0004	99
Year of birth	0.0034	93
State	0.0653	100
Direct Success	0.0511	72
Direct Failure	0.0748	69
Observed Success	0.1530	55
Observed Failure	0.1988	23

* These are unweighted averages. All other variables held at their means. The probabilities for Foreign Policy = 2 (extreme relative gains) are not included because the overall probability of this outcome was 0.001. There is only one observation coded Foreign Policy = 2 in the data.

in the data between Observed Success and foreign policy is real. The model correctly predicts 69.7 percent of foreign policy preferences, the best level of prediction among all the equations. In equation 6, the coefficients for "Realist" and "Liberal" lessons of Observed Success are in the predicted direction, and statistically significant. As shown in table 4.3, the hypothesized link between experiences of Direct Failure and Observed Success is also significant. This evidence supports my central argument: *when foreign policy elites recognize the failure of their own state's policies, they are likely to turn to foreign experiences of success as models, and these models will influence foreign policy.*

Another way to assess the importance or strength of a relationship in a probit model is to examine marginal impacts. Since the value of any variable's coefficient is dependent on the values taken by other variables, each coefficient can be interpreted meaningfully only when the others are considered. Table 4.6 shows the influence of each variable in equation 6 while other variables are held at their mean values. The analogy variables are recombined by using the average of the absolute value of the coefficients for the liberal, mixed, and realist variables in each analogy type. Consistent with the high predictive power in equation 3, Observed Success affects foreign policy more than twice as much as either Direct Success or Direct Failure. Observed Failure, although rarely cited, has an even greater impact when it is used. This clearly implies that imitation is both relatively common, and a fairly powerful source of learning in foreign policy.

CONCLUSIONS

The preferences of foreign policy elites are related to observation of other states' experiences. Lessons of Observed Success are the best single predictor of foreign policy preferences examined here, and their significant effect is robust across all models in which they are included (equations 4–6). The hypothesized link between experiences of Direct Failure and Observed Success is also supported by the data. When foreign policy elites recognize the failure of their own state's policies, they are likely to turn to foreign experiences of success as models. Generally prestigious states appear to be the most likely models for emulation. When elites use analogies to foreign models, these appear to influence foreign policy preferences more than analogies to direct experience. The data strongly support the contention that elites do imitate other states' foreign policies.

It is worth reiterating that this chapter treats the individual elite—at any given time—as the unit of analysis. A key test of my hypotheses relating to *states'* foreign policy preferences, and of my expectations based on Russian and Ukrainian schemata, will be to see if they hold when each state's elites are considered separately. The next chapter will take a step toward treating the state as the unit of analysis by comparing Ukrainian and Russian elites as two distinct groups in the data.

CHAPTER 5

STATE-LEVEL EFFECTS ON ELITE IMITATION

. . . O pointless, damned nation
When will you be free? When
Will our own Washington come to us
With a new and just law?
And someday he certainly will come!

  —Taras Shevchenko, *Iurodyvyy*

. . . But he had read Adam Smith,
And he was deeply economic,
That is he understood how to judge,
How a state becomes wealthy,
And what makes its livelihood, and why
Gold is not needed,
If it just has a product.

    —Alexander Pushkin,
    Evgenii Onegin

This chapter begins to evaluate state-level learning by separating the pooled data used in chapter 4 by country. The basic relationships established in chapter 4 now tested for Ukrainian and Russian elites separately. In chapter 1, expectations for different effects in Ukraine and Russia were suggested based on the hypothesized effects of differing "formative experiences" for each state. These expectations are elaborated and tested here and in next chapter 6.

As I explain in detail below, Russian elites should be more aware of the policy failures that led to the fall of the USSR and Moscow's loss of empire (Direct Failure); while Ukrainian elites should be more aware of the policy successes that led to national independence (Direct Success). Based on the seven hypotheses developed in chapter 3, Russian elites should therefore be

Event	Choice	
	Dichotomous	Polychotomous
Success	Continuity	Ukraine: continuity
Failure	Invert preference	Russia: choice guided by experience and observation

Figure 5.1 Expected learning patterns based on schemata

more influenced by analogies to foreign success (Observed Success) than Ukrainian elites. Drawing on the concept of schematic learning, I explain these expectations in terms of Russian and Ukrainian cognitive schemata (summarized in figure 5.1).

THE UKRAINIAN SCHEMA

Since the Treaty of Pereiaslav in 1654, this large European nation has had virtually no modern experience of sovereign statehood. Ukraine did not come to national consciousness until the nineteenth century. Most historians point to the period 1917–1920 as one of turmoil in which only minimal aspects of sovereignty were attained before Bolshevik forces reasserted Moscow's control (e.g., Subtelny, chapter 19). The fall of the USSR and the emergence of independent Ukraine were therefore major victories for Ukrainian leaders. From at least mid-1990, Ukrainian leaders appear to have pursued maximum independence from Moscow (Solchanyk 1998, 24–27). In July 1990 the Ukrainian Supreme Soviet (Verkhovna Rada) declared "State Sovereignty." In August 1991 a declaration of independence was issued by the parliament, and Leonid Kravchuk signed the Belovezh agreements in December 1991 with Russia and Belarus, dismantling the USSR. This was a victory both for President Kravchuk and other communists-turned-separatists who retained power after 1991, and for Ukrainian nationalists such as V'iacheslav Chornovil, Soviet-era dissident and leader of the independence movement *Rukh* (Chornovil, interview 11/5/97). Among the top priorities was establishing the Ukrainian military, including securing the allegiance of officers of the former Soviet military on Ukrainian soil.

The advent of complete Ukrainian independence comprises a formative event incorporating the successful achievement of a long-denied goal. It heavily influenced how Ukrainian elites framed issues once they turned to governing their new state. The former communists had achieved independence from Moscow, but saw this as ridding themselves of Gorbachev and his harmful reformist ideas. The 17-year tenure of Volodymyr Shcherbytsky as head of the Ukrainian communist party organization ensured that Ukrainian communist leaders were among the most conservative, Brezhnevite chiefs of any Soviet republic. The nationalists had achieved what must have seemed unattainable even two or three years earlier. With such a record of success regarding the issues of primary importance to each group, there was little perception of a need for further extreme change and little political will to upset important institutions of the new state. In addition, because independence was achieved through domestic compromise between leftists and nationalists who presented a relatively united front in relations with Moscow, it can be expected that domestic political stability for the sake of maintaining statehood will be part of the Ukrainian lesson of success (e.g., Nahaylo and Swoboda 1989, 331). This may also be due to the lessons of 1917–1921, when Ukrainian elites remained bitterly divided and the sparks of independence were easily extinguished by Bolshevik forces (e.g., Pipes 1968).

On the other hand, as a republic within the Soviet Union—essentially a subordinate administrative unit—Ukraine did not confront the failure of Soviet *foreign* policy directly. This had consequences for Ukrainian elites' perception of the problems of the USSR and the experiences of other states around the world. They were both less aware of the economic and other problems facing the heavily militarized Soviet economic system, and were generally denied direct contact with the world outside of the Soviet bloc.

One possible expectation based on the hypotheses developed in chapter 3 is that Ukraine will interpret its independence as an unprecedented situation and for this reason be likely to imitate foreign experience. For example, Volodymyr Horbulin (1996, 3), secretary of the Ukrainian Security Council, stated that ". . . the position of young states which do not have sufficient experience of their own statehood is extremely difficult. It is necessary to solve complex questions of the determination of priorities in foreign policy, to learn to accept with responsibility the aid of other states or to decisively refuse such aid if it does not correspond to their own national interests."

However, this effect should be diminished by the fact that Ukraine has had some brief twentieth-century experience of independence, and a more distant historical memory of being a major European polity (Kievan Rus'). In addition, Ukraine did develop its own *de facto* foreign policy before the dissolution of the USSR. Foreign Minister Anatolii Zlenko abandoned the typical subservient role of republican foreign minister and began to assert Ukrainian interests distinct from Moscow's. Ukraine had informal diplomatic relations with several states and was actively pursuing maximum autonomy from Moscow since 1990 (Zlenko 1992). These efforts contributed to the successful achievement of statehood.

Therefore, according to the theoretical framework in chapter 3, this combination of circumstances of Direct Success and no recognition of major failure would cause Ukrainian foreign policy to tend toward continuity of preferences. Imitation is unlikely (H1). The details of the formative event point to a foreign policy closer to the pole of power or *realpolitik*. Ukraine's elite achieved success in 1991 by following a policy based on the assertion of state sovereignty and the goal of independence in military, economic, and political dealings. In the wake of a major success, Ukrainian foreign policy preferences are reinforced and imitation is unlikely.

THE RUSSIAN SCHEMA

Russia's recent and distant historical legacy is dramatically different from Ukraine's. While the Russian elite gained control of an independent state with the fall of the USSR, they were acutely aware of the loss of empire. President Yeltsin and other prominent Russian republican leaders had made efforts to preserve the Soviet state in some modified form (Solchanyk 1998, 24–27). The sense of successful emergence from the communist order was significantly diluted by the sense of failure to preserve the Union with which they had come to identify. Even the architect of Russian reforms, Egor Gaidar, referred to the end of the USSR as a "heavy price to pay" (quoted in CDPSP 44, 334–337).

This sense of limited success or even failure led to a greater readiness to accept the need for further change. Simply achieving statehood was not in itself a sufficient benefit to justify the cost of dissolution of the USSR. Russian elites (and masses) therefore expected the new state to be based on different principles, in domestic politics and in relations with other states. This search for fundamentally different principles for domestic and foreign policy brought elites into conflict. However, domestic conflict over basic policy questions was seen as unavoidable, because the elites in power were convinced that continuing existing policies presented a greater danger. This perception has persisted. Egor Stroev, chair of the Council of the Federation (upper house of parliament) and one of Russia's more centrist politicians, stated in 1997 that "[s]tability today is not support of the status quo. It is anticipation of potential dangers, countering existing dangers, and support of everything that is working constructively" (1997, 4).

In addition to mixed feelings about the achievement of "independence," many Russian elites had a firm belief in the failure of the Soviet system, including its foreign relations. The source of this belief can be found in historical experience. Russia's dominant position in the Soviet Union, and the familiarity of Russian elites such as Boris Yeltsin, Egor Gaidar, Anatolii Chubais, Andrei Kozyrev, as well as more centrist figures such as Viktor Chernomyrdin, with the severe economic and political problems of the Soviet system they had inherited caused them to frame issues in terms of a drastic need for change. For example, after becoming prime minister, Chernomyrdin wrote: "We are all people of one generation and one upbringing, we grew up and received our education under a strictly centralized system, in which everything was done from the top, and we carried out [the decisions]. Today we can't behave in that way, it is necessary to seriously reconsider some of our views and approaches. . . . The failure of the oil industry [in which Chernomyrdin spent much of his career] began in 1987 . . ." (1993, 8–9).

This sense of the failure of the USSR's system and the need to create something completely different in the "new" Russia was complemented by a greater degree of direct and detailed knowledge about the experiences of states in the rest of the world. This directed the attention of the new Russian elites to models such as Poland, Czechoslovakia, Western Europe, Japan, and North America.

According to my theoretical expectations, therefore, Russian foreign policy preferences should be likely to change. Soviet autarky and the militarization of foreign relations, economics, and society were considered a failure. The USSR had fallen behind other great powers due to its isolation—economic isolation in particular. This foreign policy played a major role in the failure of the Soviet state. If those policies were continued, they would lead to even more dramatic failure, such as the collapse of the Russian state. With this experience of major failure, clearly my hypotheses predict that Russian foreing policy preferences will change, either by simple inversion for dichotomous choices (H2) or guided by additional information possibly supplied by imitation of foreign successes (H3). Also, according to this interpretation, Russian elites could be said to be in the domain of losses, and the domain of expected losses, and therefore relatively risk acceptant according to prospect theory (see chapter 3). Imitation was likely not only due to the need for additional information, but also due to the psychological impact of failure and expected continued failure if there were no change. Ukrainian elites can be seen as in the domain of gains as described by prospect theory, and therefore risk averse.

Relations with other states had to be radically recast. Assuming that the choices Russia faced were complex, recognition of past failure was insufficient to determine new foreign policy preferences. Examples of success were readily available in successful western states and east European reformers. These models would cause Russia to tend to refashion its foreign policy along liberal lines.

COMPARING UKRAINE AND RUSSIA

This chapter uses the same data set employed in chapter 4. If the data are examined separately by country, 18.8 percent of Russian observations have liberal preferences, 69.6 percent have political preferences, and 11.6 percent have realist preferences. For Ukrainian observations, the distribution is 13.9 percent liberal, 51.9 percent political, and 29.1 percent realist. The mean value of preferences for Russia is -0.0448; for Ukraine it is 0.1733. Consistent with my expectations, Russian elites are indeed more "liberal" than their Ukrainian counterparts in their foreign policy views.[1]

Due to the relatively small sample sizes of the data sets for each country, not all of the analyses undertaken for the pooled data in chapter 4 can be employed here. In particular, I use binary variables as in equation 6 (table 4.2), rather than the ordinal variables in equations 1–5 (table 4.1). This allows for all observations to be included in the analysis, even if it may dilute the effect of the "analogy" variables by coding missing values as "0"s (see chapter 4 for a discussion of this).

The results for the ordered probit estimation of effects on foreign policy preferences for Russian and Ukrainian elites are presented in tables 5.1 and

5.2, respectively. Table 5.1 indicates that the relationships within the data are basically consistent with my expectations for Russian elites. However, Ukrainian elites do not conform well to my overall expectations. In fact, the effect of Observed Success is *more* pronounced among Ukrainian elites than among Russian elites. This presents a challenge to my expectations about the results of schematic learning from formative events. I examine this in more detail, after a general discussion of the results in these two equations.

Overall, the coefficients for the "Realist" and "Liberal" analogy variables in equation 7 (table 5.1), including Russian elites only, are all of the predicted sign ("Political" variables do not have a predicted sign). The equation correctly predicts very nearly 70 percent of foreign policy preferences. The variables achieving a statistically significant effect on preferences among Russian elites are "Realist" analogies to Direct Failure and "Liberal" analogies to Observed Success. As my interpretation of Russian "formative events" would lead me to expect, analogies to Direct Success do not achieve statistical significance when controlling for Observed Success and Direct Failure.

Given the negative lessons I think Russians learned about autarky and "primacy of force." Realist-type policies, the statistically significant effect of "Liberal" lessons of foreign success is consistent with my expectations. The

Table 5.1 Ordered probit estimation of effects on preferences: Russia (equation 7)

Variable	Coefficient[a]	Standard error	Z	Significance
Direct Failure				
Realist	**1.205**	0.644	1.872	$p < 0.05$[b]
Political	0.657	0.449	1.461	$p = 0.144$
Liberal	−0.548	0.631	−0.868	$p = 0.193$[b]
Observed Success				
Realist	1.555	1.237	1.257	$p = 0.105$[b]
Political	0.418	0.438	0.954	$p = 0.340$
Liberal	**−0.912**	0.658	−1.385	$p < 0.10$[a]
Direct Success				
Realist	0.976	1.301	0.750	$p = 0.227$[b]
Political	−0.608	0.489	−1.244	$p = 0.214$
Liberal	−0.601	0.774	−0.776	$p = 0.219$[a]
Observed Failure				
Realist	1.033	0.809	1.277	$p = 0.101$[b]
Political	−0.428	0.692	−0.619	$p = 0.536$
Control Variables				
Time	0.014	0.009	1.566	$p = 0.117$
Year of birth	0.031	0.021	1.490	$p = 0.136$
Correctly predicted[c] = 69.57%				

Notes

[a] Bold type indicates statistically significant coefficient.

[b] One-tailed test.

[c] Predicted probability of 0.530 or greater used to calculate predictions for the three possible values of preferences (variable Prefsord).

$N = 61$.

significant effect of "Realist" lessons of Direct Failure is consistent with my expectations in that Russians do recognize their own state's failed foreign policies as lessons. However, I would have expected those lessons to point toward "Political" or "Liberal" policies as remedies, not toward realism. But this result is not necessarily problematic for two reasons.

First, my theory involves an interaction effect between lessons of Direct Failure and lessons of Observed Success. Direct Failure leads to an awareness of the need for policy changes. Policy prescriptions are hypothesized to come from imitation, not directly from the lessons of failure that lead to a search for alternatives. If this is the case, then including "Liberal" lessons under both Direct Failure and Observed Success in the same equation gives an estimate of which of the two is more reliably related to preferences. But the two variables should be closely related. Indeed, if the Observed Success "Liberal" variable is dropped from the equation, then the Direct Failure "Liberal" variable does become statistically significant (coefficient $= -0.840$, $p < 0.05$, $Z = -1.439$). At the same time, none of the variables for Direct Success becomes significant. This does support my contentions about the Russian "schema."

Second, "Realist" lessons of Direct Failure may be related to Russian reactions to policy failures after the formative period, for example due to the process of NATO expansion or Russia's loss of influence globally. This interpretation is also supported by the relatively strong effect that the passage of time (Time) has on preferences among Russian elites. One avenue for further research would be to conduct a case study of Russian military security policy to investigate which lessons were salient at what time. For the purposes of this chapter, however, I must leave this question open. I now discuss the control variables.

Due to the positive sign of the coefficient for Time, it appears that, as time passes, Russian preferences become more "Realist." Interestingly, just as in the pooled data overall, year of birth (YOB) is positively associated with preferences. In other words, all other things being equal, the younger an elite, the more "Realist" are his preferences. Neither Time nor YOB achieves statistical significance at the 90 percent level, but each approaches that level, and the results seem substantively significant. The positive coefficient for YOB is consistent across all equations in chapters 4 and 5. The effect of the passage of time, on the other hand, appears more important in Russia than in Ukraine (see table 5.2). For Ukrainian elites, the coefficient for Time is negative, but it does not approach statistical significance ($p = 0.445$).

In general, Ukrainian elites seem less "obedient" to my hypotheses about them than were Russian elites (table 5.2). Nevertheless, with the exception of "Realist" lessons of Direct Failure, all of the coefficients for "Realist" and "Liberal" lessons are in the predicted direction. The model is not as good a predictor of preferences as was the case in Russia, with 63 percent of Ukrainian elites' preferences correctly predicted.

Most obviously, Ukrainians seem to be *more* prolific imitators than their Russian counterparts. Both "Realist" and "Liberal" lessons of Observed

Success are statistically significant. This directly contradicts my hypothesized effects of "formative events." Further, no lesson of Direct Success achieves statistical significance; again, this is directly in contradiction to my expectations. Clearly, whatever qualifications can be introduced to explain or modify these results, the effect of my particular expectations about Ukrainian "schematic learning" from formative events is not as powerful in these data as I had hypothesized.

Regarding the control variables, as noted above the passage of time seems to have little effect on Ukrainian preferences. But the effect of age, as in the case of Russia and in all other equations in chapter five, is somewhat surprising. The younger the foreign policy elite, the more likely he is to tend toward the "Realist" pole in his preferences. In Ukraine, this effect is statistically significant. This *may* be explained by a generational effect. The achievement of Ukrainian independence came during the formative years of younger elites (born after 1939), while older elites came of age during the period of Khrushchev's "thaw" or Brezhnev's "razriadka" (détente) (see Zimmerman [1969] and Lynch [1987] for discussion of the foreign policy views dominant in these periods). Thus, controlling for analogy use and the passage of time, young Ukrainian elites are more affected by the "realist" lessons of the

Table 5.2 Ordered probit estimation of effects on preferences: Ukraine (equation 8)

Variable	Coefficient[a]	Standard error	Z	Significance
Direct Failure				
Realist	−0.198	0.478	−0.415	$p = 0.339$[b]
Political	0.144	0.390	0.368	$p = 0.713$
Liberal	−1.412	0.639	−2.209	$p < 0.05$[b]
Observed Success				
Realist	1.745	0.908	1.922	$p < 0.05$[b]
Political	0.138	0.346	0.400	$p = 0.689$
Liberal	−1.088	0.499	−2.178	$p < 0.05$[b]
Direct Success				
Realist	0.446	0.785	0.568	$p = 0.285$[b]
Political	0.142	0.397	0.357	$p = 0.721$
Liberal	−0.741	1.020	−0.727	$p = 0.234$[b]
Observed Failure				
Realist	0.850	0.422	2.014	$p < 0.05$[b]
Political	2.396	0.769	3.113	$p < 0.005$
Control Variables				
Time	−0.005	0.007	−0.764	$p = 0.445$
Year of birth	0.048	0.023	2.092	$p < 0.05$
Correctly predicted[c] = 63.29%				

Notes

[a] Bold type indicates statistically significant coefficient.

[b] One-tailed test.

[c] Predicted probability of 0.485 or greater used to calculate predictions for the three possible values of preferences (variable Prefsord).

$N = 71$.

drive for independence than their elder colleagues, whose basic views are influenced by experiences of their formative years.

Has my hypothesis about the effects of the formative experience of achieving national independence been falsified? Clearly it has to be admitted that the effects are not as pronounced as I had expected. But in the next section I dig deeper into the data on Russia and Ukraine to explore two possible qualifications to the proposition that the successful achievement of Ukrainian independence did not have the predicted effect on foreign policy preferences.

First, I divide the data from both states according to time period. This allows me to analyze relationships between types of lessons and between lessons and preferences during the actual formative period (1990–1992), and during the period following it (1993–1997) which can be considered one of "normal" rather than "revolutionary" politics. Second, I drop variables for lessons of Observed Failure from the model for both states. The reasons for doing this are that there are few cases of such analogies in either state, so outliers may drive the results, and there is little theoretical justification for their inclusion based on hypothesis 7 (chapter 3). Analogies to Observed Failure may be more rhetorical in their origins, and therefore more *caused by* policy preferences, than other types of analogies.

ANALOGY USE DURING AND AFTER
THE FORMATIVE PERIOD

A reasonable expectation based on the psychological concept of "recency" is that, as a formative event recedes into the past, its psychological effects will also weaken. Organizational theory, on the other hand, leads to an expectation that formative lessons will be institutionalized in standard operating procedures and organizational interests and culture. Therefore, while a state's policy may not diverge swiftly from preferences shaped by a formative event, the use of analogies by individuals may be quicker to change. This can be expected to happen if a significant amount of disconfirming evidence emerges indicating that the preferences resulting from a formative event may not be having the desired effect.

If this were the case, then the effects of the differing "formative events" of state-creation in Russia and Ukraine would likely be more pronounced in 1990–1992 than in 1993–1997. By January 1993 Russia and Ukraine had achieved some degree of stability, they had passed the anniversary of the fall of the USSR, and been recognized within their new borders by most of the world. The formative period can be considered to have passed, and a period of more "normal" politics—to borrow a metaphor from Thomas Kuhn—in which domestic and foreign policies are oriented toward state-building and state-maintenance, rather than state-creation, can be assumed to have begun.

Does analogy use by Russian and Ukrainian elites during the formative period conform to the expectations for the formative lessons I have developed?

Table 5.3   Direct Success over time

Direct Success	Time period		Total
	1990–1992	*1993–1997*	
Ukrainian elites			
Not used	5 (38.46%)	15 (23.08%)	20 (25.64%)
Used	8 (61.54%)	50 (76.92%)	58 (74.36%)
Total (column percentages)	13 (100%)	65 (100%)	78 (100%)
Pearson Chi-Square	1.345	$p = 0.246$	
Russian elites			
Not used	11 (57.89%)	9 (18.00%)	20 (28.99%)
Used	8 (42.11%)	41 (82.00%)	49 (71.01%)
Total	19 (100%)	50 (100%)	69 (100%)
Pearson Chi-Square	10.646	$p = 0.001$	

Table 5.4   Direct Failure over time

Direct Failure	Time period		Total
	1990–1992	*1993–1997*	
Ukrainian elites			
Not used	3 (23.08%)	23 (35.38%)	26 (33.33%)
Used	10 (76.92%)	42 (64.62%)	52 (66.67%)
Total (column percentages)	13 (100%)	65 (100%)	78 (100%)
Pearson Chi-Square	0.739	$p = 0.390$	
Russian elites			
Not used	2 (10.53%)	18 (36.00%)	20 (28.99%)
Used	17 (89.47%)	32 (64.00%)	49 (71.01%)
Total (column percentages)	19 (100%)	50 (100%)	69 (100%)
Pearson Chi-Square	4.340	$p = 0.037$	

In general, the earlier period does provide more supporting evidence for my expectations of the Ukrainian and Russian schemata than the later period.

In particular, Russian elites are much less likely to use analogies to Direct Success (table 5.3) in 1990–1992 than in 1993–1997 (chi-square= 10.646). In fact, 58 percent of the observations for Russia during the early period *did not* use analogies to Direct Success, while 62 percent of Ukrainian observations *did* use such analogies. In Ukraine, the tendency to use analogies to Direct Success does not change significantly over time (chi-square = 1.345), while in Russia the change is dramatic.

A different progression can be seen regarding usage of analogies to Direct Failure over time (table 5.4). In 1990–1992, Russian elites are highly likely to use such analogies (89 percent do so), while in Ukraine references to Direct Failure are likely, but not as likely (77 percent). Over time in Ukraine this pattern does not change dramatically (chi-square = 0.739), while in

Table 5.5   Observed Success over time

Observed Success	Time period		Total
	1990–1992	*1993–1997*	
Ukrainian elites			
Not used	6(46.15%)	27(41.54%)	33(42.31%)
Used	7(53.85%)	38(58.46%)	45(57.69%)
Total (column percentages)	13(100%)	65(100%)	78(100%)
Pearson Chi-Square	0.0945	$p = 0.758$	
Russian elites			
Not used	7(36.84%)	26(52.00%)	33(47.83%)
Used	12(63.16%)	24(48.00%)	36(52.17%)
Total (column percentages)	19(100%)	50(100%)	69(100%)
Pearson Chi-Square	1.2678	$p = 0.260$	

Russia the percentage drop (25 percent, $p = 0.037$) in usage of Direct Failure is more than double that in Ukraine (12 percent, $p = 0.390$). After 1992, Russian elites seem to be guided less by lessons of their own state's failure, and to pay more attention to their successes. This corresponds to a general shift in Russian foreign policy at the end of 1992 noted by many analysts (e.g., Dawisha and Parrott 1994, 205).

Finally, use of analogies to Observed Success is more likely in Russia in the early period: 63 percent of observations contain such analogies, while only 54 percent of observations in Ukraine do. In the later period, the situation is nearly reversed: 58 percent of Ukrainian observations use Observed Success, while only 48 percent of Russian observations do.

To sum up, during 1990–1992 Russian elites are more likely to refer to Direct Failure and to Observed Success. In the same period, Ukrainian elites are more likely to refer to Direct Success. Thus analogy usage by Russian and Ukrainian elites during this period is indeed largely consistent with my expectations based on their respective "formative events" and "schemata" discussed in chapter 4. During the period 1993–1997, the structure of Ukrainian analogy usage changes little, while it changes rather dramatically in Russia.

The average value of preferences, and its change over time, also corresponds to these observations. In Ukraine, the average value of preferences, measured on the scale from -2 to 2, in 1990–1992 is 0.08, and from 1993–1997 it is 0.18. In Russia, the value for 1990–1992 is -0.16, and in 1993–1997 it is 0.00. While foreign policy preferences in both states move towards the "realist" pole over time, those of Ukrainian elites begin closer to the pole than do those of Russian elites. This corresponds to my expectations in that Russians appear to be most affected by the "liberal" schema resulting from the formative event of the fall of the USSR closer to that event, while Ukrainians are on average always on the "realist" side of the continuum, as predicted by the "realist" content of Ukraine's formative experience. Thus there is at least some evidence that Ukrainians are affected by the formative event of independence as my framework anticipates. They continue to refer to Direct Success throughout the period 1990–1997, and their foreign policy preferences are consistent with its lessons.

It is also interesting to note that the passage of time, and therefore presumably events after the fall of the USSR, encourage elites in both states to move closer to realist foreign policy preferences. Such events might include NATO expansion, wars and interventions in the former Yugoslavia, and increasing perceptions of U.S. hegemony based on the Gulf War, the war in Kosovo, and the booming U.S. economy in the 1990s.

DROPPING "OF"

There are only 34 observations using analogies to Observed Failure in the pooled data, considerably less than half the frequency of usage of the other analogy types. Twenty of these are among Ukrainian elites and 13 among Russian elites. This low rate of usage is consistent with the fact that neither cognitive nor organizational factors provide a theoretical basis for expecting Observed Failure to be an important form of analogical reasoning (hypothesis 7, chapter 3). Variables representing Observed Failure achieved statistical significance in equations 2 and 8, but not in equations 6 or 7. Dropping them from the model can therefore be justified on theoretical and empirical

Table 5.6 Ordered probit estimation of effects on preferences: Russia (drop "OF") (equation 9)

Variable	Coefficient[a]	Standard error	Z	Significance
Direct Failure				
Realist	**1.139**	0.623	1.829	$p < 0.05$[b]
Political	0.623	0.444	1.403	$p = 0.161$
Liberal	−0.462	0.613	−0.753	$p = 0.226$[b]
Observed Success				
Realist	1.470	1.216	1.210	$p = 0.113$[b]
Political	0.319	0.420	0.758	$p = 0.448$
Liberal	**−0.963**	0.621	−1.550	$p < 0.10$[b]
Direct Success				
Realist	0.999	1.278	0.782	$p = 0.217$[b]
Political	−0.501	0.461	−1.087	$p = 0.277$
Liberal	−0.611	0.758	−0.806	$p = 0.210$[b]
Control Variables				
Time	**0.015**	0.009	1.655	$p < 0.10$
Year of birth	**0.035**	0.020	1.760	$p < 0.10$
Correctly Predicted[c] = 68.12%				

Notes
[a] Bold type indicates statistically significant coefficient
[b] One-tailed test
[c] Predicted probability of 0.530 or greater used to calculate predictions for the 3 possible values of preferences (variable Prefsord)
$N = 61$.

Table 5.7 Ordered probit estimation of effects on preferences: Ukraine (drop "OF") (equation 10)

Variable	Coefficient[a]	Standard error	Z	Significance
Direct Failure				
Realist	0.197	0.441	0.448	$p = 0.327$[b]
Political	0.035	0.371	0.094	$p = 0.481$
Liberal	**−1.180**	0.606	−1.949	$p < 0.05$[b]
Observed Success				
Realist	**1.640**	0.940	1.745	$p < 0.05$[b]
Political	−0.071	0.329	−0.217	$p = 0.828$
Liberal	−0.522	0.449	−1.161	$p = 0.123$[b]
Direct Success				
Realist	**1.039**	0.763	1.361	$p < 0.10$[b]
Political	0.430	0.380	1.130	$p = 0.258$
Liberal	−0.721	0.934	−0.772	$p = 0.220$[b]
Control variables				
Month	0.005	0.007	−0.704	$p = 0.481$
Year of birth	**0.025**	0.021	1.232	$p = 0.218$
Correctly predicted[c] = 56.69%				

Notes
[a] Bold type indicates statistically significant coefficient.
[b] One-tailed test.
[c] Predicted probability of 0.485 or greater used to calculate predictions for the three possible values of preferences (variable Prefsord).
$N = 71$.

grounds, with the proviso that the performance of these variables is something for which my theory has a hard time accounting.

If analogies to Observed Failure are dropped from the model, the results fit somewhat better with the expectations of the hypothesized Ukrainian schema. Preferences of Russian elites are again most influenced by "Liberal" lessons of Observed Success, "Realist" lessons of Direct Failure, as well as by the age of the policy maker and the passage of time (table 5.6). Lessons of Direct Success do not achieve statistical significance in this model. But, in spite of using fewer variables, the predictive power of the model is very nearly as good as the model in table 5.1. About 68 percent of preferences are accounted for.

Among Ukrainian elites, "Realist" lessons of Observed Success, "Liberal" lessons of Direct Failure, and "Realist" lessons of Direct Success achieve statistical significance (table 5.7). Of particular relevance to my expectations is the importance of lessons of Direct Success to Ukrainians, but not to Russians. These analogies are used very frequently by Ukrainians throughout the period 1990–1997, while Russians are much less likely to use this type of analogy during the formative period 1990–1992 (table 5.3). In Ukraine the impact on preferences is statistically significant, in Russia it is not. This is indeed consistent with a Russian schema focused on the lessons of the failure to preserve the Union and a Ukrainian schema based on the success of achieving statehood.

This model predicts 57 percent of preferences, a drop of more than 6 percent from the model including Observed Failure (table 5.2).

CONCLUSIONS

This chapter has established that the structure of analogy use and preferences of Russian elites does conform to expectations based on the formative events of the fall of the USSR and the emergence of the Russian Federation. Imitation and Direct Failure have an impact on preferences, while experiences of Direct Success do not. Although Ukrainian elites are apparently more prone to be influenced by observational learning (success and failure) than I would expect, a closer look at the data gives reason to suspect that experience of Direct Success—the successful achievement of independence— has a significant impact on Ukrainian preferences. This impact may be more potent during the formative period of 1990–1992, than later.

Chapter 6 further explores the hypotheses regarding state-level learning, and regarding differences between Russia and Ukraine, through a comparative case study of the sources of economic security preferences in each state.

CHAPTER 6

CASE STUDIES: FOREIGN CAPITAL
AND "STRATEGIC" ENTERPRISE
PRIVATIZATION

This chapter builds on the results in chapter 5 by examining state-level policy outcomes. I focus on policy and practice regarding foreign investment in large enterprise privatization in Ukraine and Russia, 1990–1999. The privatization (denationalization) of major industrial assets represents a fundamental economic policy choice. The decision whether or not to allow foreign capital to participate in this process represents a fundamental *foreign policy* choice. This chapter seeks to explain what seems a puzzling fact: since the fall of the USSR, Russia has had a greater preference than Ukraine for foreign ownership of large enterprises, including "strategic" enterprises designated as important for national security.

This is contrary to reasonable expectations based on military threat or perception of threat (i.e., Ukraine's desire to build relationships with other powers to balance perceived threat from Russia; traditional hostility between Russia and "the West"), and economic interests (i.e., Russia's greater capability for self-sufficiency). I advance an explanation for this based on my theory of imitation in foreign policy. Case study method provides two advantages that are complementary to the analyses in preceding chapters. First, it allows me to directly assess the process and outcome of decision-making at the state level in some detail. This should give a clearer picture of the causal role of learning and imitation. And second, it allows me to examine a number of contextually rich competing explanations for these outcomes in comparative perspective.

As discussed in chapter 1, Ukraine and Russia are appropriate for comparison because of their similarity across a number of important economic and social variables (tables 1.1 and 1.2). They have similar levels of industrial development and structure (Goskomstat 1991, 37), a similar history within the Soviet planned economic system, political and economic elites with similar education and professional experience (Burg 1990; Rigby 1990), and especially relevant here, similar post-Soviet economic crises and similar levels of corruption (Transparency International 1999). Russia and Ukraine also contain the bulk of the former Soviet military–industrial complex. The Ural Mountains area, St. Petersburg and Leningrad Region, Moscow and Moscow Region, and other parts of European Russia were home to most Soviet defense enterprises. But Ukraine contained about 25 percent of the USSR's military industry (Larsen 1997, 21). Kyiv, Kharkiv, Dnipropetrovsk, L'viv, and Mikolaiv regions were major centers of military production including aircraft, tanks, ships, missiles, radar, and military computers (Albrecht 1993).

These similarities allow for a degree of quasi-experimental control that in practice is rare in comparative case studies (Kaarbo and Beasley 1999). Variation in policies between Ukraine and Russia must be due to factors other than these constants. Following George and McKeown's (1985) guidelines for "structured, focused comparison," I ask questions about the privatization process in each case, with particular attention to how the list of "strategic" large enterprises exempt from privatization was defined and revised. Related issues of government-led marketing efforts to attract foreign investment and the creation of a legal and institutional infrastructure to facilitate foreign investment is also examined. These factors operationalize the dependent variable, economic security preferences. The process of large-enterprise privatization, related economic and security interests, leaders' analogy usage and related policy arguments serve as independent variables. I also question whether my preferred causal argument is spurious. Can the dependent and several independent variables be explained by differences in constitutional power-sharing provisions, as some authors have suggested?

The chapter is organized as follows. A section describing the dynamics of foreign participation in privatization in general is followed by an overview of economic reform in Ukraine and Russia. The issue of foreign investment in major enterprises is then examined for each case. A variety of plausible explanations for differences between the cases is then discussed, based mainly on hypotheses suggested by other authors who examine only one or the other case. Finally, I present my preferred explanation and use statements by key Ukrainian and Russian decision makers as supporting evidence. While competing explanations seem convincing when applied only to one or the other state, they encounter major obstacles when applied to both.

THE POLITICS OF PRIVATIZATION AND FOREIGN INVESTMENT

The "privatization" of state-owned enterprises has become a common aspect of public policy. FDI has also been growing rapidly in the wake of a global trend of liberalization (Bende-Nabende 1999; Chan 1995; UNCTAD 1995). The Thatcher government in the United Kingdom is usually considered the originator of the privatization trend, although Chile also was an early practitioner (Donahue 1989). In the United States, privatization often has meant running state-owned bureaucracies as if they were private enterprises (e.g., the U.S. Postal Service), or devolving government functions to private contractors. In more statist economies, privatization involves the sale of state-owned enterprises to private buyers (Donahue 1989, 6–8). The latter process is the type of privatization examined here.

I argue that such privatization necessarily presents the state with a dilemma, or *trade-off*, involving important national security questions. Many states have faced the "guns or butter" choice between military security and economic efficiency. This choice is usually framed as one between control of important assets, often necessary for military production or the functioning of society, and the vital need for productive, efficient use of resources in a competitive world.

The trade-off between security and efficiency is amplified when foreign ownership is involved. Foreign investment in privatization has been a feature of recent economic reforms from Hungary to Ghana. It can easily attract public resistance. The impression that the state is "giving away the store" to economic, political, or military competitors can require that policy makers possess strong political will to follow through.

For example, in the 1980s protest over the sale of two divisions of the British Leyland Motor Company to foreign buyers forced the deal's cancellation. "There was opposition even from Conservative MPs, led by former Prime Minister . . . Heath . . ." (Letwin 1988, 55). The privatization of British Gas led to claims that "a unique strategic asset" was being let go. A Labour Party official argued in 1985 that "[o]nly public enterprise can give Britain strategic control. . . . Without it we would have no domestically-owned company in . . . motor-vehicle and aero-engine building, ship building and computers" (cited in Letwin 1988, 56–57). In 1999, deals to sell large blocs of shares to foreign companies in a Romanian steel plant, a Lithuanian oil refinery, and a Finnish shipping company all met with strong public resistance (*The Economist* 10/30/99, 74; *RFE/RL* 11/15/99). The trade-off between major foreign investment and traditional concepts of national security is manifest and tangible for leaders facing such choices. During the economic reorientation of the 1990s, both Ukrainian and Russian leaders faced such fundamental foreign policy choices.

ECONOMIC REFORMS IN UKRAINE AND RUSSIA, 1991–1999

In October 1991, Russian President Boris Yeltsin outlined a comprehensive program of reform, the main author of which was Egor Gaidar (Aslund 1995; Gaidar 1996). The program of Gaidar and his economic team was largely modeled on Polish reforms (a.k.a., the "big bang" or "shock therapy") begun in 1989. "Following the Polish experience . . . the first [Russian] economic program [anticipated]: deregulation . . . financial and monetary stabilization . . . privatization . . . creation of a social safety net . . . structural adjustment—demilitarization of industry, integration into world trade . . ." (Kuboniwa and Gavrilenkov 1997, 4; see also Aslund 1995,

63, 83; Remington 1999, 44). In January 1992, most prices and trade were liberalized. In June, the Supreme Soviet (parliament) passed framework privatization legislation. But backsliding on reform due to political resistance was evident by April (Aslund 1995, 54).

Although the program of mass-privatization, or the transfer of state assets to the general population, continued under the direction of Anatolii Chubais, a key member of Gaidar's team, other policies were defeated or diluted. The loose monetary policy of central banker Viktor Gerashchenko, appointed by the parliament, undermined macroeconomic stabilization. In December, after the parliament failed to support his candidacy, Gaidar was removed as acting prime minister. Yeltsin then proposed Viktor Chernomyrdin, and he was easily confirmed.

Chernomyrdin had strong ties to the Russian energy sector and was often associated with the industrial lobby. He is credited with transforming the Soviet Oil and Gas Industry Ministry—which he headed from 1985—into "Gazprom," Russia's largest company. He had expressed only harsh criticism for privatization, comparing Chubais's program to collectivization under Stalin in one speech. But Chernomyrdin abandoned public opposition to privatization after reportedly being reprimanded by Yeltsin (Aslund 1995, 255; Boycko, Shleifer, and Vishny 1996, 85).

In 1993, with parliament's approval, state support for industry in the form of credits and subsidies was renewed (Boycko, Shleifer, and Vishny 1996, 6). However, Yeltsin brought Gaidar back into the government. The conflict between executive and legislative power in Russia came to a head in a violent confrontation in early October. Although the parliamentary leader Ruslan Khasbulatov and his ally, Vice President Aleksandr Rutskoi, were clearly opposed to Yeltsin's rule in general, it is also clear that Yeltsin's economic policies were among the most important specific reasons for the confrontation (e.g., Remington 1999, 44–45).

From January 1994 through April 1998 Chernomyrdin and the various cabinets he headed continued the basic policies put in place by Gaidar and his team, although their execution was inconsistent, and the original time-frame and scope of the program were retrenched. By 1995 a degree of stabilization had been achieved.[1] Inflation fell to 10.9 percent in 1997, which was also the first year of economic growth, albeit only at a rate of 0.8 percent (EBRD 1999). Chernomyrdin's government undertook a concerted effort at further market reforms, including anti-monopoly policy and reducing subsidies to utilities (Remington 1999, 203–204). In spite of the collapse of the ruble and general crisis in 1998, by 1999 growth had been restored to Russia's troubled economy.

The focus in newly independent Ukraine in 1991 was on market reform and on achieving "economic independence" (e.g., Shen 1996, chapters 2–4) from Moscow. Ukraine took a major step toward separating itself from the Soviet integrated economy with the transformation of the administrative Council of Ministers into the Ukrainian Cabinet of Ministers in April. The Supreme Rada (parliament) chose Vitold Fokin as Prime Minister. His declared intention was to dismantle the "command-administrative leadership, on which market relations get smashed to smithereens. . . ." Fokin, previously the head of the republican economic planning agency Ukrderzhplan, set out to implement the economic aspects of the recent Ukrainian declaration of state sovereignty by suspending a Soviet presidential decree's validity in Ukraine, and supporting resolutions prohibiting export of various products from Ukraine (*Izvestiia* 4/19/91).

Although the Fokin government did liberalize some prices in July 1992, most were not freed from state control; monetary emissions and especially extensions of credits to enterprises were not reduced even to the limited extent achieved in Russia. The result was wage and price inflation and a severe weakening of the Ukrainian coupon (an interim currency). Vice-Premier and Minister of Economics Volodymyr Lanovyy, then the country's senior official with a reputation as a market reformer, threatened to resign in protest of the lack of genuine economic change. When asked if President Leonid Kravchuk had expressed support, he answered "I did not receive the President's support" (*Nezavisimaia gazeta* 7/9/92).

In September 1992 Kravchuk announced Fokin's resignation, called for accelerating "radical economic reforms based on privatization and destatization," and implored legislators to unite "efforts to overcome the economic crisis, strengthen executive power and national security" (*Nezavisimaia gazeta* 10/1/92). The new government of Prime Minister Leonid Kuchma included three prominent market economists. However, Kravchuk accepted Kuchma's resignation less than a year later, not long after Kuchma had submitted his reform program to the Rada (Shen 1996, 55).

Small-scale privatization was accomplished during Kravchuk's presidency. However, other reforms were not undertaken until Kuchma became president in July 1994. Most prices and trade were then liberalized (Ash 1999). As was the case in Russia, these changes encountered strong political resistance and were modified and diluted over time. "[E]ager not to create a fissure [in] society, President Kuchma . . . sought to steer a centrist reform track. The pace of economic reform [was] moderate" (Ash 1999).[2]

Ukraine did achieve a degree of macroeconomic stabilization in 1995, and in 1996 introduced its own currency, the *hryvna*. However, privatization of medium and large enterprises was not accomplished as planned (Ash 1999). While, by 1999, 70 percent of Russia's GDP was privately produced, only 55 percent of Ukraine's production was in private hands. Russia was rated significantly higher on large-scale privatization than Ukraine, and had had more success in most areas related to market transformation (table 6.1). From 1994 through 1997, privatization revenues as a percentage of GDP were on average over twice as high in Russia as in Ukraine (table 6.2).

During the period in question, the decade from 1990–1999, neither state received a very large amount of foreign investment. For example, Poland attracted higher absolute levels of foreign direct investment (FDI) than Ukraine and Russia combined for the years 1993–1996, 1998. Nevertheless there were considerable differences between Ukrainian and Russian policies

Table 6.1   Aspects of reform relevant to privatization: EBRD ratings

	% GDP private	Cumulative progress: large-scale privatization	Trade and foreign exch.	Competition policy	Financial institutions*
Russia	70	3+	2+	2+	2/2−
Ukraine	55	2+	3−	2	2/2
Estonia	70	4	4	3−	3+/3
Moldova	45	3	4	2	2+/2
Poland	65	3+	4+	3	3+/3+
Hungary	80	4	4+	3	4/3+
Czech Republic	75	4	4+	3	3/3

Note: Russia's scores are lower than in previous periods due to policy reversals in banking, securities, price liberalisation, and trade and foreign exchange resulting from the 1998 financial crisis.

The scores ranging from 1 through 4+ rank each sector on a continuum running from no change from planned economy structure (1) to "standards and performance typical of advanced industrial economies" (4+).
* Financial Institution indicators are represented with dual scores, the first is "Banking reform and interest rate liberalisation" and the second is "Securities and non-bank financial institutions" scores.

Source: EBRD 1998.

Table 6.2   Privatization revenues as percent of GDP (private sector share of GDP as percentage given in parentheses)

	1994	1995	1996	1997	Average, 1994–1997
Russia	0.11	0.38	0.12	0.90	0.38
	(50)	(55)	(60)	(70)	
Ukraine	0.21	0.13	0.25	0.13	0.18
	(30)	(34)	(40)	(50)	

Source: Adapted from EBRD 1998, 187, 197.

Table 6.3   Total annual and cumulative foreign direct investment inflows (millions of U.S. dollars; per capita in parentheses in U.S. dollars)

	1993	1994	1995	1996	1997	1998
Russia	1,211 (8.2)	640 (4.3)	2,016 (13.6)	2,479 (16.8)	6,243 (42.4)	2,183 (14.9)
Ukraine	200 (3.8)	159 (3.1)	267 (5.2)	521 (10.2)	624 (12.3)	743 (14.8)

Cumulative FDI inflows per capita, 1993–1998: Russia $100.20; Ukraine $49.31.

Source: Adapted from United Nations Conference on Trade and Development (UNCTAD). *World Investment Report 1999*. Geneva: United Nations, 1999, 480 (FDI figures); European Bank for Reconstruction and Development (EBRD). *Transition Report Update. April 1999*, 67, 72 (population figures).

and investment levels. Ukraine received slightly less than half the *per capita* FDI that Russia did in 1993–1998 (table 6.3). I now turn to a detailed examination of privatization and foreign investment in each state's major enterprises.

FOREIGN INVESTMENT IN MAJOR ENTERPRISES
CASE 1: UKRAINE

Even before the fall of the USSR, there was some support for privatization among top officials of the Ukrainian Communist Party. At least in part, privatization was seen as a tool to diminish Moscow's role in Ukraine's economy. However, Ukrainian leaders also expressed reservations about military conversion and "boundless" privatization plans (e.g., Hurenko 1991, 6, 9).

In response to Moscow's attempt to create a USSR State Property Fund (*Pravda* 5/17/91), Ukraine took control of all Union-level enterprises and organizations on its territory and declared Moscow's directives on ownership of Ukrainian entities to have "no legal force and . . . not to be carried out." Prime Minister Fokin's cabinet issued a special statute and he "informed the [Rada] Deputies that Union ministries . . . have begun . . . knocking together joint-stock companies out of their enterprises, thereby preventing their transfer first to the republics' . . . ownership." There were 330 deputies voting in favor of revoking Moscow's authority and only one voting against (*Izvestiia* 6/7/91).

As mentioned, Ukraine had considerable success with small-scale privatization of retail and trade outlets (Ash 1999; Shvydanenko 1993, 17–24). It established a national State Property Fund (SPF) in 1992 to administer privatization. However, mass privatization, management-employee buyouts, and larger cash-based privatization projects were not implemented. Lanovyy characterized Fokin's privatization program as "the restoration of neo-socialist ways of looking at questions of property through collective forms" (*Nezavisimaia gazeta* 7/9/92). With few exceptions, Ukraine's medium and large enterprises remained wholly state property under President Kravchuk (1991–1994). This was not, however, due to a complete lack of interest in mass privatization or foreign investment.

In his 1993 budget address to the Rada, the president proposed that "privatization will be carried out on the basis of . . . an analysis . . . of individual sectors of the economy. This will . . . combine the privatization process with a structural reorganization and . . . the purposeful attraction of foreign investments. . . . [A]ll privileges will be gradually canceled and a course will be taken towards a gradual curtailment of state subsidies. . . ." (BBC SWB 11/15/93)

Kravchuk's emphasis was on a gradual change in the structure of Ukraine's economy. He placed importance on attracting foreign capital, but primarily as "purposeful" investment in certain sectors or enterprises. In July 1994 the program was completely suspended and revamped. In November, under President Kuchma, a new "voucher" program was introduced that proved more successful.

From the earliest days of Kuchma's reform program, there was pressure for the creation of financial–industrial groups (FIGs) (e.g., Moroz 1995, 3). In Ukraine (as in Russia) these proposed economic groupings were seen as attempts by state bureaucracies (mainly sectoral ministries) to maintain their economic functions, and consequent rights to budget resources (Remington 1999, 195; Zisk 1997, 67–69).

Ideas for the creation of FIGs sometimes incorporated plans for joint Russian-Ukrainian ownership of "multinational corporations" comprising enterprises previously linked within the Soviet economy. Oleksandr Razumkov, a top advisor to Kuchma, believed it was in Ukraine's interest to create FIGs combining Ukrainian and Russian enterprises. But the plans were not realized on the desired scale. In 1997, Razumkov reflected that "between Russia and Ukraine . . . non-state structures did not appear. . . . Some corporations did . . . in Kyiv . . . but they only undertook [limited] operations, not financial–industrial operations . . . We were not able to create a trans-national corporation . . . in areas like aeronautics, space, energy" (Interview 4/15/97). Ukrainian FIGs remained overwhelmingly domestic, state-owned structures.

Kuchma's mass-privatization program began in January 1995. The government declared that 8,000 companies of all sizes were to be sold in 1995. Only Ukrainian citizens or legal entities would be allowed to own privatization certificates redeemable for property (*The Financial Times* 8/30/95). The program was implemented slowly and unevenly. By the end of 1995, 25.7 million Ukrainians, only about half of the population, had claimed their certificates (ITAR-TASS 12/13/95).

Nevertheless, initial indications were that Ukraine might adopt a minimalist approach to restricting privatization in the name of security. Oleh Taranov, chair of the Rada's Committee on Economic Policy and also an economic advisor to Kuchma and former government official, announced in January that only 80 Ukrainian enterprises were on a privatization "blacklist" of firms designated to remain in state hands. All others were subject to the privatization program. The blacklisted enterprises were mainly arms manufacturers, but energy-related firms and key bread bakeries were also included. In addition, he indicated that some of the 80 firms might not be permanently banned from privatization. The number is especially low if one considers Taranov's claim that Ukraine had 2,000 defense industry enterprises (Intelnews 2/1/95). Other estimates of the size of the Ukrainian military industrial complex suggest that while there were 1,840 enterprises in the defense sector, only 700 produced exclusively for the military at the time of Ukrainian independence. By 1995, reportedly only about 100 of these were still producing weapons and other military goods (Larsen 1997, 21).

But Ukrainian industrial interests soon secured the inclusion of a wide range of enterprises on the blacklist. By August, the Rada had expanded the list to include 6,100 "strategic enterprises" exempt from privatization (*The Financial Times* 8/30/95). In addition, President Kuchma had by this time thrown his support behind the idea of FIGs modeled on, and even merging with, those in Russia (*The Financial Times* 10/30/95). In June 1995, Kuchma came out in favor of state credits to "strategic enterprises" designed to reverse GDP decline, which was 23 percent in 1994. These developments all effectively strengthened the position of the state sector (*The Financial Times* 11/4/95).

Another blow to the privatization program came in October 1995 when the Rada reduced the list of enterprises subject to mass-privatization by half, from 8,000 to 4,000, and halted the privatization of oil and gas industry firms (*The Financial Times* 11/4/95).

There is some indication that Ukrainian officials were interested in attracting foreign companies, as so-called "strategic investors," to specific investments in major enterprises not on the blacklist. However, security concerns moved to the fore in this process. In November 1995, Oleksandr Riabchenko, chair of the Rada Auditing Commission for Privatization, began to investigate privatizations involving "strategic investors" to ascertain "whether any strategic investor gained access to a restricted sector" (BBC SWB 11/25/95).

While the privatization blacklist had shrunk to 5,500 enterprises by November 1995, the Rada then added two new groups of enterprises. One group included 1,475 enterprises and the other 360; simultaneously, 224 enterprises were removed. Thus a total of 7,111 Ukrainian enterprises were excluded from privatization due to "national importance" (BBC SWB 11/25/95).

In 1996 a report from the U.S. Embassy in Kyiv assessed the position of foreign investors in Ukraine. While 7,308 medium and large enterprises had been partially privatized under the mass-privatization program, foreigners could participate only through intermediaries. They were legally prohibited from directly acquiring privatization certificates. The Rada's blacklist had effectively prevented foreigners from acquiring any shares in "thousands" of "strategic" companies in energy, communications, metallurgy, defense, and chemicals. These included "most of Ukraine's largest firms with the greatest export potential." Foreigners could legally acquire a controlling interest in any enterprise not on the Rada's list, but the process had proven difficult due to vague legislation and bureaucratic interference (Embassy of the United States, Kyiv 1996).

In April 1996 the Rada passed a foreign investment law similar to those in other former Soviet states. It was considered an improvement on three previous laws because it guaranteed registered foreigners treatment equal to that of domestic firms. Several priority sectors were designated for foreign investment including energy development, military conversion, agriculture, food processing, health care, telecommunications, transportation, information services, and banking (Embassy of the United States, Kyiv 1996). However, foreign investment in key enterprises remained difficult. In June 1996 the SPF announced that fourteen metallurgical enterprises were scheduled for privatization, with shares from 25 to 51 percent offered. But, after an attempt by the Rada to block sales of such "strategic enterprises" to foreign investors, the SPF announced that the state would retain controlling blocks of 51 percent or more in strategic firms (*The Mining Journal* 11/14/97).

In July, President Kuchma called for an acceleration of the privatization program (Kuchma 1996, 4). In early 1997 the proponents of privatization of major enterprises made a concerted effort to overcome the Rada's oppo-sition. Riabchenko announced that the ban on privatization of strategically important enterprises was expected to be lifted in April. His commission was preparing a new law "On . . . privatization of strategically important enter-prises" to replace the blacklist (BBC SWB 2/11/97).

At the same time Prime Minister Pavlo Lazarenko revived the idea of attract-ing "strategic" investors to selected sectors and enterprises not on the blacklist. He announced to an EBRD delegation that the government intended to com-plete planned sales of "strategic" enterprises in the first half of 1997. A list of 228 enterprises existed, and the state would retain no more than 26 percent of the shares (BBC SWB 2/21/97). However, for most of 1997 the State Property Fund languished without a director approved by the parliament. Acting director Volodymyr Lanoviy was unable to gain the Rada's approval after his appointment in March, and Oleksandr Bondar was only approved in the position in late October 1997 (RFE/RL 11/10/97, 10/23/98).

In the fall of 1997 further legal infrastructure was established to support foreign investment. The Cabinet of Ministers enacted a decree protecting foreign investors against expropriation, giving them the right to repatriate profits, and some exemptions from customs duties. A five-year exemption from the profits tax was also included for enterprises with foreign investment registered by 1995 (*The Mining Journal* 11/14/97). Potential "strategic" investors from Russia were especially encouraged. Meeting with Yeltsin in February 1998, Kuchma signed documents on economic cooperation and stated Ukraine's desire for increased investment by Russian businesses in the privatization of "strategic" enterprises in Ukraine. He stated that the Russian share of 7 percent of the total $2 billion of cumulative foreign investment in Ukraine was too low (Deutsche-Presse-Agentur 3/3/98).

The government planned to sell 14 of 25 energy distribution companies in 1998. However, following the victory of communist and other leftist candidates in Rada elections in April, Prime Minister Pustovoytenko ordered the SPF to cancel their sale. Although the official reason for this was lack of investor interest, during the election campaign leftist candidates had vigor-ously protested the cheap sell-off of the country's "strategic enterprises." By July 1998, only 9,600 of the 18,000 medium and large enterprises in the mass privatization program had been partially privatized (*West LB Country Profile:Ukraine* 1999).

The parliament's approach seemed to change in October 1998. The idea of attracting individual foreign investors to key projects again seemed to gain support. The Rada instructed the government to draw up a list of "strategic enterprises" in order to improve both government management and the pro-cedure for privatization of these enterprises (Info-Prod Research (Middle East) 10/13/98). In October the Rada finally agreed to the appointment of a new SPF head, Oleksandr Bondar. It was likely that the Rada was respond-ing to the serious economic crisis brought on by crisis in Russia. The gov-ernment needed funds in order to avoid default on its debt payments, support the *hryvna*, and address mounting wage and pension arrears.

In December, Serhiy Tyhypko, Deputy Prime Minister for Economic Affairs, announced that the government would give priority to "strategic" investors in large enterprises. According to Tyhypko, the Cabinet had taken this decision in the expectation that "privatizing a Ukrainian enterprise, such an investor can adapt it to its system." He announced that the major telecommunications company Ukrtelekom would be privatized by a strategic investor, who would then be required to invest in expanding the Ukrainian telephone system (UNIAN News Agency 12/5/98).

However, even with what seemed a new momentum for privatization of large enterprises driven by an immediate need for revenues, by February 1999 only 51 of 301 planned tenders had resulted in sales. The government placed blame on a lack of proper legislation and regulation. However, Bondar stated that the main reason was a lack of buyers. Tyhypko voiced his dissatisfaction with the SPF, noting its weak marketing efforts on behalf of Ukrainian strategic enterprises. According to Tyhypko, there were *no* presentations held abroad to attract strategic investors (UNIAN News Agency 2/2/99).

Then, in a major blow to large-enterprise privatization, in July 1999 the Rada failed to approve the government's plan to sell Ukrtelekom. As Timothy Ash observes, privatization had not moved to the major Ukrainian utilities by 1999. In assessing the causes of the general lack of progress in large-scale privatization, Ash noted the fine balance of power between president and parliament in the Ukrainian constitution. He also cited the priority placed by many Ukrainian politicians on "state-building," which led to the "fear that many of the privatized assets (particularly oil and gas pipelines) may be acquired by Russian investors, which will undermine the process of state building. The sale of strategic enterprises has thus often run into the opposition of an 'unholy' alliance of Ukrainian nationalists on the one hand, who fear domination by Russian investors, and left-wingers who oppose privatization in principle" (Ash 1999).

This case study brings several trends to light. Most obviously, the blacklist restricting privatization of major enterprises expanded in Ukraine to several times even the largest estimate of the size of the military–industrial complex. By late 1995 the list included 7,111 firms, while the most generous estimate of the military–industrial complex is 2,000 firms (and the most restrictive would be 100). Clearly, the definition of "strategic enterprise" in Ukraine has been broad and aimed at least in part at excluding foreign capital from most of Ukrainian industry. The major beneficiaries of this are likely to be the industrial sectoral ministries and managers of major state enterprises. They have retained control over valuable assets, as well as the ability to exploit those assets without outside scrutiny. They have also retained the state-centered system of enterprise administration which they are expert at manipulating, while avoiding independent audits, shareholder pressures, and other measures restricting autonomy that would accompany a market environment.

It is nevertheless also clear that there was some movement toward attracting foreign investment to major enterprises, especially after 1994. A legal and institutional framework to support such investment exists, but there has been only sporadic support from the president or government, usually in carefully chosen sectors of the economy. It appears that Ukrainian leaders sought to channel foreign capital to certain sectors, and protect other sectors. So-called "purposeful" investment was pursued during the administrations of both Kravchuk and Kuchma. As will become apparent, there was more of an emphasis on this strategy in Ukraine than in Russia.

It is telling of the limited enthusiasm for foreign investment that foreigners were not allowed to buy privatization certificates. Rather, potential foreign investors were required to seek Ukrainian partners who legally could buy certificates from the population. The absence of any evidence of a marketing effort by the SPF aimed at foreign capital is also striking.

Finally, it is clear that the Ukrainian parliament played an important role in limiting the privatization plan and in restricting participation in it through the blacklist. In Russia, the State Duma attempted to play a similar role, but was largely ineffective. This raises the possibility, noted by Ash (1999), that differences in policy and practice between Russia and Ukraine can be explained by differences in the constitutional division of power between executive and legislative branches. I return to these issues in the discussion section following examination of the Russian case.

CASE 2: RUSSIA

Russian laws and decrees in December 1990 and 1991 developed basic legal provisions for foreign investment (Aslund 1995, 229). In late 1991 Chubais was named to head the Russian State Property Committee and a Cabinet session discussed the basic principles of Russian privatization. In February and March of 1992, the first small-scale privatization auctions were undertaken and the process gained momentum.

In June 1992 a framework mass privatization program was approved by parliament, but passage involved a basic compromise with the industrial lobby and labor unions. "Insiders"—employees and especially managers— were given clear advantages in the privatization of their enterprises (Aslund 1995, 245; Zisk 1997, 29). Subsequently, all legal provisions for privatization were made through presidential decrees until June 1997, when the State Duma (the lower house of the Russian parliament established by the 1993 constitution) passed a law on cash-based privatization involving the sale of the remaining shares of medium and large enterprises through cash auctions.

As mentioned, Russia's overall economic reform plan was modeled on Polish reforms. But, Polish privatization through state-sponsored mutual funds had not enjoyed much success (Boycko, Shleifer, and Vishny 1996, 12–13). Chubais and Gaidar preferred a mass privatization program based on the experience of Czechoslovakia. "Through . . . discussions in eastern Europe, the idea of free distribution of property gained popularity . . . The Polish failure to privatize because of attempts to make discrete sales was illuminating, while the Czechoslovak attempt at voucher privatization looked promising" (Aslund 1995, 227, see also 235–236).

"The Russian decision makers looked at privatization in Poland primarily to learn what pitfalls to avoid and at that of Czechoslovakia to learn how to do it" (Aslund 1995, 229). "Thus, exactly as in Czechoslovakia, enterprises in selected sectors were compelled to privatize, but they were given a choice on how to go about it. . . . The Russian reformers carefully avoided the situation . . . in Poland, where the privatization law . . . gave several interested parties the right to veto privatization" (247). In this way Russia avoided the situation in Ukraine, in which the industrial lobby and the parliament seemed able to veto the government's privatization plans on several occasions.

Announcing the program to the public in a televised speech, President Yeltsin indicated that some key industrial and economic assets would remain in the hands of the state. "Russian enterprises that will be offered for privatization checks in 1993 [do] not include . . . atomic power stations, certain defense installations, pipelines and land-reclamation systems" (CDPSP 44, 331–334).

But there was no public mention of the exact number of enterprises included. As in Ukraine, in order to ascertain how Russia defined "strategic" enterprises, it is important to estimate the size of the military industrial complex. The number of defense enterprises in Russia was put at 1,800 by a former head of the State Committee on Defense Industries (cited in Denezhkina 1998, 130). A report by the Bonn International Center for Conversion estimated 2,000 Russian defense enterprises, of which 269 were "bankrupt" by June 1994 (Izyumov, Kosals, and Ryvkina 1995, 14). Similarly, the Russian magazine *Ekspert* (2/16/98, 51), citing data from the Economics Ministry, put the military–industrial complex at 1,794 enterprises.

Foreign investment was not initially considered a central element of privatization. Foreigners were considered potential sources of major investments needed in highly unprofitable firms, or to complete unfinished construction projects (Aslund 1995, 231). This is similar to the Ukrainian emphasis on "purposeful" foreign investment. Unlike in Ukraine however, if foreign investment was not central to the privatization strategy, neither was there a desire or willingness among its authors to exclude foreigners in order to appease the domestic industrial lobby. Nondiscriminatory rules were established and foreigners were allowed to purchase privatization vouchers directly from the population. This was hoped to make vouchers more liquid, raising their market value and enhancing the appeal of mass privatization for the population (Aslund 1995, 236).

At least among some officials, there was a sense of threat to Russia's economic security. For example, Minister of Foreign Economic Relations and Trade Petr Aven (1992, 51), a member of Gaidar's team, wrote in 1992 that U.S. nontariff barriers were designed to destroy Russia's technological potential (51–52, 60). For Chubais, real security threats did exist from foreign capital, but his perception of this type of threat was minimal. "[T]hrough front men foreigners could get access to enterprises banned from being privatized. There is such a danger and work really does need to be done on this, including by the Federal Security Service [FSB, a successor organization of the KGB], with which we are collaborating. But I think these are more like unique cases than some kind of mass process" (BBC SWB 9/25/95). Chubais was also sensitive to the political implications of foreign investment, he "worried about foreign investors buying big Russian companies for almost nothing, because that would arouse public hostility to privatization" (Aslund 1995, 231–232).

Gaidar was dismissed by Yeltsin in December 1992. One influential group in opposition to him and the privatization program was the Russian Union of Industrialists and Entrepreneurs headed by Arkadii Vol'skii. This organization, along with its parliamentary arm Civic Union, was the major representative of the industrial lobby. "[T]hey were hostile to early Western investment, fearing that Western companies would oust them" (Aslund 1995, 234; see also Zisk 1997, 29). Although there was some degree of mutual recognition of threat, the policy preferences of the government and the parliament on privatization were in conflict. In an atmosphere of extreme confrontation, the privatization program for 1993 was never adopted. The 1994 program was enacted by presidential decree. More than previously, it favored outsiders at the expense of managers of state enterprises. Rather than appeasing the industrial lobby, Yeltsin proved unyielding.

Eventually the ranks began to break. Managers of large enterprises had been waiting to acquire capital to buy the firms they ran, but in spring 1994 many apparently decided it was in their interests to participate in the voucher privatization. It became clear that the government would move on to cash-based privatization auctions, and firms' valuations were likely to rise, possibly out of the price range of Russian mangers (Aslund 1995, 257).

During the final months of voucher privatization, there was also an increase in foreign participation as some of Russia's most attractive enterprises came up for auction. "For the first time, foreigners actively participated in voucher auctions" (Boycko, Shleifer, and Vishny 1996, 104). Over $2 billion in foreign investment entered Russia in this period (102, 114), demonstrating that significant foreign investment in Russian industry was not only technically legal (as in Ukraine), it was politically feasible as well. With the completion of voucher privatization in July 1994, 15,052 medium and large enterprises were partially privatized, representing 80 percent of the industrial workforce. After being twice rejected by parliament, a post-voucher cash-based privatization program was decreed by Yeltsin (EBRD 1995).

In March 1995, leading Russian banks made a proposal to the government to secure a privileged role in cash privatization. Variously called the "consortium scheme" or "loans-for-shares," the banks' proposal was described positively by privatization officials as a plan "to mortgage . . . [shares of enterprises of national importance for] . . . funds . . . considered as earnings from privatization. . . ." (Federal Information Systems Corporation 4/13/95). In fact this was an opaque, noncompetitive process for privatizing many of Russia's most important industrial assets (e.g., Gustafson 1999, chapter 2).

As the loans-for-shares deal was being negotiated, privatization officials announced the list of enterprises scheduled to be privatized in 1995. Vladimir Sokolov, chair of the Russian Federal Property Fund, detailed efforts to attract foreign investors: "[W]e will step up our advertising abroad. . . . [W]e are studying lists of both Russian and foreign partners so that we could . . . bring . . . revenue to the budget. . . ." Sokolov raised the issue of strategic enterprises: "strategic enterprises or enterprises of national importance. . . . operate in the areas of . . . the country's defense capability, strategic materials. . . ." These would remain unitary firms under state ownership and control. This is consistent with Yeltsin's 1992 speech announcing the privatization program. However, Sergei Beliaev, head of the State Property Fund, also made it clear that any enterprise not considered "strategic" would eventually be privatized.

This was not always the case in Ukraine. In 1995 the Rada reduced the number of enterprises subject to privatization by half. Also, as had been the case initially in Ukraine, in Russia it emerged that some defense enterprises were not considered "strategic," and that many of the enterprises initially on the list might eventually be removed (Federal Information Systems Corporation 4/13/95). According to Zisk (1997, 28), a "large number of state defense enterprises . . . were privatized by 1995."

Stephan Haggard (1990, 199) makes the distinction between restrictive "positive-list" and permissive "negative-list" systems of restricting foreign investment. Russian officials repeatedly emphasized the negative-list approach. Enterprises not explicitly exempted were to be privatized and were open to foreign investment. In Ukraine it appears that only enterprises specifically designated as both scheduled for privatization *and* available to foreign investors were so in practice. Ukraine therefore can be seen as using an informal positive list approach.

Russian officials actively marketed Russian firms to foreigners. Sokolov stated that "we have been sending abroad a good deal of sales information . . . delivered by Reuters . . . there are over 200,000 recipients. . . . We are expanding the network of our offices. . . . We do not say that we are doing everything possible at the expense of Russian investors. . . . We are trying to create equal conditions for both of them. . . . Let us note that foreign investors buy very few shares in this country. Not more than ten percent of the shares have been bought by foreign investors. This is woefully inadequately [*sic*] for implementing economic reform and for meeting the [budget] targets" (Federal Information Systems Corporation 4/13/95).

Final approval of the loans-for-shares scheme had not yet been given. Budget revenues of 9.1 trillion rubles were expected from the privatization program in 1995, and Sokolov referred to the choice faced by the government regarding "strategic enterprises. . . . We have already touched upon the dilemma of whether they would be sold or transferred in trust to banking groups. These are the main sources of revenue" (Federal Information Systems Corporation 4/13/95). Thus the question of which enterprises were "strategic" and what exactly "strategic" meant was entangled in 1995 in the political struggles between the Russian bankers, the privatization bureaucracy represented by Beliaev, Sokolov, and, ultimately, Chubais (then First Deputy Prime Minister in Chernomyrdin's government), interests which would benefit from increased budget revenues, and certainly the managers of major enterprises themselves.[3]

In May Chubais appeared to gain the upper hand in this struggle. He was selected to head the newly created Federal Commission for Budget Privatization Revenues which was to include representatives of the Russian secret services (ITAR-TASS 5/12/95). In June a list of 2,809 "strategic enterprises" banned from privatization was first announced, including defense firms, big oil companies, the telephone giant Rostelekom, and many other Russian "blue-chip" companies (*The Moscow Times* 6/21/95).

In July 1995, Beliaev announced a finalized list of 3,054 "strategic enterprises," including Gazprom. These were either not to be privatized, or were to be held back until 1996 or 1997. Transportation Minister Vitalii Efimov voiced strong opposition to the decision to privatize over twenty transport companies because foreign competitors would "buy off stocks in order to remove Russian transport companies from the Russian market."

But the list was not expanded to include these or other firms. In September 1995 the Russian government adopted Executive Order 949, which classified "3,000" enterprises as strategic.[4] Chubais explained that the list had been prepared over a long time with "much dispute and debate." "This means also that anything not on the list . . . can be freely privatized" (Federal Information Systems Corporation 3/5/98).

A second list contained enterprises included in loans-for-shares. Chubais described them: "These are fantastically attractive enterprises . . . [in] the petroleum sector, steel, transport enterprises, river and seaports, and much else. This is . . . very exciting for Russia and indeed for foreign investors" (BBC SWB 9/25/95). The scheme allowed for limited participation by foreigners (Federal Information Systems Corporation 9/25/95), although it is generally considered a closed, noncompetitive transfer of valuable assets at bargain prices to Russia's wealthiest private interests. Eventually it is the case that foreigners gained some stake in these companies.

In early November 1995 the "loans-for-shares" auctions began. The Duma called on the government to halt privatization, citing the threat posed to national security (Agence France Presse 11/28/95). In December, forces aligned against loans-for-shares scored victories. Sergei Burkov, chair of the Duma's Committee on Property, Privatization, and Economic Activity (dubbed the "deprivatization panel" in the Russian press), was the leading opponent in parliament. His petition to Yeltsin resulted in the cancellation of eight auctions (*Segodnia* 12/22/95, 2) of firms Yeltsin described as "of strategic importance for national security," including Sukhoi Aircraft Design, Progress aviation company (combat helicopters), and the Irkutsk aviation plant (jet fighters) (*The Moscow Times* 3/14/96).

The negative political reaction to the extensive and uncompetitive sale of major industrial assets, as well as presidential elections scheduled for June, probably contributed to the absence of progress in privatization in 1996 (EBRD 1997). In March, a presidential decree established a commission under the State Committee on Defense Industries tasked with developing a new approach to privatization of the defense sector, "taking into account national interests." Vasilii Zhigulin, head of the privatization department of the Sate Committee declared "it is evident that the previous policy of total sell-offs is damaging for the country."

The commission was to consider the role of foreign investors in privatization and to review and expand the list of "strategic enterprises." Another function of the commission was to determine the maximum proportion of shares that could be held by foreigners for each enterprise. According to *The Moscow Times's* Anton Zhigulsky, the "government sought to lighten the huge financial burden of its defense complex by selling off state shares in defense enterprises . . ., but strong opposition from the powerful military-industrial lobby thwarted most attempts" (3/14/96; also see Zisk 1997).

The new commission was headed by First Deputy Prime Minister Oleg Soskovets, a former USSR Minister of Metallurgy. He named the five largest oil companies, pledged to banks under loans-for-shares, as enterprises that should not yet be privatized (*Russia and Commonwealth Business Law Report*, 5/8/96; see also Aslund 1995, 325).

Challenges to privatization continued, usually with an emphasis on "strategic" enterprises. In April 1996 Burkov's committee began investigating the privatization of strategic enterprises (*Kommersant-Daily* 4/12/96). In May, the Communist Party—the largest Duma faction—called for protection from foreign competition as well as the state's resumption of control of "strategic" enterprises and "the leading role" in the economy: "Privatization was conducted in violation of the laws. . . . [T]he country has lost food security and is doomed to be dependent on foreign countries" (*The International Herald Tribune* 5/29/96).

Nevertheless, by 1996 a significant portion of defense production was already privatized. Thirty percent was undertaken by joint-stock companies with no state ownership; companies with partial state ownership accounted for another 34 percent. FDI in defense enterprises was one of the methods used by these firms to secure access to export markets for their products (Denezhkina 1998, 132; Zisk 1997). Export by defense firms of civilian goods was an attractive alternative to producing for the Russian state, which was chronically late in payment (Denezhkina 1998, 128).

After Yeltsin's reelection, banks received the right to buy the shares they had been managing under loans-for-shares (EBRD 1997). In November, Economics Minister Yasin announced a new policy of limited support and protection for selected "strategic enterprises." There were fears that banks were pressuring the Kremlin for "a new corporatist policy restricting competition and limiting foreign investment." However, November also saw the announcement that a 25 percent stake in Sviazinvest telecommunications holding company would be sold in 1997 with no restrictions to foreigners. Communications Minister Vladimir Bulgak stated that the expected revenues from this sale were $2–4 billion (Thornhill 1996, 3).

By the beginning of 1997 there were 123,000 private enterprises and 88,000 state enterprises, compared to 205,000 state enterprises in 1992.

While foreigners owned less than 2 percent of all of Russia's medium and large enterprises, *they owned 12 percent of the shares of the largest 100 companies.* Some restrictions applied. In some enterprises, mostly in the energy sector, foreigners were limited to 15 percent ownership (EBRD 1997). However, after the privatization of major oil companies, a presidential decree removed this provision (*Ekspert* 11/17/97, 5; also see *Business Central Europe* 12/97–1/98, 12). In the defense sector, *502 of approximately 1800 defense enterprises were completely in private hands as of January 1997,* and an additional 509 had been corporatized (transformed into joint-stock companies) with the state retaining all or some shares (Russian Economic Ministry cited in *Ekspert* 2/16/98, 51).

In March 1997 the government initiated a new comprehensive reform program including continued privatization of major enterprises. An 8.5 percent share of Unified Energy Systems (UES) was sold (EBRD 1997). In June, the Duma adopted a law to regulate cash-based sales. Pavel Bunich, of the pro-government "Our Home is Russia" faction, who authored the law, stated that the definition of a "strategic enterprise" should remain narrow. "[A] list of strategic enterprises is drawn up. . . . [W]e should not arbitrarily expand the interpretation of the notion of strategic enterprises. *If we arbitrarily expand the list, we will not have an effective economy.* You must remember that private enterprises perform better than state-owned ones" (Federal Information Systems Corporation 6/24/97, emphasis added). The law included the idea of the "golden share," a single share giving the state a veto right over some major decisions. Retention of this right by the state was designed to further the privatization of strategic enterprises, although it also clearly limits the rights of the private shareholders to some degree (Interfax 6/24/97). Following this the State Property Committee was upgraded to Ministry status, reflecting the reality of the political backing that the privatization process now had (RFE/RL 1/10/97).

The government's push to privatize major enterprises continued in 1998. Foreigners were not restricted from participating in these offerings (Federal Information Systems Corporation 3/5/98). First Deputy Minister of State Property Aleksandr Braverman described "an absolutely amazing tendency. While previously we saw that defense enterprises were clearly opposed to privatization, now we can give the Duma an additional list of 400 enterprises which have provided information on each of the 21 criteria required by the Duma [for corporatization as a prelude to privatization]."

Braverman also implied that the list of strategic enterprises had already been shortened. "If you are talking about the privatization of strategic enterprises which ensure national security, we, like any other country, have the right to protect ourselves. . . . We have a list of enterprises which the government decided to cut on December 23, 1997 . . ." (Federal Information Systems Corporation 2/19/98). In May, he announced a draft plan to cut the list by more than 70 percent, to approximately 800 (*The Moscow Times* 5/8/98). This suggests a behind-the-scenes battle within the government. In June he said that a presidential decree reducing the number of strategic enterprises would be ready by mid-July. The new policy would use the "golden share" option (ITAR-TASS 6/29/98).

With the 1998 financial crisis the privatization program was severely hampered. In June, after the failure to sell Rosneft due to lack of interest at the given minimum price, Braverman announced that the suspension of the sales of the TNK and VNK oil companies. But, he also suggested that a 5.87 percent stake in Gazprom would be offered (Federal Information Systems Corporation 6/11/98).

In July, Deputy Prime Minister Viktor Khristenko announced that the government had cut the number of strategic enterprises to 1,000 and would now push for further privatization (*The Financial Times* 7/21/98). This represents somewhat more than half of the military–industrial complex. The battle over the list had apparently been won by the Privatization Ministry and its allies.

Responding to pressure from international financial institutions to break up the natural gas monopoly, in February 1999 the Duma passed a law authorizing further and extensive privatization of Gazprom. Gazprom, involved in intense competition for the European market, had formed a partnership with Germany's Rurhgas, which owned a small stake (*Ekspert* 11/17/97, 42–53). The new law provided for 25 percent plus one share to remain state property, and privatization of an additional 13.5 percent. Previously, a presidential decree had limited foreigners to 9 percent ownership. Now, foreigners would be allowed to own a maximum of 25 percent minus one share. Russian journalist Sergei Beregovoi (1999, 7) commented that Gazprom believed it could survive intact more easily with Russian *or* foreign private owners than with government officials on the board of directors.

DISCUSSION

The policies and outcomes described here demonstrate that Ukraine retained its state-owned large enterprises, while Russia achieved considerable privatization of them. Foreign investors played a moderately important role in the process in Russia. In Ukraine, foreign capital was largely shut out. By 1999, Russia's economic security preferences on the question of foreign ownership of "strategic" enterprises had evolved. There was no longer a significant resistance to partial ownership, but full control by foreign owners of a major company was still unlikely to gain much support. Gustafson (1999, 75) reaches a similar conclusion, "at least in the so-called 'strategic industries,' such as metals and oil." Foreigners owned 12 percent of the shares of Russia's 100 largest companies. The support of the "leftist" Duma for 25 percent minus one share foreign ownership of Gazprom—the jewel in the crown of Russian industry— marks a considerable willingness to allow foreign capital into the commanding heights of industry. It is a stark contrast to the Ukrainian Rada's rejection of the privatization of Ukrtelekom at roughly the same time.

One way to represent the dependent variable of this chapter, economic security preferences, is with the parallel lists of "strategic" enterprises banned from privatization in each state. While Ukraine's list had grown to 7,111 by 1998, Russia's had been whittled down to 1,000 enterprises (figure 6.1). Considered as a percentage of the military–industrial complex of each state, the contrast is even greater (figure 6.2). The definition of "strategic enterprise" was broadened in Ukraine to include the defense sector and almost all major enterprises. In Russia, firms in the energy and metallurgical sectors, as well as in transportation, and perhaps 800 firms of the military–industrial complex were removed from the list. The contrast in policy outcomes is as stark as are the similarities in basic economic and political variables in Ukraine and Russia. How can these differences be explained? A comparative perspective will help eliminate several possible explanations, including some proposed by analysts examining only one of the cases.

The possible explanations for differences in Russian and Ukrainian approaches to foreign investment in strategic enterprises include the influence

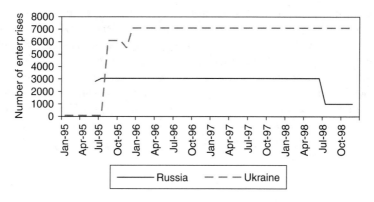

Figure 6.1 "Strategic" enterprises restricted from privatization

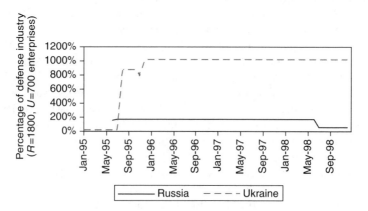

Figure 6.2 "Strategic" enterprises restricted from privatization: percentage of defense industry

of military threat, perceptions of threat, economic interests, domestic politics, and the psychological effects of lessons of historical experience.

There is no mention by opponents or proponents of foreign investment in either case of any *immediate* military threat. There are perceptions of *potential* threat in both Ukraine and Russia expressed by opponents of foreign investment in strategic enterprises in the legislature, and occasionally by government officials. The officials involved directly with privatization, such as Riabchenko in Ukraine and Chubais in Russia, evince a more limited sense of possible, isolated threats from foreign access to specific defense-related information or resources. But, the key point is that there is little difference in the level of threat perception between Ukraine and Russia.[5] There is a certain level of perceived threat in Ukraine from Russia, but, as seen below, Presidents Kravchuk and Kuchma consistently call for *expansion* of economic cooperation with Russia. The level of threat perception was not high enough to prevent Ukrainian presidents from publicly advocating close economic cooperation with Russia. In Russia, in most instances threats are assumed to originate from the United States and other Western powers. Statements by Minister of Foreign Economic Relations and Trade Aven, Transportation Minister Efimov, and of course the Communist Party demonstrate this. As is apparent in the next section, among both groups of elites, the major "threat" is seen to be domestic instability.

It seems evident that the need for budget revenues drove the Russian privatization process to a significant degree. The government's marketing efforts aimed at potential foreign investors can be seen in this light. Chubais and his team of privatization officials understood that the participation of foreign investors in auctions was likely to raise the price of the enterprises being sold, and therefore budget revenues. This was also the logic behind the decision to allow foreigners to purchase privatization vouchers. *Russian preferences were for increasing budget revenues even if shares of major enterprises fell into foreign hands. Ukrainian preferences were the reverse.*

A Rubicon was crossed with the Duma's passage of the 1997 privatization law. Initial resistance to privatization of major enterprises by the sectoral ministries and enterprise directors had been overcome as a critical mass of members of these groups began to consider privatization in their interests. Zisk (1997) also presents an argument along these lines.

Nevertheless a purely "economic interest"–based explanation such as Zisk's is inadequate because both the need for budget revenues and the economic interest of directors in holding on to their enterprises surely obtained in Ukraine as well. There is no evidence to indicate that the Ukrainian industrial lobby was *more* threatened by privatization in general or foreign investment in particular than its counterpart in Russia. And if anything, Ukraine had a greater need for budget revenues than did Russia.

States with insufficient domestic investment capital, or balance of payment difficulties, have been hypothesized to be more likely to prefer FDI (Haggard 1990, 197; UNCTAD 1995, 271). In transition economies in general, "[f]iscal pressures appear to have played a large role in encouraging states to move towards cash-based privatisations and international tenders of 'strategic' enterprises to raise much-needed budgetary revenues. This has motivated many governments to increase private sector participation in infra-structure" (EBRD 1998).

Although both Russia and Ukraine were short on investment capital and budgetary funds, Ukraine certainly had fiscal problems at least as severe as Russia's, achieving 10,000 percent inflation in 1994. Russia at least had significant revenues from energy exports.

Neither is it the case that Russia's general economic interests were more conducive to an open investment policy than Ukraine's. Ukraine has a pop-ulation roughly one third that of Russia, an economy of similar proportion, and fewer natural resources than Russia. Theories of international political economy (Katzenstein 1985, 39–40; Pomfret 1991, 5–8) argue that smaller states have greater incentives for international openness than larger states. Larger states, especially those with sufficient natural resources, have a greater incentive to attempt self-sufficiency or autarky. Katzenstein (1985, 85) pres-ents data showing that small European states tend to have a higher propor-tion of foreign direct investment than do larger European states. *The relative tendencies in Ukraine and Russia are the opposite of those predicted by economic interests.*

Domestic political coalitions against foreign investment are another pos-sible explanation. Ash's (1999) explanation for Ukraine's resistance to for-eign investment based on an "unholy alliance" between nationalists opposed to Russian investment and leftists opposed to any private investment (espe-cially Western) seems convincing to a degree; but it is easy to see how simi-lar forces in Russia could have aligned to resist major foreign investment. Indeed, they initially did. The design of the mass-privatization program was compromised to accommodate workers, represented by Soviet-era trade unions, and the industrial lobby. Sergei Pavlenko (1996) gives a good description of the powerful anti-privatization forces in Russia. He writes that the *political* motivations for including enterprises on the list exempt from pri-vatization included (1) stopping privatization, (2) excluding foreign investors from the Russian market, and (3) gaining access to budget resources. The political forces behind it were the Communists who wanted to renationalize the economy, the managers of large enterprises fearing loss of control, Russian financial circles who feared losing income from enterprises, and federal and regional officials who oversee enterprises and benefit from rents.

It seems difficult to argue that in Russia there were not substantial polit-ical interests, comparable to those in Ukraine, opposed to privatization in general, and foreign investment in strategic enterprises in particular.

A related explanation is institutional. Ash (1999) notes the fine balance of powers between the executive and legislative branches of the Ukrainian state. In contrast, the "dominant" Russian presidency is invested with powers allow-ing it to manipulate or ignore the legislature on many issues (e.g., Remington 1999, 46). Yeltsin was able to use his power of decree to accomplish most of the privatization program over the Duma's objections, while in Ukraine the Rada seemed to be the major roadblock to privatization.

There are two problems with this argument. First, because each society was in the process of creating the institutions of the state, a causal connection between these and policy outcomes is likely to be spurious. The institutions are being created in order to further the various goals of the political forces involved. Second, before the 1993 Russian constitution and the 1996 Ukrainian constitution, the executive–legislative relationships were similar: based on Brezhnev-era constitutions as amended in each republic. The balance of constitutional power was similarly fluid in each state immediately after the fall of the USSR. The new constitutions are therefore best seen as results of struggles over power and policies, including the central question of economic reform.

Not surprisingly, in both cases the executive did indeed prefer a constitution with a strong presidency, while opposition forces preferred a strong legislature. In Russia, Yeltsin resisted this and forced (literally) a referendum on his preferred constitutional draft. In Ukraine, Kuchma also planned a referendum and was in conflict with the parliamentary group proposing its own draft with more legislative powers. However, Kuchma agreed to an eleventh-hour proposal to cancel the referendum and consider the parliamentary draft (Het'man 1996, 45, see also 48–52, 64–65).

The Rada seemed to gain the power to drive the process of expanding the privatization blacklist. "Economic restructuring and modernisation depends on the divestiture of enterprises, for example Ukrtelekom, that have been deemed strategic. . . . However, such moves have been delayed by legislative conflict. . . " (*West LB Country Profile: Ukraine* 1999). But, there is scant evidence of concerted executive resistance to this trend. Indeed, if the Ukrainian president had had the political will to enact privatization by decree, legally he could have done so. For example, President Kuchma did use his constitutional decree power to order the privatization of between 50 and 75 percent of the shares of 20 regional power companies in May 2000 (RFE/RL 5/16/00).

Finally, the attractiveness of a given country to potential investors may lead to higher levels of foreign investment. Foreign investors can be attracted by a high level of economic development and exportable resource endowments (Krasner 1985, 179; Dell 1991), economic growth (UNCTAD 1995, 271), a large domestic market, and general export potential (Chan 1995, 1). It is worth considering whether outside interest, and the resulting pressure, was much greater in one case than in the other.

The most significant difference between the Russian and Ukrainian economies is Russia's wealth of energy resources. However, there is little evidence that Russia was willing to open this sector up to significant foreign investment until at least 1997 or 1998, if then. Any advantage Russia may have had in terms of the size of the domestic market is likely to be counterbalanced by Ukraine's higher population density and favorable location closer to the western European export market and Black Sea ports. Indeed, in the final years of the USSR and the earlier years of independence, there was optimism about Ukraine's economic prospects and the opportunities for foreign investors (e.g., *Journal of Commerce* 10/16/91, 8A and 10/21/91, 4A). Although it needs to import energy from Russia and Turkmenistan, Ukraine has 60 percent of the former USSR's oil refineries, a wealth of mineral resources, accessible sea ports, extremely fertile soil, and rail links between east and west (*The Financial Times* 8/30/95). If Ukrainian leaders had placed a higher priority on attracting foreign investment, it seems that there was sufficient interest among potential investors.

Haggard (1990, 194) proposes that "[v]ariations in the role of foreign capital among countries . . . must be explained by the political and economic threats foreign firms pose, the level of development of local firms when MNCs enter, and the political links between the private sector and government." However, when these factors do not vary, "national policy," including "basic property rights, . . . the structure of incentives, . . . discrete policies toward particular sectors or firms, [and] regulations such as restrictions on equity," can be expected to play a key role in explaining variation in foreign investment levels (192). It seems clear that it is just such variation in "national policy" that remains to be explained. The question therefore is what remains to explain variation in Ukrainian and Russian national policies regarding foreign investment in "strategic" enterprises? My answer throughout this book has been to look to the patterns of Russian and Ukrainian "schematic learning".

As noted in chapter 5, Ukrainians' dominant schema based on the formative event of the successful drive for independence shaped their perception of the USSR's failure as well. It was much more comfortable to believe that the policies already jettisoned—control from Moscow, suppression of national self-determination—were the root of the USSR's failure. It was easy to overlook the fact that the political and especially economic systems of independent Ukraine were still largely "Soviet" in form and substance.

Russia's historical legacy held lessons much different than those learned in Ukraine. Known options from direct experience had been exhausted, "new" policy options had to be found. This pointed elites to foreign experiences. The models of Polish "shock therapy" and Czech voucher privatization seemed attractive and relevant. Lessons of economic interdependence and openness to investment incorporated in the success of Japan, Western Europe, and North America after World War II also attracted attention. The Cold War, after all, seemed to offer evidence of the superiority of such policies.

Consistent with prospect theory and my expectations based on formative events including major failure, these direct and observed historical lessons gave birth to the political will in Russia to make political and even security-related sacrifices. The goal of privatization, combined with the belief that economic openness was a fundamental element of successful statecraft, led to the pursuit and defense of foreign investment in strategic enterprises. The Russian leadership tenaciously resisted abandoning this policy because it would mean a return to failed Soviet policies of autarky. The Ukrainian frame of reference, in contrast, left little room for the political will necessary to pursue difficult, radical change, *nor was such change perceived as vitally necessary.* Ukrainian leaders felt that history argued for preservation of a political consensus and that economic planning appropriate to Ukraine's interests (rather than those of Moscow) could pull their state out of its crisis.

EVIDENCE OF ELITE SCHEMATA IN UKRAINE AND RUSSIA

Before the fall of the USSR, Kravchuk commented on the lessons of the Soviet experience for Ukraine. "The desire for independence is . . . the hope that a state of their own will be closer to them, will protect their interests. They say: If we had a state of our own, would it have built the Chernobyl Atomic Power Station so near Kiev? Never!" (*Izvestiia* 11/26/91).

Vitold Fokin explained his approach in the following terms. "Ukraine was a state in the overall system of the Soviet Union. . . . There was a very carefully thought-out system of resource distribution . . . functions, and responsibilities. . . . When the USSR existed, *this was correct.* It was dictated by the desire to achieve . . . optimization. . . . When Ukraine became independent, then the first thing we needed to do was . . . to decide what was needed for the Ukrainian economy. Do we need metallurgy? How much metal do we need for our interests, and . . . do we need to extract coal? How much? Which machine building branches do we need? What to do with agriculture? That is, we needed to create a base which would be optimal for the needs of Ukraine . . ."(Interview 11/18/97, emphasis added).

After Fokin's resignation, Kravchuk maintained his focus on building political consensus and achieving economic progress through better administration by the state. Kravchuk's new premier, Leonid Kuchma, was considered a "compromise candidate acceptable to both Parliament and Ukraine's large industrial lobby." Although he identified attracting foreign investment and increasing the proportion of manufactured exports as priorities, Kuchma also considered Russian-style shock therapy "unacceptable" and believed "[w]e need gradual evolution. We cannot privatize all major industries today" (*Russia and Commonwealth Business Law Report* 10/16/92).

Kravchuk also repeatedly stated that Ukraine must maintain or reestablish its links economic links with Russia. "I promised . . . that we would do everything [possible] so that there would not be confrontation amongst our people. . . . [T]his together with our relations and our implementation of agreements with Russia . . . and others will give us the opportunity [for] survival . . ." (BBC SWB 11/13/92). In 1993, Kravchuk discussed the basic Ukrainian international economic orientation. "[T]oday not a single state in the former union will be able to solve the crisis unless we create a common economic space and common . . . market within the CIS [Commonwealth of Independent States]. Why? Because links with the West and its economy are links of a qualitatively new level. They include world prices, payments in currency, new technologies, new banking, financial and credit systems and new relations in all aspects of economic life . . ." (BBC SWB 8/23/93). And in September 1993: "The fact is that Western European states have formed a common market. The United States, Canada and Mexico are moving towards economic integration. . . . But . . . movement towards economic integration had always been a gradual process . . . *and without fail had advantages and the strengthening of one's own state, sovereignty and independence.* . . . This is self-evident . . ." (BBC SWB 9/3/93, emphasis added). It is clear that Kravchuk's policy preferences included first restoring the functioning of the existing economy, which he believed depended in part on reestablishing ties with other former Union republics, and only then moving forward with market reforms. At least in part this seemed to be driven by a concern over civil accord and the ability of the population to survive the winter. As will be seen, Russian leaders had almost identical concerns about civil peace and food supply, but took a markedly different approach.

My argument hinges on the generalization of the impact of formative events on the political elite of a country over time and across individuals. Ukraine's second president, Leonid Kuchma, differs from Kravchuk in important ways. He is usually considered more supportive of close relations with Russia, less interested in issues of Ukrainian national identity like language, and more open to market economics (e.g., Lukanov 1996, 89–112). If, in spite of the differences, formative events have had an impact on Kuchma and his administration's policies similar to that they had on his predecessor, this would support the schematic learning explanation.

In a December 1994 address to parliament, Kuchma outlined his historical perspective and policy priorities. "As the experience of many countries that have been able to overcome a systemic economic crisis indicates, the decisive factors were connected to the strengthening of the state's administration of stabilizing processes, with the decisive administrative use of macroeconomic factors. That is the way it was for us, too, after the Civil War [1918–1921], and during the Great Depression in the United States. . . . For us today the situation is really almost analogical—the state is weak, society is unstructured, and the economy is practically unguided. . . . And we have only one way out—to strengthen the state. . . .

Without a strong government it will not be possible to effectively administer the state sector of the economy, which in Ukraine still comprises more than 85 percent [of the economy]. . . . In this issue we have . . . even allowed regressive tendencies, the deindustrialization of the country. . . .

And for this reason it is especially important that . . . we will succeed in overcoming the confrontational mood, to begin a [domestic] dialogue, which can conclude in a joint victory over the conditions in which we find ourselves" (*Uriadovyy Kur'er* 12/24/94, 1, 3).

Kuchma's emphasis on strengthening the state and domestic political consensus for economic reform is strikingly similar to Kravchuk's, although he is more aware of a crisis and the need for change.

Although Kuchma remained president past the end of the period of this study (1999), a general policy shift seemed to occur after his reelection in

November 1999. The most-often cited indicator of this shift was the appointment of Prime Minister Viktor Iushchenko, a younger figure usually associated with market reform policies during his tenure as Central Bank director. Did this policy shift indicate that the dominant schema of top Ukrainian decision makers had been modified or replaced?

Because Iushchenko had relatively little to say publicly about the privatization of major enterprises, it is difficult to assess how much his approach differed from previous practice. Regarding domestic politics, Iushchenko still expressed a desire for consensus, but seemed willing to risk more conflict than his predecessors. He stated that "[i]n the period of nine years of the modern history of Ukraine it has become an obvious truth that the further we keep away from consolidation [of political forces], the harder it is for us to resolve pragmatic economic tasks. . . . In my opinion, the importance of the need to form a democratic majority grows every day. . . . In fact this consolidation is Ukraine's only choice for the future. If the government manages to make the national-democrats believe that our course may lead to victory, so that they can and must unite their efforts around this course, we could consider our task accomplished . . ." (BBC SWB 6/2/00). Iushchenko seemed to indicate that he was interested in cooperation with only one of the major factions in the Rada—the national-democrats such as the *Rukh* party (now divided into two factions). Apparently he had discounted any chance of cooperation with the other major group, the leftists. Iushchenko seemed to imply that the national-democrats should be prepared to join his program, rather than expect compromises from the government. In an earlier statement, Iushchenko was more explicit: "Our programme is [appropriate] for both our political forces and the executive. However, I'll be honest: there will be no disaster if the parliament disagrees with our point of view" (BBC SWB 4/4/00). This may have signaled a change in approach for Ukraine.

In Russia, the frame of reference regarding economic reform and economic openness was significantly different from that in Ukraine. Gaidar made his first major public defense and explanation of reforms in the newspaper *Izvestiia* in 1992. It is clear that neither political consensus nor protection from the global economy is as important to him as immediate destruction of the Soviet economic system, including in foreign economic relations.

"The main thing with which I must categorically disagree is the myth that it is possible to get out of the crisis and save Russia without radical market reforms. . . . In the summer of 1991 the Soviet Union's economy was unmanageable, in a state of free fall. . . . Indeed, we were faced with the questions of whether . . . society would survive. . . .

The breakup of the Union was a heavy price to pay for an unsuccessful attempt to reverse the course of history [the August 1991 putsch]. . . .

The process of structural reorganization that has begun will be painful, but it will have to be undergone all the same. [P]rivatization has been set in motion. . . . The center of gravity regarding the choice of paths . . . is shifting from yesterday's question of whether to enter the market . . . to tomorrow's alternative: Where do we go with the market? . . .

Today, having worked out and implemented in practice an active, open and future-oriented structural policy, we can form competitive production facilities, enter the community of the world's developed countries as equals, and finally overcome our humiliating backwardness. . . . But the forces of inertia . . . are . . . pulling the country into the past, into a completely closed defensive position and self-isolation behind high customs fences and toward the same old abundant financial injections that make for the reproduction of inefficiency. The first path led postwar Japan into the ranks of the world's economic superpowers. The second path threw Argentina—one of the richest countries at the beginning of the 20th century—into the embraces of underdevelopment.

Now . . . the traditional power elite are once more reaching . . . for excessive military appropriations. . . . [But] there is no united front of adversaries of reform among the directors of defense enterprises. . . ."

For Gaidar, there is no doubt of the need for change. Nor does he harbor any illusion about the possibility of achieving meaningful reform through political consensus. Like Kravchuk, he too wants to join the world market "as equals," but continuation or rejuvenation of the Soviet integrated economic system is not an option for doing so. Rather, Soviet domestic and international economic principles are squarely to blame for the dire economic circumstances of the post-Soviet period. In his memoirs, Gaidar (1996) describes the origin of his approach to economic and political reform.

"Taking on the work of preparing a program of reform . . . I . . . recalled the Sopron [Hungary] economic conference of 1990. . . . For me the discussion of Russian economic problems . . . with Professor[s] William Northaus of Yale University and Rudiger Dornbush from the Massachusetts Institute of Technology was the most interesting. . . . For us [Gaidar and his team] in the fall of 1991 the results of the Sopron discussions on such key questions as the synchronization of . . . various aspects of reforms, the opening of the economy, currency exchange policy, were important starting points" (88–90).

"[T]he experience of colleagues undertaking reforms in eastern Europe indicated that the most difficult and conflictual area would be privatization" (198).

". . . In the summer of 1992 . . . Poland was already beginning to emerge from the crisis, showing the route along which other countries would travel" (244).

Gaidar was aware of foreign experiences with reform and applied their lessons in Russia. His expectations for the political battles to surround privatization indicate his belief that political confrontation and conflict would inevitably follow market reform.

President Yeltsin's major statement on privatization was given as a national television address in 1992 (CDPSP 44, 331–334). "At this point, a very elementary thing has to be comprehended. We are taking just the very first steps toward a normal human life, and we are stumbling and falling. . . . Difficult as it may be, the majority of people understand . . . we cannot go back to the old ways. . . .

At the most critical moments, you and I did not allow ourselves to cross that line that cannot be crossed under any circumstances. Civil peace is the most precious thing that Russia has. . . .

In the next few months, we will begin . . . the distribution of . . . privatization checks among the people. . . . The privatization check is a unique ticket for each of us to a free economy. The more property owners there are in Russia, . . . the sooner prosperity will come to Russia, and the more likely its future will be . . . safe. . . ."

Although Yeltsin's emphasis on preservation of civil peace is consistent with statements by Kravchuk and Kuchma, the Soviet past is seen as a mistake, both for its political beliefs and undemocratic nature, and also for its failure as an economic system.

Viktor Chernomyrdin was prime minister until April 1998 (and again briefly after the 1998 financial crisis). His statements provide evidence that elites are indeed socialized into dominant policy preferences and schemata. As noted in the case study, Chernomyrdin was compelled by Yeltsin to adopt preferences consistent with those of the general reform line of Gaidar and his associates. In 1998, the former Soviet industrial bureaucrat and one-time vocal opponent of privatization stated that "much has been said about whether privatization has gone right or wrong, but there has been no other way for us. . . . [P]rivatization of big companies will be continued" (Xinhua News Agency 11/23/97).

In his 1997 presentation to the Duma's plenary budget meeting, Chernomyrdin argued for continuing structural economic reforms, continuing cash-based privatization of major firms, further opening the Russian economy to the rest of the world, and attracting more foreign investment to Russian companies. His argument to the legislature hinged on the limited successes already achieved by Russian reforms.

"There is another litmus test for the change in the economic situation. That is the behavior of foreign investors. In only the first half of this year [1997], around $7 billion of foreign investment entered the Russian economy, which is 3.3 times more than in the first half of last year. . . .

I will say a few words about the priorities of the 1998 budget. Along with traditional social goals . . . there are new tasks, such as military reform. . . . Encouraging growth means leaving more money within the economy itself, while at the same time creating conditions for that money to be transformed into investment. [W]e are forcing ourselves by economic means to work single-mindedly to encourage private investment. . . .

It should be frankly admitted that we are making poor use of the potential for attracting foreign investment. . . .

The policy of economic growth cannot but be based on our country's active integration into the world economy. . . .

I cannot fail to react to the initiative . . . on a vote of no confidence in the government. . . . If we start a fight, we will ruin next year and the following years" (BBC SWB 10/10/97).

Chernomyrdin outlines a plan for continued major privatizations, military reform to free up investment resources, and continued opening to the world economy. If the deputies choose to oppose him, he promises them not compromise, but a lengthy fight.

The other prime minister to make a major impact on Russian domestic and foreign policies was Vladimir Putin, who became acting President of Russia in January 2000 and was elected to the office in March. Putin has been a controversial figure among Russian and foreign analysts and observers because of what are often seen as his anti-democratic, backward-looking tendencies. The largely successful violent repression of Chechen resistance made him at once popular among the electorate, and suspect in the eyes of those concerned with Russian democracy and development. The former KGB agent seemed to cannily use the powers of the state to silence domestic criticism, especially in the mass media, and bring most major political forces under his sway. There was also suspicion that Putin would seek a new confrontation with the West in order to justify dismantling democracy and the private sector in response to a foreign "threat."

There were certainly signs that he favored a more protectionist approach to foreign economic relations. In November 1999 as prime minister he seemed to signal a new autarkic tendency, telling the Coordinating Council of Domestic Producers that "[i]ntegration into the world economy has led to considerable losses for Russia. . . . Russia is not ready to successfully enter the world economy. . . . The Russian government plans to protect Russian producers that are subject to discrimination from foreign partners. . . . The Russian economy annually loses $2–2.5 billion due to discrimination of domestic goods in the West . . ." (Interfax 11/23/99).

However, at the same time Putin's government was considering the sale of an additional 2.5 percent of Gazprom's shares to a "strategic investor," an offer of nine percent of Lukoil's shares "on Western stock exchanges in 2000," as well as introduction of the "golden share" option for Lukoil. Privatization auctions continued to channel significant revenues into federal coffers (Interfax 11/23/99).

In a November 1999 radio broadcast, Putin addressed economic issues. "I am absolutely convinced that whoever gains power in Russia, they will be committed to the principles of market economy, and that no-one is likely to pull off a large-scale change—even those who are now loudly proclaiming they will. . . .

I am not sure that [privatization of the fuel and energy sector] was done in full accord with the interests of the state. . . . But this does not mean that we now have to rush back and start revising everything. By doing this, we would inflict even greater damage because it would create total uncertainty in the minds of domestic and foreign investors" (BBC SWB 11/2/99).

While Putin was clearly more apprehensive about the effects of the market, especially the global market system, than Gaidar or Chubais, or even Chernomyrdin, there was nevertheless no indication that he advocated a return to highly protectionist foreign economic relations. Indeed, under

President Putin the Property Ministry proposed further *narrowing* the definition of a "strategic enterprise." According to *Interfax* (cited in RFE/RL 7/31/00) "[a]t present, there are approximately 700 [strategic] corporations in which the government is required to maintain a share. The ministry would like to divide those companies into four categories; in one of those categories the state would maintain 100 percent of the stock and in the three others smaller amounts."

In both Russia and Ukraine it appeared that leaders with preferences somewhat at odds with dominant schemata came to power in 1999. However, in the absence of a new formative event to shock the state organization, they were constrained to work within the parameters of "normal" politics, and can only amend dominant policy preferences gradually and incrementally. This raises the interesting question of how, why, and to what extent dominant schemata are modified or amended in the absence of a formative event. This question, however, falls outside the scope of the present study.

CONCLUSION

In Russia, the list of "strategic" enterprises exempt from privatization and foreign investment was shortened and the definition made more restrictive, excluding a large portion of the military industrial complex. In Ukraine, the list grew longer and the definition apparently expanded to include the entire defense sector and almost all other major enterprises. Russia undertook extensive marketing efforts to promote its enterprises among potential foreign investors, while there is no evidence that Ukraine did so. Both Russia and Ukraine developed a legal and bureaucratic infrastructure to support privatization and foreign investment. But, while the Russian the State Property Committee was eventually upgraded to ministry status, in Ukraine the State Property Fund languished for a considerable period without a director.

Although explanations for either Russian or Ukrainian policies based on economic interests, domestic politics, or security concerns may seem plausible when considered in isolation, comparative method draws attention to the striking similarities between Russia and Ukraine across important independent variables, and undermines such explanations. The most plausible remaining explanation is psychological: a process of schematic perception based on learning from history's formative events. Ukrainian and Russian elites responded differently to similar circumstances because *their perceptions were framed by different schemata based on different historical experiences*, both direct and observed. These perceptions are consistent with my theoretical framework and imitation is apparent in the formation of Russian economic security preferences.

In Russia, the economic and foreign policies of the USSR were seen as abject failures by 1991. I argue that this recognition of failed protectionism and autarky leads Russian elites to search for foreign models of success. The case study demonstrates that Russian policy makers based their new policies on observed lessons of success, specifically Polish shock therapy and Czech mass privatization. More broadly, the roots of Russian policies extend to an understanding of Japanese post-war economic success and general knowledge of Western-style thinking on domestic and international economic policies. It is noteworthy that Russians draw lessons from foreign failures as well as successes. The decision to allow foreigners to purchase Russian privatization certificates was a policy innovation based on observed shortcomings of reforms in eastern Europe. Gaidar was also aware of the dangers of Argentine-style corporatist and protectionist policies (i.e., import substitution).

The result of these lessons of direct failure, observed success, and observed failure is the formation of a foreign-policy schema which values the benefits of interdependence over those of military security, butter over guns. Russia's interests are perceived to be better served by allowing considerable foreign investment in major enterprises. This is expected to integrate Russia into the system of mutual interests and interdependence represented by the global market economy. Russian elites state that this serves the vital long-term function of increasing the efficiency of Russia's industry. In the short term, this policy is perceived to provide the important benefits of increasing budget revenues and decreasing the management burden on the state. The benefits are worth the trade-off in terms of foreign influence, vulnerability to espionage, infringed sovereignty, domestic political conflict, and reduction of the state's short-term potential for military production.

In Ukraine, elite statements, policy, and practice indicate that military security was valued over interdependence. The USSR was considered a failure in some important respects, but not in those directly relevant to foreign economic policy. Rather, the formative event of successful achievement of independence dominated the elite schema and set the parameters of policy options. Ukrainian elites valued economic independence and sovereignty above openness or efficiency. This policy cannot be understood by considering actual threats, domestic political factors, or economic interests. However, it is quite understandable given the lessons of Ukrainian history. Emerging from the Soviet empire, Ukrainian elites proceeded on the assumption that maximizing sovereignty and independence took pride of place.

The economic and other failings of the new Ukrainian state were perceived not as symptoms of major flaws in policy, but as temporary side effects of the colonial past. The perception was that with sovereignty and statehood, all other things would come in time. Progress in the economic sphere was expected to eventually emerge as the result of the strengthening of the state. Once decisions were being made in Kyiv rather than Moscow, better state administration of major enterprises could make them internationally competitive. There was no urgent need to fight risky and destabilizing political battles over foreign (or domestic) economic policy. Domestic political stability was worth the price of policy stagnation because it was perceived to further state building and consolidation of sovereignty. This was the lesson of both the achievement of independence in 1991 and the failure of Ukrainian state-building in 1918–1921.

Ukrainian leaders recognized some foreign successes, but these were perceived through the lens of the dominant schema based on Ukraine's successes. Basic policy preferences were already set by the formative event of independence, and references to observed success were consistent with existing policy. President Kravchuk believed it was "self evident" that models of economic cooperation such as the European Union or NAFTA had the effect of strengthening sovereignty and independence. But such institutions are usually considered to pose fundamental challenges to sovereignty. President Kuchma cited U.S. New Deal policies as evidence that strengthening the role of the state was appropriate in order to pull Ukraine out of crisis. Perhaps telling of his perception of successful Soviet economic management, he also referred to the period after the Bolshevik victory in the civil war as teaching the same lesson.

This emphasis was a result of the particular historical lessons learned by Ukraine's elites, and not simply of the real and obvious need to build an effective sovereign state strong enough to resist whatever desire Moscow had to reassert imperial power. States such as Latvia, Lithuania, Estonia, Georgia, and Moldova were able to reconcile divisive market reforms, a higher degree of economic openness, and the strengthening of sovereignty to maintain real independence from Moscow in spite of significant ethnic Russian populations, and even serious military threat in the cases of Georgia (Abkhazia) and Moldova (Pridnestrovia), including actual combat with forces closely associated with Moscow. *Post-Soviet state building and economic protectionism do not necessarily go together.* Rather, Ukrainian elites' perceptions of the lessons of history led them to prefer this policy.

The evidence here largely confirms the findings of the quantitative analysis in chapters 4 and 5. There can be little doubt that Russian elites were open to learning from foreign experience in the area of economic security. Key decisions were guided by these lessons. The case studies provide direct evidence that observational learning from both foreign successes and, perhaps in exceptional circumstances, foreign failures like Polish privatization or Argentina's decline, does indeed occur. And the patterns of learning revealed in the cases fit my hypotheses fairly well.

Now I turn to summing up the arguments and evidence presented in this book, and examining their implications.

CHAPTER 7

CONCLUSIONS: IMITATION AND TRANSITION IN INTERNATIONAL RELATIONS

HAWKS, DOVES, OWLS, AND MOCKING BIRDS

Do states learn from other states' experiences in international relations? This book has established the fact of imitation in foreign policy. But the book has also advanced a general theory of foreign policy learning and imitation that predicts when state-level learning is likely to occur, and what the likely sources of "lessons" will be. This theory finds considerable support in the quantitative and case-study data evidence. Finally, the book has outlined a general framework for studying preferences and interests in foreign policy and international relations. These elements combined, I believe, comprise this book's contribution to general understanding of foreign policy and international relations.

MAJOR FINDINGS

I find that the answer is yes, states do learn from other states' experiences in international relations. It is of course possible, though I think unlikely, that the evidence presented here for Russia and Ukraine is completely anomalous. But it is also possible, even likely, that the basic findings are generalizable. The brief look at cases such as Japan in the introduction seems to support this. The quantitative evidence in chapters 4 and 5 is that there is a discernable structure to analogy use along the lines predicted by my hypotheses. If analogies were not causally related to preferences, such relationships would be unlikely. A correspondence with preferences would exist if analogies were used rhetorically to advocate preferences; but if analogies were used in this way—either consciously or as the involuntary product of a cognitive process—there is no apparent reason why different types of analogies are related more or less strongly to preferences and to each other. However, this kind of variation clearly exists.

Observational learning in world politics usually takes the form of imitation, or learning from observed success, rather than learning from observed failure. A formative experience including a lesson of direct failure makes imitation likely. However, there is also evidence that astute policy makers—those who make use of more types of relevant information—do learn from others' mistakes, as Democritus and Benjamin Franklin would have them do. Russian policy makers, for example, drew lessons from the shortcomings of privatization in Eastern Europe that led them to allow foreigners to buy privatization certificates—a policy innovation.

Overall, prestigious models are more likely to be imitated than those that are seen as generally similar, or technically relevant. This does not bode well for the efficacy of policies developed through imitation, and should provide a caution to policy makers undertaking analysis of foreign experiences. The most prominent or attractive examples might not be the most relevant models. In Russia in the early 1990s a politically charged debate developed between those who thought that Russia should choose to build a state more like Switzerland than like the United States. Chair of the parliament Ruslan Khasbulatov was an advocate of the socially oriented Swiss approach. Egor Gaidar (1996, 72) argued that both of these models were largely irrelevant, and that the more appropriate model of choice would be between successful and unsuccessful states in Latin America, in order to avoid what he termed "latinamericanization" or descent into an ineffective, impoverished bureaucratic state. If policy makers had focused more on similar and relevant models and less on prestigious or high-profile models, the experiences of countries like Argentina, Brazil, or Chile might have been more instructive for Russia. In Ukraine, similar models would have been quite useful; and the model of Taiwan might have been very instructive, given both a sense of threat and close economic ties in its relations with China. During my 18 months of field research and in the hundreds of documents I have read by Ukrainian policy makers, I have never once heard or seen this analogy mentioned as instructive for Ukraine, probably because of the lack of prestige as well as cultural distance, as suggested in chapter 4.

Finally, due to cognitive and especially organizational factors, it appears that the policy priorities set in place by formative events do indeed have significant staying power. Evidence for this is found both in the quantitative analysis in chapter 5 and in the case studies in chapter 6. In chapter 5 analogy use in both Ukraine and Russia in 1990–1992 conforms well to the expectations regarding Russian and Ukrainian formative lessons. Elite analogy usage and preferences, especially in Russia, change somewhat in the later period 1993–1997. However, in chapter 6 it becomes clear that, by 1993, the basic parameters of foreign policy were set. Attempts to diverge from them ran into established expectations and interests; such divergence appears to happen gradually and incrementally, if at all. It is not much of an oversimplification to state that Chernomyrdin inherited Gaidar's policies, Kuchma inherited Kravchuk's. Both Putin in Russia and Iushchenko in Ukraine seemed restricted to incremental changes in foreign and domestic policies. The learning framework developed here is based on formative events, but it does not directly address issues of incremental learning from setbacks short of major failures. Under what conditions might observational learning be likely in the absence of a formative event of major failure?[1] Future research might focus on different patterns found in incremental learning versus learning through major shocks or other formative events.

But, the conclusions reached here might be challenged on several fronts. First, as mentioned, it is of course possible, though I think unlikely, that Russian and Ukrainian elites during the 1990s had highly atypical cognitive patterns. The only way to address this through research on other cases. Second, the patterns found here are of variation in foreign policy preferences of individuals, given three control variables. But it would be useful to include other variables such as economic factors, military threat, and aspects of domestic politics, especially for data aggregated at the state level. The case studies in chapter 6 go some way toward countering such arguments. But future research with more extensive state-level data would certainly be useful. Third, are the results for H1–H7 robust to other coding schemes and research designs, as I anticipate in chapter 3? This also must await future research. While these potential challenges cannot be fully answered here because they require additional data, none provides an obvious counter-explanation for the striking patterns of analogy use that emerge in the analysis above. It is to the wider implications of these findings for policy and theory that I now turn.

IMPLICATIONS FOR FOREIGN POLICY DECISION MAKING

This study advances our understanding of bias in decision-making by pointing to the circumstances under which different types of selection bias will operate based on the *source* of information. One clear implication is that relevant foreign evidence may be disregarded when it is overshadowed by perceptions of direct success. As mentioned in chapter 1, Khong (1992) convincingly argues that the Johnson administration's Vietnam decisions were largely shaped by the analogy to U.S. experience in the Korean war—an analogy that would be classified as Direct Success according to the framework developed here, and discourage vicarious learning. There was no major lesson of Direct Failure to make Lyndon Johnson's decision group receptive to George Ball's warnings based on French experience. After the failure in Vietnam, I would expect arguments such as Ball's to be more persuasive for American decision makers. The key for wise decisions, however, is to overcome cognitive bias in order to recognize and consider relevant information, regardless of the source.

A second implication for policy is that, even if decision makers consider vicarious experience, the most appropriate evidence may often be overlooked because it does not originate from a prestigious source. This may provide a caution for what often seems to be eager imitation of the United States by many states today.

Finally, when policy makers are acutely aware of their own state's failure(s), the opposite tendency may emerge: they may ignore relevant direct experience in favor of more cognitively appealing observed successes.

Social scientists are well aware of the powerful implications of selection bias for the conclusions we reach, but I do not know of any decision-making procedures or policy studies that focus on guarding against the type of selection bias outlined here, which has its root not in the content, but the source of information.

IMPLICATIONS FOR FOREIGN AID POLICIES

Foreign aid can have many goals, such as preventing starvation, providing incentives for reform, or buying influence or allegiance (Hook 1995). However, in the case of "technical aid," the goal is to change the way officials or other important elites of a given country think. In other words, the goal is psychological. It is in the case of technical aid—the provision of knowledge as opposed to goods, services, or funds—that the findings of this study are especially relevant. When the goal of aid is to change minds, there is an implicit assumption on the part of the aid giver that the recipient is in need of learning. A major problem for technical aid programs arises when the recipient does not share this perception.

One example of this seems to be the Canadians' program to aid Ukraine in its relations with Russia mentioned in the introduction. Even though the Ukrainians requested the aid themselves, they nevertheless did not seem open to changing the way they thought about foreign policy. The clear conclusion of the research in this book is that policy preferences are very unlikely to change absent a recognition of direct failure. One important question for technical aid programs, therefore, can be stated bluntly. If the recognition of direct failure is absent for the recipient, then technical aid might have little or no impact, or even a backlash effect. If technical aid is given in these circumstances, it must be conveyed to the recipients that they have been mistaken, that they have failed. This must not only be conveyed, but it must also be accepted and internalized by the recipient. If this message is not effectively communicated first, it is unlikely that any of the "good advice" coming from the donor's highly paid consultants will be heeded, or even heard.

How can technical aid programs be designed to communicate such a message? Simply telling the targets of the aid that they are "wrong" is likely to fail. The words will fall on deaf ears and the lecturer will likely be told that he simply doesn't understand the "real situation" in the recipient's country. In fact, this is likely to be true. How many USAID or World Bank officials have had to depend on bribes to feed their family, or to join the Communist Youth League in order to go to University?

In the cases examined here, one of the hypothesized reasons why Russian elites were more open to radical change is that they had had greater exposure to the world outside of the USSR and the socialist bloc. They were able to see Soviet policies as failures *relative to* the glaring successes of western policies, which they had seen first hand. It seems logical that direct contact with and study of the successful policies that are intended as "lessons" of technical aid is a potentially effective way to communicate to aid recipients that policy options superior to their own exist. This means that programs of study or practice outside of the home country are likely to have a greater impact on technical aid recipients than are programs that provide foreign consultants, advisers, or experts in-country. This will be the case unless the recipient is already convinced of the need for policy change. Another alternative is to expose elites from one country to high-level policy makers from a variety of countries that face, or have faced, similar problems. In this way, the relative failure of one's own policies may become apparent.

During my field research, I only heard positive stories of the impact of technical aid from officials and academics who had been on such programs of foreign study (e.g., former Deputy Prime Minister Roman Shpek; parliamentary "Reforma" faction leader Serhiy Sobolev; Trade Ministry official Valeriy P'iatnyts'kyy). I only heard of negative experiences of technical aid from Westerners working in Ukraine and Russia. In particular, technical consultants working in Kyiv for various U.S. and multilateral programs consistently complained of how obtuse, arrogant, and insincere Ukrainian officials were. And of how ineffective they felt their programs were. In other words, the Ukrainians just weren't listening. They didn't "get it."

Although all of this evidence is of course anecdotal, the following excerpt from an interview with Valeriy P'iatnyts'kyy (1997), at the time Deputy Head for Multilateral Economic Relations of the Ukrainian Ministry of Foreign Economic Relations and Trade, is suggestive. He describes the effect of participation in two such technical aid programs on his understanding of foreign economic policy.

> Over these years, my approach to foreign ties, in particular to foreign trade has changed. . . . [M]y views on economic policy . . . underwent a period of formation. First taking in the events which were happening, when I worked in the University [as an economics instructor]. In 1994 I was actually among the first teachers to teach [market] economics and I studied in the Institute of International Development of the World Bank in Washington. A two-month course on market economics. That had a certain impact on me. And in 1995 I was in a course for a half year in Vienna, the United Vienna Institute . . . [T]here was a big course on economic policy; not theory but policy. [T]he professors and lecturers [were] from all over the world, from the IMF . . . [I had] the knowledge of a university professor plus the experience of a state servant working directly in some aspects of foreign policy, economy, trade policy. [T]hey were advisers of the minister, advisers of the prime minister, . . . It was necessary to expand my approach with some sort of knowledge and experience. [My] views changed in the direction of liberalization in general, of everything . . . in the direction of understanding and becoming aware of those economic processes which on one hand brought us to the fall of the USSR and to the crisis at which we have arrived, and what happened outside of [the USSR], the states which

existed, the systems which existed. . . . That is today, the . . . path of development is the same for everybody. . . . And the most important thing that in general was for me a sort of opening was . . . the orientation on the needs of
concrete consumers. That is the theory of . . . consumption. . . . For us [in the
USSR] it was understood that we had an orientation towards production.
Production for the sake of production. Trade also for the sake of trade. It was its
own type of, in theoretical terms, a theory of mercantilism . . . To trade for the
sake of saving, not for the sake of improving your condition.

Clearly the message of the two aid programs P'iatnyts'kyy participated in
was effective. He came to reinterpret the experience of his own country by
expanding his knowledge of the experiences of other countries, in part
through direct contact with other policy makers. These programs were conducted in the West, away from P'iatnys'kyy's normal policy and intellectual
environment. The relative failure of Soviet foreign economic policy was
brought home to him in this way.

The implications of my research are that technical aid programs that
remove participants from their typical environment and expose them to a
wide range of authoritative knowledge have a higher chance of success.
Another such program, besides the two economic programs mentioned by
P'iatnyts'kyy, is the International Visitors program for mid- and high-level
officials run by the U.S. Information Agency (USIA).

Indeed, a kind of "study abroad" program was apparently not unimpor-
tant to Japan's early success in emulating China. Prince Shotoku sent Japan's
best young minds to study China as members of a "large official embassy" in
A.D. 607 Reischauer (1974, 20) argues that "[t]his embassy, and many others
that followed it during the next two and a half centuries, played a vital role
in the great period of learning from China. . . . The result was, in a sense, the
first organized program of foreign study in the world."

DOES THE JAPANESE EXAMPLE FIT THE THEORY?

Returning to the case of Japan, it can now be asked whether the theory
developed in chapter 3 helps illuminate why Japan imitates foreign experience when it does, including in foreign policy priorities. The expectation
clearly is that Japan will imitate others in the wake of major failures, and
ignore foreign experience when things are going well.

In 1945, Japan had clearly suffered a major foreign policy failure—perhaps
the most damaging such failure any state has ever experienced. But, couldn't
it be true that what Reischauer describes as the eagerness to learn from the
United States in post-war Japan is really nothing more than giving in to the
inevitable, since the United States did occupy Japan after an unconditional
surrender. Reischauer (1974, 242–243) does not think so, and cites the
"special postwar Japanese psychology" as one of the factors, along with previous experience with democracy and other institutions, that made Japan
receptive to the lessons brought by the Americans.

In earlier periods, Reischauer (18) notes that at the time Japan began deliberately imitating China, in the sixth century, it had just become aware of the level of China's development. The sudden discovery of a superior civilization in geographic proximity to their own may have created a sense of relative failure among the Japanese, or of an unprecedented situation of competition or threat. In addition, China was indeed a prestigious model of success: "the richest, most powerful, and technologically most advanced country in the world. . . . It is small wonder that the primitive Japanese in their isolated island country felt the reflected glory of the new Chinese empire and awoke to a new awareness of Chinese civilization. The result was a cultural surge forward in Japan that stands in sharp contrast to the slow, fumbling progress of Northern Europe at this time. The difference lay not so much in the somewhat similar tribal peoples of Japan and Northern Europe, as in the attractiveness of their respective models. While Rome was falling completely to pieces, China was rising to new heights of grandeur" (Reischauer 1974, 18–19).

In foreign policy, emulation of China was also evident. "Under the influence of Chinese ideas, the Japanese for the first time thought of the Yamato state as an empire, and at that, an empire on equal footing with China. Prince Shotoku even dared to phrase a letter to the Chinese as coming from the Emperor of the Rising Sun to the Emperor of the Setting Sun" (Reischauer 1974, 21–22). In domestic politics, "the Japanese created an elaborate central government, patterned after that of T'ang China, the most highly developed and complex governmental structure the world had as yet seen." But the success of Japan's policies allowed its leaders to cease looking outward for models to emulate. Japan continued to develop, but in isolation, and without suffering another major shock until Admiral Perry's arrival in 1853. Then, this clear failure of Japan's isolationist foreign policy led to a reordering of foreign policy preferences, and Japan emulated the policies of the liberal western empires that threatened it.

This successful imperial foreign policy was not abandoned until it in turn led to disaster. In 1945, as noted, the Japanese were again acutely aware of policy failure, and in search of a new model. The case of Japan does seem to fit my theoretical expectations based on psychological and organizational dynamics. Imitation leads to change in foreign policy preferences only in the wake of a shock. Imitation does not occur, or at least has no effect on policy, in the absence of such a shock. Once a new policy is set in place, it may change incrementally but will not change drastically in the absence of a major failure or unprecedented challenge. This is quite consistent with my theoretical framework and provides some initial support for my claims of generalizability.

THEORETICAL IMPLICATIONS

I hope this study's most important contribution to international relations theory is to suggest a mechanism for moving foreign policy preferences in either direction along the cooperation–conflict continuum. Several authors

have advanced concepts including such a continuum. They include Arnold
Wolfers's (1962) ideas about discord and collaboration, poles of power and
indifference, Karl Deutsch's (1968 [1957]) concept of a security community,
Robert Keohane and Joseph Nye's (1989) concepts of complex interdependence and realism, Richard Rosecrance's (1986) concepts of the worlds
of the trading state and the military–political state. These authors all posit
not only two possible poles of a continuum, but the likelihood that the characteristics of the international system change as states' foreign policies range
along the continuum.

But what moves foreign policy in one direction or another? Rosecrance
argues that it is the relative cost of conquest, influenced by technological
change and the spread of nationalism, but he also expects that "social learning" influences perception of these realities. Keohane and Nye also cite various objective factors, but recognize that it is perception of these factors that
actually leads to change in policy. Kenneth Waltz (1979) also makes an argument for movement along the continuum, and imitation is an important part
of this movement, but in the neo-realist conception of things socialization will
be unidirectional, toward and not away from "primacy of force" policies.

These authors also recognize the likelihood that the characteristics of the
international system change as states' foreign policies range along the continuum. Sorting out the implied feedback loop is one area of interest for further
investigation. Changing preferences should lead to change in the strategic setting, which should cause more change in preferences by providing new lessons of direct and observed experiences of success and failure. Foreign policy
elites can be assumed, as a rule, to be interested in the success of their policies. But their understanding of the formula for success can change. The
greater the degree of perceived policy failure, it can be assumed, the more
likely that preferences will shift as a result of observational learning.

The theory of learning in foreign policy advanced here, and the evidence
supporting it, make the case that major formative events have the effect of
moving a given state's foreign policy preferences along this continuum. The
process of imitation or emulation provides a mechanism for the spread of
"trends" or norms regarding foreign policy. One such trend is the issue studied in chapter 6: economic liberalization including opening to foreign investment in major enterprises. This policy has spread around the globe,
beginning with Thatcher and Pinochet, who both faced serious economic
failures. Equity markets and FDI regimes have now been liberalized world-
wide, and a wave of privatizations has also taken place. It seems extremely
unlikely that these policies are all based on myopic, self-focused processes
and not on imitation and emulation of observed success. This is suggestive
of a systemic learning process, of which imitation is a central component.

A Systemic Perspective

If it is assumed that the "shape" or rules of the international system are
unknown to states, then systemic learning can represent a process of

discovering the shape of the system, and learning from foreign experience can play a role in this process. Dan Reiter (1996) tested a systemic learning hypothesis and found that small states generally did not learn systemic lessons about alliance behavior from the two world wars. However, if systemic learning is possible, this has theoretical and policy implications for understanding and influencing foreign policy change, especially when choices are not dichotomous.

If systemic learning involves lessons that change policy preferences of a considerable proportion of states in the system, it can conceivably take two forms: similar lessons learned by states from their individual experiences, or shared lessons drawn by some or all states from events which some states do not experience directly.

It can be assumed that a stable international system is one in which all states have adapted Pareto-optimal foreign policy mixes. These policies provide some balance of preferences, perhaps characterizable in terms of absolute or relative gains. For simplicity, I'll assume that preferences do not vary greatly among states in this system. If something in the international system changes so that states' policies are no longer optimal, they will experience some degree of immediate policy failure and learn that something is wrong. In this way, direct individual experience can provide a systemic lesson of failure for states.

However, learning about the new optimal policy mix is likely to be a process of trial and error. Presumably, all states will not react to objective change in the same way. This can be represented by assuming random policy variation in reaction to the new systemic environment. A state that finds the new optimal policy mix will be likely to provide an example, or model, for others through its relative success. Similarly, states which stumble onto poor policy mixes may provide lessons of what not to do in these new conditions for some astute policy makers. Therefore, systemic policy innovation has two fundamental stages. First, all or some states learn from direct experience (significant policy failure) that they are doing something wrong. Second, one or some states may stumble onto the "correct" new policy mix, but many are likely to learn about the new optimal policy mix through observation of others' successes in combination with their own relative failures.

Such a systemic model connects observational learning with socialization into the international system while allowing for systemic change.[2] It may help explain why and how different systems with different dominant norms emerge in different historical periods (e.g., colonialism, balance-of-power, national self-determination, global economic interdependence). Harold Lasswell (1950[1936], 153) has made similar observations: "Passing time includes the rise and fall of skill combinations of every description. It seems that during the feudal age in Europe skill in fighting was a major avenue to power. Later, skill in organization was essential to the consolidation of the national monarchies. Skill in bargaining brought the private plutocrat into his own during the nineteenth and early twentieth centuries. The insecurities of the world of the twentieth century, manifested in world war and revolution, have fostered the chances of the man of skill in propaganda (witness Lenin, Mussolini, Hitler)."

After 1991, Russia and Ukraine can be seen as states in search of optimal foreign (and domestic) policies. In Russia's case, the Soviet experience was a clear example of foreign policy failure for most elites who were initially in power. In Ukraine's case, this was not so. According to the systemic perspective, they both should be open to learning from foreign experiences because the environment has changed, although the specific nature of Ukraine's formative experiences of independence will cause it to search for policy options later than Russia, once disconfirming evidence mounts. This fits well with the evidence from chapters 5 and 6.

FAILURE, LUCK, AND WISDOM

It may be true that, in world politics, the state that fails badly is luckier than the others that muddle through. Costly failure appears to be the source of profitable reform. On the other hand, if policy makers would be wise, they would do well to learn to recognize their own state's *relative* shortcomings, as well as the successes *and* failures of others. In addition, the results of this study indicate that an essential element of effective relations with other states is understanding how an interlocutor perceives the successes and failures of his or her own state.

In this book I have found that imitation does occur in international relations and I have drawn theoretical and policy implications based on my schematic learning framework. I have used quantitative and qualitative methods to evaluate the role of analogies to direct and foreign experience in the shaping of foreign policy preferences. And I have attempted to point to the importance of preferences and change in preferences for understanding the international system. I believe foreign policy learning and preference change in the international system are topics that deserve greater investigation and a more central role in the study of international relations. Most scholars and policy makers would agree that they are difficult topics to study; I hope this book helps promote further research in these areas and provides some of the tools with which to do this rigorously and productively.

APPENDICES
APPENDIX A: TECHNICAL NOTES

This appendix contains additional technical notes regarding the data collection, data coding, and statistical analysis.

DATA COLLECTION AND CODING PROCEDURE

The data is assembled from publications of the Ministry of Foreign Affairs of Ukraine, the Ministry of Foreign Affairs of the Russian Federation, and from interviews with foreign policy elites. The following volumes were used: *Polytika i chas* [Politics and Time (Ukrainian)] 1990–1997; *Mezhdunarodnaia zhizn* [International Affairs (Russian)] 1990–1997; *Diplomaticheskii vestnik* [Diplomatic Courier (Russian)] 1993, 1995, 1997. Interviews were conducted by the author in 1997 and early 1998.

Five Ukrainian interviewees were sufficiently senior to include in the data set: Vitold Fokin—prime minister; Roman Shpek—deputy prime minister; economics minister; Vadim Hetman—central bank head; Oleksandr Razumkov—presidential adviser; first-deputy security council secretary; and V'iacheslav Chornovil—opposition (*Rukh*) leader.

No assumptions are made about the importance of the frequency of usage of various analogies. Even if the same analogy is used more than once in a given text, it is counted once only. And each text can have only one value for each type of analogy and for policy preferences. If there is an apparent contradiction, the coder is instructed to consider the statements together and use his or her judgment to resolve the conflict. In practice, some analogies and analogy types occurred more than once in a given article, but it was rare that these seemed contradictory. There was a strict rule that conflicts over values assigned to one variable could not be resolved by reference to another variable.

INTERCODER RELIABILITY

There was complete agreement among coders about the categorization of analogies as either "direct" or "observed" and either "success" or "failure." Not surprisingly, coding analogies and policy preferences along the five-point scale proved more difficult. Scott's *pi* statistic for intercoder reliability involves calculating both the rate of complete agreement between coders, and the rate of agreement expected by chance given the number of categories and their overall frequency of use (Holsti 1969, 140; Scott 1955). For the five-point scale, chance would produce 39 percent agreement, while the coders' judgments were in total agreement 60 percent of the time. Using 15 observations coded by both myself and another coder hired for this project, I have calculated Scott's *pi* as.0.32. It is also worth noting that in only three instances, out of 75 total pair of coding decisions tested, was the difference between the coding for any given analogy or policy preferences greater than 1.

Holsti (1969, 142) argues that as coding complexity increases, the results may be both "more useful and less reliable." In the present context, the achievement of complete agreement in three fifths of the coding is a fair result, significantly higher than expected by chance; although a higher rate of agreement is of course desirable. The data are not perfect, but complete agreement is not a necessary condition for inclusion in the analysis.

One reason for using multiple coders is simply to expand the size of the data set. For this, maximum agreement is the only important criterion. Another reason, however, is to guard against coder bias. I have separated summary statistics of each coder's data to determine whether there are any systematic differences (table A.1). Nearly 70 percent of the observations coded by the hired coder were Ukrainian elites, while data coded by me included an even division of Russian and Ukrainian observations. This largely explains why the average values assigned for foreign policy preference, Observed Success, and Direct Success were consistently closer to the negative pole of the scale in my coding. For the hired coder, the mean score for Russian elites is -0.0000 while that for Ukrainians is 0.4000. Similarly, in the data I coded, the mean scores are -0.0862 and 0.0909, respectively. The Ukrainians are more intuitive realist than the Russians in both coders' data. But, when a variable for "coder" is included in equation 6, it is insignificant ($p = 0.945$) and does not change the significance or direction of any other variable. Finally, if equation 6 is run without the hired coder's data, the results are similar to those in table 4.2. Even though the sample size is reduced, Direct Failure: Liberal, Observed Success: Liberal, and Observed Failure: Mixed retain significance. Observed Failure: Realist ($p = 0.186$) Observed Success: Realist ($p = 0.354$) and state ($p = 0.153$) do not, but no other variables become significant either.

In sum, while coding complexity may lead to noise in the data, and decrease the statistical significance of the results, it does not appear to bias the analysis.

Below I give further details of the coding process, but first I discuss some aspects of the quantitative analysis.

QUANTITATIVE ANALYSIS

Ordered Probit

The primary statistical method used to analyze the quantitative data is ordinal or ordered probit, a form of maximum likelihood estimation. Ordered probit is

Table A.1 Characteristics of data by coder

	N=	% year of birth after 1939	% state = Russia	Mean of foreign policy=	Mean of OS=	Mean of DS=
Coder 0 (BG)	119	31.1	50.4	-0.0000	-0.2188	-0.0602
Coder1 (CD)	29	27.6	31.0	0.3448	-0.0556	0.0833

appropriate for my data set because the dependent variable is represented by ordinal categorical rather than continuous data. Ordinary least squares (OLS) regression is not appropriate with such data because the dependent variable cannot be assumed to plausibly take on any possible value, nor can it be assumed to be interval data in which the values assigned measure the distance between points on a consistent scale (Aldrich and Nelson 1984, 11–12; Long 1997, 114–115). Maximum likelihood estimation techniques such as ordered probit involve determining the probability that the dependent variable takes on a certain value, given values of the independent variables (Aldrich and Nelson 1984, chapter three). For samples with 100 or more degrees of freedom, maximum likelihood estimation approximates the properties of OLS as an unbiased, efficient estimator with normal distribution of errors (53). This is important for the reliability of hypothesis testing.

Ordered probit analysis rests on several assumptions about the data. Long (1997, 119) discusses these in detail. Among these are an assumption of some relationship between exogenous and endogenous variables, although not necessarily a linear one, independence of observations, and the normal distribution of residuals. There is no indication that data used in the analyses violate these assumptions.

INDEPENDENCE OF OBSERVATIONS

Because 91 observations are articles, speeches, or statements by the 27 individuals represented more than once, the assumption of the independence of observations is challenged (Long 1997, 119). An ordered probit estimation (table A.2) for lagged foreign policy preferences (in the most recent prior observation for that individual) shows that the relationship is statistically insignificant.

DATA CODING: DETAILED EXPLANATION AND EXAMPLES

The data are coded based on the analogies and preferences they contain. I have drawn on the content analysis literature for guidance in developing and implementing the coding scheme (e.g., Krippendorf 1980). Content analysis is defined by Holsti (1969, 14; see also Weber 1990, 82n1) as "any technique for making inferences by and systematically identifying specified characteristics of messages." Axelrod (1976) employs procedures similar to content analysis in order to determine "cognitive maps" of decision makers. In the present context, Axelrod's seminal study is especially informative in that his focus was on decision-makers' perceptions of causal relationships and how these maps (similar to schemata) are used to interpret new information.

In my study, the unit of analysis for coding purposes is the individual article, policy statement, or interview. The type of content to be coded is a selection of text that either indicates a foreign policy preference (dependent variable) or a foreign policy relevant analogy (independent variable). All preferences and analogies relevant to

Table A.2 Ordered probit estimation of lagged preferences effects on preferences

Variable	Coefficient	Standard error	Z	Significance
Policylag	0.11	0.28	0.40	$p = 0.35$

foreign policy in the articles, statements, or interviews are used. There are four possible types of analogies that must be coded, as well as the foreign policy preferences expressed in each observation unit. The analogy types are Direct Success, Direct Failure, Observed Success, and Observed Failure.

The implications of the analogies must be assessed to determine coding. The coder must ascertain not only which of the four types of analogy is being used, but also what the stated or implied meaning of the analogy is for foreign policy. This necessitates some knowledge and judgment. Coding preference is more straightforward and involves identifying statements of what should be done or what is correct to do. Examples are given below of how preferences and analogies are coded along the five-point scale (figure 3.3).

No assumptions are made about the importance of the frequency of usage of various analogies. Even if the same analogy is used more than once in a given text, it is counted once only. If there is an apparent contradiction between two statements of preferences, or the same type of analogy (e.g., observed failure) or the same analogy used more than once, the coder is instructed to consider the statements together and use his or her judgment to resolve the conflict. In other words, there is a rule that each text can have only one value for each type of analogy and for preferences. In practice, many analogies and analogy types occurred more than once in a given unit, but it was fairly rare that these were contradictory. It was especially rare that the same analogy or analogy type was coded as both negative and positive within the same unit. Coding contradictions usually involved differences of a value of one on the five-point scale, and were resolved as the individual coder saw fit based on his or her knowledge of the context of each analogy (for a discussion of coding techniques in general see Weber 1990, 21–40).

The coding task here involves a certain degree of judgment as well as language skills and some knowledge of Russian and/or Ukrainian politics. Use of a degree of judgment is necessary because, as noted by Morrow, preferences are not directly observable, and success and failure must be understood as subjective assessments of events by the foreign policy elites. Although judgment is a necessary part of coding, objectivity can be preserved if the personal beliefs of coders are not expected to influence coding outcomes (Shapiro 1997).[1] The coding rules alone must determine scores. In the case of observations coded by the author (80 percent of the total), in order to avoid bias due to my preexisting beliefs about the views of individual elites and knowledge of the content of their writings, I first recorded all statements indicating policy preference, then I separated the statements from reference to their authors in order to code them. Analogical references (the independent variables) were coded in the same way. In this way, I was coding "blind," unaware of whose statements I was coding and the corresponding analogies/preferences.

A five-point scale represents ordinal points ranging from pure absolute gains preferences to mixed preferences to pure relative gains preferences. It incorporates preferences for interdependence, political cooperation, and autarky, treating these as the poles and mid-point of a continuum of possible preference rankings. As discussed in the main text, this definition of the dependent variable in the study of foreign policy is intended to allow for the analysis of "foreign policy" as a single object of study. Regardless of the validity of my particular continuum, if it is not possible to think about foreign policy as a single variable, I would argue that the term itself really has no analytical meaning and should be abandoned by students of politics and international relations.

How do coders determine the value of a particular analogy or preference on this scale? I have relied as much as possible on existing international relations literature for coding instructions. Examples from well-known works served as prototypes for coding. In this way, I hoped to maximize the chance that the coding reflects generally accepted categories of foreign policy types.

The discussion of intercoder reliability above indicates an acceptable level of reliability in the data. The validity of the coding scheme is more difficult to assess than its reliability. Does my coding measure what it is intended to, "lessons" and "preferences"? The empirical analysis in the main text is one test of whether my data as coded have what Weber (1990, 18–21) calls *hypothesis validity* and *predictive validity*. The former requires that analysis establish relationships between variables as expected by theory; the latter that events outside of the data correspond to expectations established in the study. Although these criteria for validity clearly are not definitive, this is a function of the fact that this is the first application of my coding scheme. There is no external prior standard with which the coding here can be compared. In the absence of such a measure of validity, I briefly discuss the variables and present several examples of coding of preferences and analogies from the data set.

Dependent Variable

My dependent variable is foreign policy preferences. To measure these, I use elite statements of goals or policy priorities. There are several reasons why it is possible to consider elite statements representative of actual foreign policy preferences. First, there is some evidence of continuity between public and private statements of foreign policy elites (Khong 1992). Second, there is evidence that prevarication in public statements on foreign policy is rare (Axelrod and Zimmerman 1981). Third, most of the statements used here are better seen as inter-elite communication than as "public" statements. The journals of the Russian and Ukrainian foreign ministries are simply not widely read. The audience is a narrow group of practitioners and specialists. Statements by foreign policy elites in these journals are likely to be seen as statements of official policies or intentions by those executing the foreign policy of each state. Declaring basic foreign policy preferences at odds with actual goals or strategy would likely be counterproductive in these fora.

Examples of Preference Coding from the Data Set

Coded as "−1": Andrei Kozyrev, Foreign Minister of the Russian Federation, *International Affairs* 3–4, 1992, Speaking at a February 1992 conference of the Ministry. "The drastic changes in internal development that we are living through today, possibly for the first time in Russian history, are taking place not in a hostile environment, as was the case in the past, but in an overall favorable external environment. And this substantially eases reformist activities, giving an added chance for democracy. Now there is really no source of danger for Russia whatsoever. There are no potential enemies, or the military threats to Russian interests associated with them" (93). "The goal is a broad one: the thorough economization of our policy and diplomacy. . . . The most important criterion here is achievement of an organic commonality with the world economy, speedy entry into the IMF and other institutions." (97)

Kozyrev's comments are coded as "−1"—a moderate preference for economic interdependence. The selection indicates no perception of foreign threat or immediate concern with relative gains, and the primacy of economic integration with the rest of the world. References to international support for political development, and the goal of membership in an international organization, indicate that political cooperation is expected to accompany economic cooperation, thus moderating his seemingly categorical "trading state" views.

Coded as "0": Leonid Kuchma, Ukrainian President, former Prime Minister, speaking to the General Assembly of the UN, November 21, 1994, *Politics and Time* 12, 1994. "In particular, the attempt to form a viable Agenda for Development is today the highest priority not only for Ukraine, but certainly for all member states of the United Nations. . . . Among these tasks, as we understand them in Ukraine, is the guarantee of a strong peace and political stability through socio-economic reform and development in the interests of man" (3). "We have a firm intention to . . . eventually join the GATT/ WTO system. We hope that the system's activity will encourage the creation of an open, transparent trade system and create additional opportunities to expand the access to the world market of export products from states with transition economies, including Ukraine" (6).; "We propose . . . a 'Partnership for Development'. . . . for stable economic growth . . . , to declare solidarity in the task of strengthening of international security, justice, and equal rights, to voice the importance of creating real partnership and equal rights in all areas of international life." (7)

Kuchma's comments are coded as "0"—a preference for negotiation and political cooperation. It is political cooperation, likely through an international organization, that will promote a range of goals including peace, stability, growth, equality, justice, and access to markets. The political values of international solidarity and partnerships are primary, implied necessary conditions for favorable outcomes in economic and military areas.

Coded as "1": Iurii Skokov, chair of the National Council of the Congress of Russian Communities, former Secretary of the Russian Security Council; *International Affairs* 11–12, 1995. "Russia needs to undertake a strong foreign policy based primarily on national interests and on the interests of global stability. We must clearly define the priorities of Russian foreign policy. Naturally, one of the most important priorities is relations with the former Soviet Republics. Here, unquestionably, a course toward integration and cooperation is necessary. Nevertheless we must decisively, harshly [*zhestko*] defend the interests of millions of our compatriots, who have become foreigners by the will of fate in what used to be a single country." (13)

Skokov's preference is coded as "1"—a moderate preference for military security. The emphasis in his comments is on protecting Russia from implied threats, and the need to defend national interests unilaterally. Cooperation within the former Soviet space is not a goal in itself, but a means for defending interests, including integration of territories previously ruled from Moscow and possible harsh measures in defense of Russians' or Russophones' rights outside of Russia. Neither political nor economic cooperation is a priority, but there is no direct mention of imminent military threat to Russian "national interests," so this statement is coded as a moderate leaning toward the primacy of force.

Independent Variables

The variables Direct Success (DS), Direct Failure (DF), Observed Success (OS), and Observed Failure (OF) correspond to the four possible types of analogy I have identified. These are coded according to their content using the five-point scale in figure 3.3. Using the same scale for dependent and independent variables is theoretically appropriate because the meaning of an analogy is assumed to be literally "analogous" to whatever foreign policy issue the decision maker is grappling with. Examples are provided to illustrate how coders judged the content of these analogies and assigned each a value on the scale.

Examples of Independent Variable Coding

Direct Success

Coded as "−1": Evgenii Primakov, Russian Foreign Minister, speaking to the Argentine Council on Foreign Relations, November 24, 1997, *Diplomatic Courier* 12, 1997. "Life has shown clearly that Russia has moved along the path of market economics and democracy, and is becoming an increasingly attractive partner. There has been a major privatization program, inflation has been controlled . . . , production has stabilized, the Russian ruble feels confident. The Russian economy is weathering the test connected with the international financial . . . turbulence. The government and the parliament are taking even more measures aimed at creating attractive conditions for . . . investment" (33).

Coded as "1": Iurii Shcherbak, Ukrainian Ambassador to the U.S., *Politics and Time* 11, 1996. "In the mass media of the USA in 1992 and 1993 there appeared a series . . . of openly anti-Ukrainian publications, often originating from enemies of Ukraine in foreign propaganda centers. . . . [I]f the excess and noise of this black propaganda campaign is disregarded, it was easy to identify two points of criticism. (1). Nuclear disarmament (non-disarmament) of Ukraine. (2). The absence of detectable economic reforms, the conservation in Ukraine of a series of characteristics of the Communist-Soviet regime. . . . Today it is possible to note with pride that young Ukraine's diplomacy honorably resisted the 'onslaught and pressure' from the USA and Russia, played the 'nuclear card' brilliantly, and received the maximum possible political profit from 'denuclearization.' " (6–7)

Direct Failure

Coded as "0": Anatolii Zlenko, Ukrainian Foreign Minister, *International Affairs* 11, 1990. "The skins, as they say, are old, but the wine is new. We have no doubt that a full use of their constitutional rights [1978 USSR Constitution] by all of the Union Republics from the very start would not only not have contradicted the interests of the Soviet Union in the past, but would have saved it many difficulties today" (6). "We have studied the experience of Ukrainian foreign relations of 1917–1922, the proposals of the USSR [Ukrainian Soviet Socialist Republic] 1922–1923 for the organization of a joint foreign political service of the USSR [Union of Soviet Socialist Republics], which would have incorporated the interests of Ukraine. . . . Aren't we working on the same problems today?" (13)

Observed Success

Coded as "−1": Henadii Udovenko, Ukrainian Foreign Minister, "Priorities of Foreign Policy Speech of H. Y. Udovenko at the Session of the Supreme Rada of Ukraine 15, September [1994]." *Politics and Time* 10 1994. "There has been some movement . . . the recent economic agreements with Kazakstan and Uzbekistan, based on the principles of GATT. That is, there is a basis for development of normal, civilized relations." (4)

Observed Failure

Coded as "−1": Roman Shpek, Minister, Head of the Ukrainian Agency for Reconstruction and Development, former Deputy Prime Minister, former Minister of the Economy, former Finance Minister, Interview November 28, 1997. "For us instructive today is the experience of Northern Korea, Cuba, this is the memory of our past . . . we were building socialism for 75 years . . . millions of people died . . . nobody saw socialism, as they called it, 'with a human face' " (question 7).

Appendix B: List of Interviews

Ukraine

Top-Level Elites Included in the Data Set

Chornovil, Viacheslav Maksymovych. Kyiv, 11/5/97
Fokin, Vitold Pavlovich. Kyiv, 11/18/97.
Het'man, Vadym Petrovych. Kyiv, 11/3/97.
Razumkov, Oleksandr Vasyl'ovych. Kyiv, 4/15/97.
Shpek, Roman Vasiliovych. Kyiv, 11/28/97.

Mid- and Low-Level Elites

Chumak, Vasyl Asenovych. Kyiv, 4/17/97.
[Senior Researcher, ISEMV]

Haran, Oleksiy Vasil'ovych. Kyiv, 4/17/97.
[Head of the Center for Political Analysis, newspaper Den]

Hrach, Leonid Ivanovich. Yalta, 6/20/97.
[Head, Communist Party organization, Crimea.]

Hrechaninov, Vadim Oleksandrovych. Kyiv, 4/29/97.
[President, The Atlantic Council of Ukraine; and Chief of the Military Experts Group, Ukrainian Center of Economic and Political Research; former positions: 1994–1996—Assistant to the President of Ukraine for Military Questions; 1993–1996 Deputy Minister of Defense for Military Policy and Deputy Director of the National Center of Disarmament; 1991–1993—Head of the Center for Operations and Strategic Research, Ministry of Defense of Ukraine]

Iatsenkovskyy, Volodymyr Volodymyrovych. Kyiv, 4/25/97.
[Head, Information Section, Ministry of Foreign Affairs]

Leshchenko, Leonid Ovdiyovych. Kyiv, 4/10/97.
[Leading Researcher, ISEMV; former position: 1993–1996, Minister-Counsellor in Embassy in China]

Myroshnychenko, Viacheslav Iuriyovych. Kyiv, 4/14/97.
[Assistant to the Minister of Information, Head of the Secretariat of the Ministry]

Odarych, Serhiy Olehovych. Kyiv, 4/11/97.
[President, Ukrainian Perspective; former position: Rukh Secretariat and Tsentr Provodu NRU until 1995].

Pakhomov, Iuriy Nikolaevich. Kyiv, 11/6/97.
[Director of ISEMV; adviser to the President of Ukraine]

P'iatnyts'kyy, Valeriy Teziyovych. Kyiv, 4/18/97.
[Deputy Head for Multilateral Economic Ties. Ministry of Foreign Economic Relations and Trade]

Pohrebyns'kyy, Mykhaylo Borysovych. Kyiv, 4/24/97.
[Director, Kiev Center for Political Research and Conflict Studies]

Potekhin, Oleksandr. Kyiv, 11/18/97.
[Director, Ukrainian Center for Peace, Conversion and Conflict Resolution Studies; Professor, Institute of Sociology, Acad. of Sciences of Ukraine; former position: Head, USA and Canada section, Ministry of Foreign Affairs of Ukraine, 1993–1994]

Sobolev, Serhiy Vladyslavovych. Kyiv, 11/4/97.
[Rada deputy, Head of Rada fraction "Reforma"; vice-chair of privatization committee].

Zherebets'kyy, Evhen Petrovych. Kyiv, 4/23/97.
[People's Deputy of Ukraine, member of Foreign Affairs Commissions; former position: Member of orgkomitet of Rukh during founding, second, third congresses, and was member of Secretariat of the Kyiv NRU]

Russia

Mid- and Low-Level elites

Kortunov, Andrei, Moscow, 2/12/98.
[President, Moscow Social Science Foundation.]

Prokhanov, Aleksandr. Moscow, 2/4/98.
[Editor, *Zavtra* newspaper; considered the father of post-Soviet Russian nationalism.]

Trenin, Dmitrii V. Moscow, 2/11/98.
[Carnegie Center, Moscow.]

Appendix C: Interview Questionnaires

English

Ben Goldsmith
Ph D Candidate
Department of Political Science
University of Michigan
March 1997. Updated October 1997
Draft Questionnaire - English

Ukrainian/Russian Foreign Policy

I am conducting research on Ukrainian/Russian foreign policy after the fall of the Soviet Union. I am especially interested in the reasons for continuity or change in policy. I have 7 questions. In order not to take up too much of your time, I propose that your answers be limited to 4-6 sentences. My goal is to learn your real opinions. If you would prefer that I not make reference to you, I of course will agree. I will also have a few demographic questions after the interview.

1) Independent Ukraine/The Russian Federation has been conducting relations with other sovereign states for over 5 years now. In your opinion, what is the major positive experience of Ukrainian/Russian foreign policy changed during this time? Why?

2) How has your personal approach to foreign affairs changed in these years? Why?

3) There are various opinions on the degree of interdependence between foreign economic relations and state security. Some specialists believe that a country can engage in open trade and investment, even with a country which is a possible military threat. Other specialists believe that there should be a policy of minimizing economic interaction with such a country. In your view, what should be Ukraine's/Russia's approach to foreign economic relations with a country which is a possible military threat?

4) At times, international norms or rules can conflict with the laws or interests of individual states. Some specialists believe that international norms should have precedence over laws or interests of individual countries. Other specialists believe that the laws or interests of each country, or in other words sovereignty, should have precedence. In you opinion, is it worth it to infringe Ukraine's/Russia's sovereignty in some way for the sake of international norms or rules? In other words, is it worth it for Ukraine to relinquish some part of its sovereignty in order to take part in international organizations?

5) This is a question about priorities for Ukraine/Russia today. Should Ukraine/Russia place more importance on the goal of full political participation in European and other international organizations, or should Ukraine/Russia consider increasing international trade and investment to be more important?

6) In your opinion, which experience in international affairs has been the most important, that is instructive, for Ukraine/Russia. Give 2-3 examples if possible.

7) Someone said that a wise person studies the experience of others. In your opinion, which experiences of foreign countries might be especially useful for the young Ukrainian/Russian state?

UKRAINIAN

Бенджамін Голдсміт, кандидат політичних наук   02.11.97 анкета 4
Університет Мічигану-Департамент Політології

Зовнішня Політика України

Моє дослідження стосується української зовнішньої політики після розпаду Радянського
Союзу. Зокрема мене цікавлять причини безперервності або змінюваності політики. У
мене до вас 7 запитань. Щоб не гаяти вашого часу, я пропонував би, щоб відповіді не
були більші, ніж 3-4 хвилини. Моя мета - узнати ваши справжні думки. Якщо ви
хочете, щоб я не посилався на вас, я звичайно був би згоден. У мене також буде
декілька демографічних запитань на прикінці інтерв'ю.

1. Незалежна Україна вже понад 5 років веде відносини з іншими суверенними
країнами. На вашу думку, який головний позитивний досвід української зовнішньої
політики в цей час? Чому Ви так уважаєте?

2. Як змінювався ваш особистий підхід до закордонних справ у ці роки? Чому?

3. Є різни думки про ступінь взаємозалежності між зовнішніми економічними
зв'язками та державною безпекою. Одні спеціалісти вважають, що можна вільно
торгувати, а також вкладати та приймати інвестиції, навіть якщо якась країна
становить потенційну воєнну загрозу для держави. Інші спеціалісти вважають, що
економічні стосунки з такою країною краще зводити до мінімуму. Як вважаєте ви,
якщо якась країна становить потенційну воєнну загрозу для України, якими повинні
бути економічні стосунки з цією країною?

4. Інколи буває суперечність між законами чи інтересами якоїсь країни та
міжнародними нормами чи правилами. Одні спеціалісти вважають, що міжнародні
норми повинні переважати над законами чи інтересами окремих країн. Інші
спеціалісти вважають, що повинні переважати закони чи інтереси кожної країни, тобто
принцип суверенітету. На вашу думку, чи варто обмежувати суверенітет України
заради міжнародних норм та правил? Іншими словами, чи варто віддати частину
суверенітету, щоб брати участь у міжнародних організаціях?

5. Ще одне запитання про пріоритети. Що найважливіше для України сьогодні:
політична участь у європейских та інших міжнародних організаціях чи дальший
розвиток економічних відносин з європейскими та іншими країнами?

6. На вашу думку, який досвід у міжнародному житті є для України важливим, тобто
повчальним? Наведіть 2-3 приклади, будь ласка.

7. Хтось сказав, що мудра людина вчиться на досвіді інших. Який досвід зовнішніх
країн, на вашу думку, може бути особливо корисним для молодої української держави?

RUSSIAN

Бенджамин Голдсмит
Ph.D. Candidate, Department of Political Science
University of Michigan (updated to 10/97 version. 1/22/98)

Внешняя политика России

Мое исследование касается российской внешней политики после распада Советского Союза. Меня особенно интересуют причины стабильности или изменений этой политики. У меня к Вам 7 вопросов. Чтобы не тратить ваше время, я предлагаю, на ответы не больше чем 2-3 минуты. Моя цель - узнать ваши настоящие взгляды. Если Вы предпочитаете, чтоб я не ссылался на Вас, я конечно был бы согласен. У меня тоже будет несколько демографических вопросов.

1. Российская Федерация уже более чем 6 лет ведет отношения с другими странами в контексте пост-советского мира. На ваш взгляд, какой главный **позитивный** опыт российской внешней политики за это время? Почему?

2. Как изменился ваш личный подход к международным делам за это время? Почему?

3. Есть разные мнения о степени взаемозависимости между внешними экономическими связями и государственною безопастностью. Одни специалисты считают, что можно свободно торговать, а также класть и принимать инвестиции, даже если какая-то страна становиться потенциальной военной угрозой для государства. Другие специалисты считают, что экономические отношения с этой страной лучше доводить до минимума. Как считаете Вы, если какая-то страна становиться потенциальной военной угрозой для России, какими должны быть экономические отношения с этой страной?

4. Иногда бывает противоречие между законами или интересами какой-то страны и международными нормами или правилами. Одни специалисты считают, что международные нормы должны **стоять над** законами или интересами отдельных стран. Другие специалисты считают, что **законы и интересы каждой страны** должны стоять над международными нормами, то есть принцип суверенитета. На ваш взгляд, стоит ли ограничить суверенитет России во имя международных норм и правил? Другими словами, стоит ли отдать какую-то часть суверенитета чтобы принимать участие в международных организациях?

5. Еще один вопрос о приоритетах. Что важнее для России сегодня: **политическое** участие в европейских и других международных организациях или **дальнешее** развитие экономических отношений с европейскими и другими странами?

6. Как вы считаете, какой опыт в международной жизни является для России значительным, то есть поучительным? Приведите 2-3 примера, пожалуйста.

7. Кто-то сказал, что мудрый человек изучает опыт других. Какой опыт других стран, по вашему мнению, может быть особенно полезным для Российской Федерации сегодня?

Appendix D: The Data Set

article y	ob	indivd	source	coder	state	month	df
Kravchuk, L. PIC 17190 (Sept), pp. 5-9	34	1			0		2
Zlenko, A.M. MZ 1190, pp5-17.	38	2	3		0		11
Hurenko, S.I. PIC 1191, pp3-18.	36	3	4		0		13
Hyrenko, A.M. PIC 291							14
Hurenko, S.I. PIC 291, 3-12.	36	3	4	4	0		15
Kravchuk, L.M. PIC 1191, pp3-8	34	1	1	4	1		23
vyetug hokov VR... No11 1991, 3-8	34	1	2		1		23
Zlenko, A. PIC No11 19927, 3-8	38	2	5	4	0		27
Belous, O. PIC 392, pp35-38	39	5	5		1		27
Belous, O. PIC No3 1992, 35-38	39	5	6	4	1		32
Zlenko, A.M. PIC 7-892, pp25-29.	38	2	6		0		32
Pavlychko, D. PIC 7-892, pp3-4.	29	6	7		1		32
Shcherbak, Iu. PIC 7-892, pp5-8.	34	1	7		1		38
Kravchuk, L. PIC No2 1992, 4-9	34	1	8		1		38
Tarasiuk, B. PIC No3 1992, 4-8	49	9	9		1		39
Hotsulin, V. PIC No.3 (Berezen) 1993, 40-45	39	9	17		1		39
Lytvyn, V. PIC No3 1993, 26-31	56	11	56		1		39
Durdynets, V. PIC No4 1993, 4-11	37		11		1		40
Kryzhanivs'kyy, V. PIC No.4 1993, 17-19			54		0		40
Hal'chyns'kyy, A. PIC No4 1993, 12-16	56		55		0		40
Lytvyn, V. PIC No4 1993, 43-47	34	1	56		0		50
Kravchuk, L.M.. PIC 2-94, p86	49	9	1	4	0		50
Tarasiuk, B.I.. PIC 2-94, pp3-6	34	1	2	4	1		51
Kravchuk, L.M.. PIC 3-94, pp67-69	38	1	2	4	1		52
Zlenko, A. PIC 394, pp 69-70.	48	10	2	4	0		53
Kravchuk, L.M.. PIC 4-94, pp70-71	38	2	9	4	0		55
Zlenko, A.M. PIC 4-94, pp92-93	38	2	11	4	0		57
Pyrozhkov, S. PIC 594., 22-21.	37	12	13	4	1		57
Zlenko, A. PIC 7-94, p87	28	13	13	4	0		57
Zlenko, A. PIC 9-94 pp85-86, 87	31	13	13	4	0		58
Durdynets, V.V.. PIC 9-94, pp15-20	31	9	13	4	1		58
Masol, V. PIC 9-94, pp82-83	49	14	13	4	1		59
Udovenko, H.Y., PIC, 10+94, pp3-5.	54	15	14	4	1		59
Udovenko, H.Y., PIC, 10+94, pp77-79	38	15	17	4	0		60
Udovenko. H.Y., PIC, 10+94, pp81-84	39	17	17	4	1		62
Tarasiuk, B.. PIC 11+94, pp76-78	31	13	13	4	0		64
Udovenko, H.Y., PIC 11+94, pp3-8	38	15	13	4	0		68
Udovenko, H.Y., PIC 11+94, pp74-75	31	13	13	4	1		70
Shpek, R., PIC 11+94, pp9-14.	31	13	13	4	1		70
Kuchma, L.D.. PIC 12+94, pp3-7	44	16	16	4	1		71
Moroz, O.O.. PIC 1+95, pp3-6	39	5	10		1		72
Hotsulin, V.P.. PIC, 2+95, pp3-8	48	13	13		0		73
Udovenko. H. PIC No4 1995, 3-8	31	17	17		0		73
Udovenko, H. PIC No6 1995, 7-13	31	13	15		0		75
Kuchma, L. PIC No8 1995, 3-6	38	15	15		0		75
Zlenko, A. PIC No10 1995, 17-21	38	15	16		1		76
Udovenko, H. I., PIC, 7?No9? 1995, 5-9	31	13	16		1		77
Udovenko, H. I., PIC No10 1995, 3-9	44	16	16				
Moroz, O. PIC No11 1995, 10-13	39	5	10				
Bilorus, O & V Vlasov, PIC No.12 1995, 31-36	48	13	13				
Pyrozhkov, S. and O. Kramarevs'kyy, PIC 196, pp14-24.	31	17	17				
Udovenko, H., PIC I+96, pp. 9-13	39	17	17				
Hotsulin, V. PIC I+96, pp3-8	38	15	15				
Kuchma, L.D. PIC 3+96, pp3-8	44	16	16				
Moroz, O. PIC 3+96, pp74-75	63	16	16				
Tabachnik, D.V., PIC 3+96, pp55-66	38	18	18				
Kuchma, L.D., PIC 4+96, pp3-7	38	15	15				
Kuchma, L. PIC 596, pp. 3-8							

Horbulin, V. PIC 5/96 pp84-86
Herman, V. PIC 6/96, pp. 16-20
Udovenko, H. PIC 7/96, 73-74
Kuchma, L. PIC 7/96, 3-7
Kuchma, L. PIC 7/96, 81-85
Tabachnik, D. PIC 7/96, 59-67
Kuchma, PIC 8/96, pp3-8
Kuchma, L. PIC 8/96, pp77-78
Tabachnyk, D. PIC 8/96, pp67-74
Iushchenko, V. PIC 8/96, pp56-61
Kuchma, L. PIC 9/96, pp3-4
Udovenko, H. PIC 10/96, pp. 3-6.
Shcherbak, Iu. PIC 11/96, pp. 3-17.
Udovenko, H. PIC 1/97, pp3-13.
Razumkov, O. Interview, 4/15/97.
Udovenko, H. PIC 7/97, pp3-7.
Shpek, Interview 1/28/97
Herman, V. Interview 11/3/97.
Chomovol, V. Interview, 11/5/97
Fokin, V. Interview 11/18/97.
Belov, O. F. PIC 7/77, 27/31
Shevardnadze, E. MZ 2/90, pp14-16.
Karaganov, S. A. (et al) MZ 3/90, pp 3-14.
Karaganov, S. MZ 5/90, pp49-22.
Karaganov, S. MZ 7/90, pp85-94.
Kozyrev, A & Gaidov, G., MZ 11/90, pp. 91-101
Karaganov, S. MZ 4/91, pp49-59.
Silaev, I. MZ 5/91, pp5-14
Shevardnadze, E. MZ 10/91 pp5-14.
Pankin, B. MZ 1/191, pp5-12.
Gareev, M MZ 2/492 pp15-26
Kozyrev, A. MZ 3-4/92, pp91-98
Khasbulatov, R. MZ 3-4/92, pp86-91.
Lukin, V. MZ 3-4/92, pp98-101
Primakov, E. MZ 3-4/92, pp102-104.
Stankevich, S. MZ 3-4/92, pp107-110.
Karaganov, S.A., MZ 7-8/92, 134-6.
Kozyrev, A. MZ 7+92, pp5-11
Dobrynin, A. MZ 7/92, pp54-68.
Kozhokin, E. MZ 8 9/92.
Kozyrev, A. DV 1-2/93, pp. 32-34.
Kozyrev, A. DV No3-4 1993, 25-27 (coder Christina D)
Kozyrev, A. V., DV 3-4/93, pp. 25-27
Kozyrev, A DV 3+/93, pp. 27-28.
Kozyrev, A. DV 3+/93, pp35-36.
Chernomyrdin, V. MZ No4 1993, 8-12 (coder BG)
Shaposhnikov, E. MZ 9/93, pp. 5-15.
Dubinin, Iu. MZ 9/93, pp. 24-43.
Kozyrev, A. MZ No11 1993, 3-14 (coder Christina D.)
Kozyrev, A. MZ No5 1994, 5-15 (coder Christina D.)
Kozyrev, A.V., PIC. 10+94, pp81-84.
Kozyrev, A. DV 1/95, pp. 59-60.
Yeltsin, B. DV 1/95, pp. 4-6
Ivanov, I. MZ No1 1995, 11-13 (coder Christina D.)
Ivanov, I.S. DV 1/95, pp. 60-62.
Kozyrev, A. DV 2/95, pp. 63-64.
Ivanov, I. S. DV 2/95, pp. 61-62.
Kozyrev, A. MZ No4-5 1995, 8-14 (coder BG)
Yeltsin, B. DV 3/95, pp. 3-7.
Kozyrev, A. DV 4/95, pp. 24-25.

Notes

1 Introduction

1. Moravcsik (1997) addresses the theoretical role of preferences across many issue areas. Frieden (1999) provides a useful summary of the literature on defining preferences.
2. Frieden (1999, 66–75) reviews other approaches to deducing states' international economic preferences.
3. Levy (1994) reviews the literature on learning in foreign policy. Cederman (2001) explores the liberal peace itself as a partially learned effect.
4. See also, Rosecrance (1986, 160, 185, 186, 212–213, 215) and Waltz (1979, 77, 118, 181). Keohane and Nye (1989, 12) discuss "contagion effects" and "social" sensitivity. Discussions of international norms usually rely on implicit or explicit assumptions about imitation (e.g., Finnemore and Sikkink 1998; Ray 1989; Raymond 2000, 295).
5. In the social psychological literature, there are distinctions made between "imitation," "identification," and "modeling." Bandura's (1986, 48) preferred term, "modeling," incorporates both imitation and identification. I have chosen to use the term imitation because it has gained some currency in the study of international politics (Waltz 1979) and its meaning is readily grasped by those unaware of the psychological terminology.
6. But see case studies in Resende-Santos 1996 and indirect evidence in Cederman 2001.
7. While Eckstein's logic informs my case selection, I do not believe that case studies can be valid *tests* of theories (Achen and Snidal 1989). A single case, or even a small-N comparative case study, cannot provide sufficiently generalizable evidence to justify discarding a theory or accepting it as a general proposition. However, in the search for provisional support, indications of possibly significant independent variables, and illustration of hypothesized causal effects, "crucial case" methodology is appropriate.
8. But it should be stressed that such an interpretation of Russian history, while perhaps common, is certainly open to question. And my argument and case selection don't hinge on it.
9. A study of the U.S. Security Council for the explicit purpose of learning from its structure and operation is found in the journal of the Ukrainian Ministry of Foreign Affairs (Baranovs'kyy 1995).
10. In explaining the new (1997) Russian strategic doctrine, Ivan Rybkin, then head of the Russian Security Council, went so far as to cite the English language terms "first-use" and "first-strike" and say that Russian policy was now equivalent to the former, not the latter—just like American policy. Russian ORT news, February 1997.

11. Another example is the Ukrainian government's study of the U.S. Securities and Exchange Commission as well as similar bodies in major European states. The chair of the then-newly formed State Commission of Ukraine for Securities and the Stock Market wrote: "Similar organs, regulating the stock market, exist in many countries of the world. In the creation of the Commission the experience of the analogous body in the USA was used. . . . However, there is no need to worry that, having taken the American example, Ukraine might not gain entry to the European stock market system: there is little substantive difference between the American Commission and . . . the French, German, English, and others . . ." (Mozgovoi 1997).

12. At the time of the interviews, Markevych was Director of the Canada-Ukraine Partners Office in Kyiv and Waschuk was Counselor at the Canadian Embassy there.

2   Choice, Learning, and Foreign Policy

1. Reiter (1996) perhaps comes closest, but recognizes that his framework applies with difficulty, if at all, to major powers or to complex choices.

2. "Utility" and "preference" are used interchangeably in formal decision theory (Pratt, Raiffa, and Schlaifer 1995, xvi–xvii).

3. Kimura and Welch (1998, 214) equate "interests" with "preferences-over-outcomes" within specific issues; although they distinguish between such single-issue preferences and a more general understanding of preferences, this distinction seems to me to be one of degree, rather than kind. Any issue-specific preferences involve trade-offs with other values, as they recognize in claiming that Japan suffers opportunity costs due to its policy on the Northern Territories. Their study and its conclusions are open to at least two basic criticisms. First, they do not attempt to develop a theory of interests which might guide them in understanding their case. Second, they base their conclusions about interests as a general concept on a single case study. If $N = 1$, there can be little confidence in the general nature of the result.

4. The difficulty of defining the term apparently stems from the difficulty of finding criteria which are not related to behavior. For example, a text on learning, Hilgard and Bower's *Theories of Learning*, warns "learning must always remain an inference from performance, and only confusion results if performance and learning are identified" (20). But three pages earlier these same authors present their definition of the term "Learning refers to the change in a subject's behavior to a given situation brought about by his repeated experiences in that situation, provided that the behavior change cannot be explained on the basis of native response tendencies, maturation, or temporary states of the subject (e.g., fatigue, drugs, etc.)" (17). This definition is unsatisfactory for two reasons. First, it commits the error of defining learning as a change in behavior which the authors themselves warn against. Excluding changes in behavior which can be understood as products of some other causes does not solve the problem, it simply defines learning as all changed behavior which we can't otherwise explain. Second, it fails to distinguish between simple memory (e.g., learning the alphabet) and insight or understanding of causal linkages (e.g., learning that studying more helps students get better grades).

5. For example, Lloyd Etheridge (1985, viii, see also 66) defines learning as "a record of increasing intelligence and effectiveness across return engagements." He continues, "Often, however, such government learning has not occurred. . . ." His goal is not to explain a phenomenon called foreign policy learning, but rather to explain "blocked learning" (ix) caused by the dominance of cognitive factors over rational or analytical decision making. It is curious that by Etheridge's definition learning and cognition are antithetical. Other works which take the same normatively-based approach to learning include Breslauer 1991, 830; Larson 1991, 351, 362, 390; Thies 1991, p. 187 (all in Breslauer and Tetlock, eds. 1991). In a review of the organizational learning literature, Huber (1991, 125–126) discusses the problems associated with narrowly defining organizational learning in terms of "effectiveness" or intentionality.

6. Jervis (1976) and Khong (1992) both discuss schemata and analyze the policy implications of different schemata held by policymakers. This is one straightforward way to "operationalize" learning. My approach does not contradict theirs, but I do want to define precisely how different schemata affect policy. Why focus on schemata? Khong (10) provides 6 functions which analogies may serve, but these do not include a specification of how an analogy leads to certain conclusions in the 6 "diagnostic tasks" he identifies. I seek here to make explicit what is implied in this approach analogies provide guidelines for arranging and rearranging preferences over strategies and/or outcomes.

7. This statement can be somewhat qualified. At least theoretically, it is possible that behavior can change by chance or as a side-effect of other events before it is learned to be preferable by the actor. In major policy decisions, I do not believe this is likely to be relevant.

8. Steinbruner's concept of "cybernetic learning" (78–79) is much different.

9. Haas might not accept my characterization of his definition of learning. However, given that he sees learning as the triumph of "substantive rationality" and the construction of "new nested problem sets" based on new knowledge (3), and that such "analytic" thinking overcomes "[r]outines [which] seek to limit the complexity of the real world" (38), I assume that he associates learning with cognitive and organizational complexity, as he himself seems to recognize (193). He (1997, 16–17) maintains the "new knowledge" requirement for learning, and calls it "more complex" (56). Tetlock (1991, 34) also makes an explicit connection between accuracy and complexity in learning.

10. An extension of Wolfers's theory is found in Zimmerman (1973, 1987). He links the variation in domestic political salience of various "issue areas" with variation in the character of foreign policy based on Wolfers's poles of power and indifference.

11. For debate on the use of neorealism as a theory of foreign policy, see Elman (1996a and b) and Waltz (1996).

12. Huber (1996 [1991], 141–143) focuses on mechanisms of information distribution through which organizational learning may occur, and across which it may vary. In order to benefit from experience or observation, the relevant information must be available and members of an organization must know how to get it. For nation states, this may cause more open societies to learn differently than closed societies, which restrict information, often without even knowing the exact content of the information to which they are

denying themselves access. This is consistent with Reiter's (1996, chapter 8) expectations about learning and political structure.

3   A THEORY OF IMITATION IN FOREIGN POLICY

1. The same can be said for Reiter and Meek (1999), even though they attempt to study three types of military strategy. In fact, the dependent variable is dichotomous, measuring whether or not a "maneuver" strategy was used. Also, in both Reiter (1996) and Reiter and Meek (1999), the "cognitive" factors noted below of prestige and similarity are not considered (they do measure policy success). I would argue that any test of vicarious learning excluding "prestige" in particular is likely to be inconclusive.

2. Reiter (1996, 64, 183) seems to use the terms "beliefs" and "preferences" interchangeably. See Morrow (1994) for a discussion of the distinction, such as it is, between these terms. Beliefs are considered assumptions about facts. Although many game theorists (see Lake and Powell 1999) attempt to draw clear distinctions between these terms, I believe the distinction is one of degree. What seems a fundamental preference in one situation (e.g., wealth) can be a belief in another context (e.g., the belief that wealth brings happiness). Trying to make qualitative distinctions between beliefs and preferences leads to a logical infinite regress. Any given "fundamental" preference can be transformed into a belief by proposing a prior assumed preference that justifies pursuit of the first. I "prefer" the term preference because it implies choice among competing options.

3. This is not a novel argument: see Aron 1967, 195; and Keohane and Nye 1977, 224. "Survival," used by Waltz (1979) is perhaps the least vague. It can distinguish between offensive and defensive realists (Jervis 1999), although I think not between defensive realists and liberals. If offensive realists always expect expansion (not survival), the picture of a system full of revisionist states is simply too far from the reality we seek to explain. The theoretical vapidity of these assumptions becomes clear when their alternatives are considered. Could useful competing theories be built on assumed state preferences for extinction, national insecurity, or weakness? If not, then what meaningful insights follow from them?

4. For an alternative using two axes and four values (isolationism/internationalism, militarism/accommodationism), the "MI/CI scheme," see Wittkopf 1990, Holsti and Rosenau 1993, 1996; Holsti 1998.

5. Gowa and Mansfield 1993; Grieco 1988; Jervis 1988, Waltz 1979. This is not to say that all realists posit that states exclusively seek relative gains nor that all liberals assume that relative gains never matter. Jervis (1999) and Powell (1991) both point out that there may be varying degrees of concern for the two different types of outcomes. Glaser's (1994/95) "contingent realism" recognizes the importance of relative gains, but he believes the relative gains concerns and thus the security dilemma can be mitigated without violating other realist assumptions. Relevant recent discussions of international relations theories and include Powell and Lake (1999), who argue that "microfoundations" are underspecified, and Jervis (1999) and Martin and Simmons (1998) provide insightful recent surveys.

6. For example, Wittkopf's ("MI/CI," see chapter 2 and note 4 above) categories of hardliners and isolationists should correspond roughly to concern for relative gains, while his categories of accommodationists and internationalists should correspond roughly to absolute gains concerns. As preferences move toward the midpoint, various balances of the four values would be observed. The advantages of the scheme used here are that it is not restricted to security issues, it is theoretically rather than inductively developed, and it involves only one axis so it can be included in ordinal quantitative analysis.

7. Grieco, Powell, and Snidal 1993; Jervis 1999; Powell 1991; Snidal 1991a and b.

8. I have included some prominent textbooks on the assumption that these provide more basic and consensual characterizations.

9. Considering various issue areas in a single framework is advocated by Jervis 1988, Keohane 1984, Powell 1991 and applied in studies including Gowa 1989, Gowa and Mansfield 1993, Keohane and Nye 1989, Mansfield 1994, Rosecrance 1986, Waltz 1979 (chapters 7–9). Recent work incorporating both domestic and international politics includes Huth 1996, Jacobson, Evans, and Putnam 1993, Milner 1997.

4   ARE ELITES INFLUENCED BY FOREIGN ANALOGIES?

1. Data collection and coding are discussed in greater detail in the appendix.

2. Since the topic addressed is always "what should our foreign policy be?" I assume that any substantive example from the international experience of one's own state or another state used by an elite is considered relevant to, and an analogue for, foreign policy.

3. Strategies for overcoming the problems of listwise deletion are developed by King et al. (2001). I choose two specifications of the equation because I have theoretical reasons to expect nonusage of an analogy type is meaningful (i.e., H1–H3, H7) and values should not be imputed for these missing data.

4. Observed Failure: Liberal is dropped from the equation. It has almost no variation because this type of analogy was used only twice. The coding procedure for the dummy variables, using zero to indicate *either* a value in another category or nonusage of the analogy type greatly reduces the problem of collinearity among dummy variables for a single analogy type (e.g., Direct Success), so reference categories are not omitted and meaningful coefficients result. As a further check, if the "Mixed" category is dropped from each analogy type, all the analogy variables that were significant in equation 6 remain so, and no others gain significance; nor do the relative levels of significance change.

5. Discrepancies between the total number of observations using an analogy type and the total number included in equations 1–6 are caused by missing data. Some observations could not be coded for foreign policy preferences (6) or year of birth (10).

6. This assumes that rhetorical or instrumental analogy use is "noisier" than substantive analogy use. Analogies used for effect (perhaps as the "Hitler" analogy is sometimes used by U.S. leaders) should have less to do with actual preferences than analogies that really shape those preferences.

7. On Gaullist foreign policy see, for example, Van Oudenaren 2000, 37–38. For more on Dubinin's own characterization of the Gaullist approach to

Europe, see his memoirs (1997, 152–153) in which he notes de Gaulle's position against any "foreign interference" or "outside forces" being involved in Europe and his "policy of independence" for France with military forces directed "at all azimuths."

8. All references to pre-1992 Soviet experiences are coded as "direct" experience for Russians and Ukrainians. All elites in the data set were Soviet citizens prior to 1992 and almost all were mid- to high-level Soviet political or diplomatic officials, and Communist Party members.

9. On the USSR and the CSCE see, for example, Donaldson and Nogee 1998, 83. Dubinin discusses his experience as a Soviet negotiator in the Helsinki process in great detail in his memoirs (1997, chapter 6). It is clear that he recognizes the necessity of including the United States in European security and that he believes a negotiated agreement is the best way to achieve Soviet goals. He recognizes persistent "contradictions" between East and West and Western European fears of the USSR in particular (214). He believes that building on what was achieved through negotiation and compromise would have been the best option for Soviet policy toward the West. If the large role Dubinin recognizes for the United States in Europe is considered, the contrast between the CSCE and Gaullist analogies is especially clear.

10. Here the prestige and issue-success factors may be convoluted. Sorting them out must remain a task for future inquiry. However, I think it would be difficult to argue that the creation of the European Community really shared much with, say, the creation of the Commonwealth of Independent States. It is more likely that advocates of the CIS are attracted by the status of the EU today, rather than its actual similarity to their tasks. There also could be overlap between analogies to Central and East European states and the former Soviet Bloc when discussing H5 and H6.

5 STATE-LEVEL EFFECTS ON ELITE IMITATION

1. It is important to note that this is not an artifact of differences between coders. If a binary variable for coder is introduced into the model for equation 6, the effect of differences between coders does not have a statistically significant effect on preferences (coefficient = 0.1247916, $p = 0.694$). Intercoder reliability is discussed in the appendix.

6 CASE STUDIES: FOREIGN CAPITAL AND "STRATEGIC" ENTERPRISE PRIVATIZATION

1. Kuboniwa and Gavrilenkov (1997) question the sustainability of this stabilization.

2. Due to the nature of the Lexis-Nexis Academic Universe database through which this source was accessed (see bibliography), it is not possible to cite page numbers for direct quotations. The full text of the source is searchable, however, for easy location of any referenced information, including quotations.

3. In 1994 some strategic enterprises were approved for privatization, "under tremendous pressure from the managers who wanted to privatize" (Boycko,

Shleifer, and Vishny 1996, 99). Zisk (1997) discusses the complex and evolving role of the defense industry enterprise directors in Russian politics and economic reform.

4. Chubais stated that it contained 3,000 enterprises and had the written consent of the president. Although previous references to the list had indicated that 3,054 enterprises were included, it is unclear whether 54 enterprises had actually been dropped from the list, or if Chubais was simply using a round figure for convenience. The latter appeared to be the case because the figure of 3,054 was subsequently referred to by government officials.

5. Some might argue there is no *real* threat to Russia from the United States or NATO, while Russia *really* did pose a threat to Ukraine. Such a view must be treated with skepticism, not least because the classic measure of threat—capabilities—clearly support's the Russian perception. Western intentions also become highly suspect after NATO expansion—at least in Russian eyes. If we know nothing else about international relations, we know that states tend to underestimate the threat they pose to others and overestimate the threat others pose to them. This is the logic of the security dilemma.

7   Conclusions: Imitation and Transition in International Relations

1. Farkas (1998) presents a model of incremental direct state learning.
2. Rosenthal and B. Zimmerman (1978, 77) give a similar description of how observational learning can manifest itself in individual behavior. "Three major effects of vicarious experience have been identified: inhibition-disinhibition, facilitation, and novel learning. Inhibition refers to suppression of a known response because vicarious experiences indicate that it will be punished. . . . Disinhibition refers to the manifestation by an observer of a formerly punished response because of the model's fearless behavior. . . . Facilitation refers to vicarious instigation of a known but not punished response . . . Finally, novel behavior can be vicariously acquired. . . ." Socialization into a (changeable) social system is the logically expected result, I contend.

Appendix D: The Data Set

1. Shapiro (231) makes the point that computer coding is also vulnerable to problems of judgment and subjective bias because the coding program must be written by people. Subjectivity and judgment are necessary aspects of any coding procedure for "representative" information that intends to discern the meaning of statements, but not for "instrumental" information that is only concerned with describing an aspect of a text such as the frequency of occurrence of certain words (228).

REFERENCES

Achen, Christopher H. and Ouncan Snidal. 1989. "Rational Deference Theory and Comparative Case Studies," *World Politics* 41, 2: 143–169.

Adler, Emanuel and Michael Barnett, eds. 1998. *Security Communities*. Cambridge, U.K.: Cambridge University Press.

Agence France Presse. (Lexis-Nexis Academic Universe).

Albrecht, Ulrich. 1993. *The Soviet Armaments Industry*. Philadelphia, Pa.: Harwood Academic Publishers.

Aldrich, John H. and Forrest D. Nelson. 1984. *Linear Probability, Logit, and Probit Models*. Sage University Paper series on Quantitative Applications in the Social Sciences, 07–101. Thousand Oaks, Calif.: Sage.

Allison, Graham T. 1969. "Conceptual Models and the Cuban Missile Crisis," *American Political Science Review* 63, 3: 689–718.

Anderson, Richard D., Jr. 1991. "Why Competetive Politics Inhibits Learning in Soviet Foreign Policy," in George W. Breslauer and Philip E. Tetlock, eds. *Learning in U.S. and Soviet Foreign Policy*, 100–131. Boulder, Colo.: Westview Press.

Argyris, Chris. 1992. *On Organizational Learning*. Oxford, U.K.: Blackwell Business.

Argyris, C. and Schon, D. A. 1978. *Organizational Learning: A Theory of Action Perspective*. Boston, Mass.: Allyn and Bacon.

Aron, Raymond. 1967. "What is a Theory of International Relations," *Journal of International Affairs* 21, 185–206.

Artisien-Maksimenko, Patrick and Yuri Adjubei, eds. 1996. *Foreign Investment in Russia and Other Soviet Successor States*. New York: St. Martin's Press.

Ash, Timothy. 1999. "Ukraine: Policy Environment (August 3)," *Quest Economics Database*. *West LB Country Profile*. [N.p.:] Janet Matthews Information Services. (Lexis-Nexis Academic Universe).

Aslund, Anders. 1995. *How Russia Became a Market Economy*. Washington, DC: The Brookings Institution.

Aven, P. 1992. "Vneshneekonomicheskie sviazi Rossii: kakimi im byt?" [Foreign Economic Ties: What should they be?] *Mirovaia Ekonomika i Mezhdunarodnaia Otnosheniia* [World Economy and International Relations] 7, 44–47.

Axelrod, Robert, ed. 1976. *Structure of Decision: Cognitive Maps of Political Elites*. Princeton, N.J.: Princeton University Press.

Axelrod, Robert. 1986. An Evolutionary Approach to Norms. *American Political Science Review* 80, 4: 1095–1111.

Axelrod, Robert and Michael D. Cohen. 1999. *Harnessing Complexity: Organizational Implications of a Scientific Frontier*. New York: The Free Press.

Bandura, A. 1977. *Social Learning Theory*. [N.p.:]Prentice Hall.

Bandura, Albert. 1986. *Social Foundations of Thought and Action: A Social Cognitive Theory*. Englewood Cliffs, N.J.: Prentice-Hall, Inc.

Baranovs 'kyy, Oleksandr. 1995. "Amerykans'ka stratehiia bezpeky" [American Security Strategy] *Polityka i chas* [Politics and Time] 3: 72–76.

Beike, Denise R. and Steven J. Sherman. 1994. "Social Inference: Inductions, Deductions, and Analogies," in Robert S. Wyker, Jr. and Thomas K. Srull, eds. *The Handbook of Social Cognition. Volume I: Basic Processes.* Hillsdale, N.J.: Lawrence Erlbaum Associates.

Beissinger, Mark R. 1992 "Elites and Ethnic Identities in Soviet and Post-Soviet Politics," in Alexander Motyl, ed., *The Post-Soviet Nations: Perspectives on the Demise of the USSR, 141–169.* New York: Columbia University Press.

Bende-Nabende, Anthony. 1999. *FDI, Regionalism, Government Policy and Endogenous Growth.* Aldershot: Ashgate.

Bennett, Colin. 1991. "How States Utilize Foreign Evidence," *Journal of Public Policy* 11, 1: 31–54.

Beregovoi, Sergei. 1999, "Duma Passes Law on Privatizing Gazprom," *Kommersant,* 1/21/99, 7 (Lexis-Nexis Academic Universe).

Bermeo, Nancy. 1992. "Democracy and the Lessons of Dictatorship," *Comparative Politics* (April), 273–291.

Berry, Frances Stokes and William D. Berry. 1999. "Innovation and Diffusion Models in Policy Research," in Paul A. Sabatier, ed. *Theories of Policy Process.* Boulder, Colo.: Westview Press.

Blacker, Coit D. 1991. "Learning in the Nuclear Age: Soviet Strategic Arms Control Policy, 1969–1989," in George W. Breslauer and Philip E. Tetlock, eds. *Learning in U.S. and Soviet Foreign Policy,* 429–468. Boulder, Colo.: Westview Press.

Boxwell, Robert J. 1994. *Benchmarking for Competitive Advantage.* New York: McGraw-Hill.

Boycko, Maxim, Andrei Shleifer, and Robert Vishny. 1996. *Privatizing Russia.* Cambridge, Mass.: The MIT Press.

Breslauer, George W. 1991. "What Have We Learned About Learning?" in George W. Breslauer and Philip E. Tetlock, eds. *Learning in U.S. and Soviet Foreign Policy,* 825–856. Boulder, Colo.: Westview Press.

Breslauer, George and Philip Tetlock, eds. 1991. *Learning in U.S. and Soviet Foreign Policy.* Boulder, Colo.: Westview Press.

British Broadcasting Corporation. *Summary of World Broadcasts* (BBC SWB). (Lexis-Nexis Academic Universe).

Bueno de Mesquita, Bruce. 1994. "Political Forecasting: An Expected Utility Method," in Bruce Bueno de Mesquita and Frans N. Stokman, eds. *European Community Decision Making: Models Applications and Comparisons,* 74–104. New Haven: Yale University Press.

Burg, Steven L. 1990. "Nationality Elites and Political Change in the Soviet Union" in Lubomyr Hajda and Mark Beissinger, eds. *The Nationalities Factor in Soviet Politics and Society,* 24–42. Boulder, Colo.: Westview Press.

Business Central Europe. (Dec. 1997–Jan. 1998).

Campbell, Donald T. and Julian C. Stanley. 1966 [1963]. *Experimental and Quasi-Experimental Designs for Research.* Boston: Houghton Mifflin Company.

Canadian Embassy in Ukraine. [N.d.] Document A.

Carr, E. H. 1939. *The Twenty Years' Crisis, 1919–1939: An Introduction to the Study of International Relations.* New York: Harper & Row.

Cederman, Lars-Erik. 2001. "Back to Kant: Reinterpreting the Democratic Peace as a Macrohistorical Learning Process," *American Political Science Review* 95, 1: 15–31.

Chan, Steve. 1995. "Introduction: Foreign Direct Investment in a Changing World," in Steve Chan, ed. *Foreign Direct Investment in a Changing Global Economy*. New York: Macmillan.

Chernomyrdin, V. 1993. "Rossiiskie reformy i sibir" [Russian reforms and Siberia] *Mezhdunarodnaia zhizn* [International Affairs] 4: 8–12.

Chornovil, Viacheslav Maksymovych. Interview with author, Kyiv, Ukraine, November 5, 1997.

Clark, William Roberts. 1998. "Agents and Structures: Two Views of Preferences, Two Views of Institutions," *International Studies Quarterly* 42: 245–270.

Clarke, Michael. 1989. "Comparing Foreign Policy Systems: Problems, Processes and Performance," in Michael Clarke and Brian White, eds. *Understanding Foreign Policy: The Foreign Policy Systems Approach*, 185–215. Hants, England: Edward Elgar.

Cohen, Michael D. and Lee S. Sproull, eds. 1996. *Organizational Learning*. Thousand Oaks, Calif.: Sage Publications.

Congressional Quarterly. 2000. *The Middle East*. Washington, DC: CQ Press.

Cracraft, James. 1988. "Opposition to Peter the Great," in Ezra Mendelsohn and Marshall S. Shatz, eds. *Imperial Russia 1700–1917: State, Society, Opposition. Essays in Honor of Marc Raeff*, 22–36. DeKalb, Ill.: Northern Illinois University Press.

Current Digest of the Soviet Press (CDSP).

Current Digest of the Post-Soviet Press (CDPSP).

Cyert, Richard M. and James G. March. 1963. *A Behavioral Theory of the Firm*. Englewood Cliffs, NJ: Prentice Hall.

Dallin, Alexander. 1991. "Learning in U.S. Policy Toward the Soviet Union in the 1980s," in George W. Breslauer and Philip E. Tetlock, eds. *Learning in U.S. and Soviet Foreign Policy*, 400–426. Boulder, Colo.: Westview Press.

Dawisha, Karen and Bruce Parrott. 1994. *Russia and the New States of Eurasia: The Politics of Upheaval*. Cambridge, U.K.: Cambridge University Press.

Dawisha, Adeed and Karen Dawisha. 1995. *The Making of Foreign Policy in Russia and the New States of Eurasia*. Armonk, N.Y. : M.E. Sharpe.

Deardorff, Alan V. 1995. *Determinants of Bilateral Trade: Does gravity work in a neo-classical world?* Cambridge, Mass.: National Bureau of Economic Research

Dell, Sidney S. 1991. *International Development Policies: Perspectives for Industrial Countries*. Durham, N.C.: Duke University Press.

Denezhkina, Elena. 1998. "Russian Defence Firms and the External Market," in Ian Anthony, ed. *Russia and the Arms Trade*. Stockholm: SIPRI: Oxford University Press.

Deutsche-Presse-Agentur. (Lexis-Nexis Academic Universe).

Deutsch, Karl W. et al. 1968 [1957]. *Political Community and the North Atlantic Area: International Organization in the Light of Historical Experience*. Princeton, N.J.: Princeton University Press.

Divine, Robert A. 1985. *Since 1945: Politics and Diplomacy in Recent American History*. Third edition. New York: Alfred A. Knopf.

Donahue, John D. 1989. *The Privatization Decision: Public Ends, Private Means*. New York: Basic Books.

Donaldson, Robert H. and Joseph L. Nogee. 1998. *The Foreign Policy of Russia: Changing Systems, Enduring Interests*. Armonk, N.Y.: M.E. Sharpe.

Dubinin, Iurii. 1995. Ot Vladivostok do Vankuvera [From Vladivostok to Vancouver], *Mezhdunarodnaia zhizn* [International Affairs] (11–12): 86–87.

Dubinin, Iurii. 1997. *Diplomaticheskaia byl: zapiski posla vo Frantsii* [Diplomatic Past: Notes of an Ambassador in France]. Moscow: ROSSPEN.

Eckstein, Harry. 1975. "Case Study and Theory in Political Science," in Fred Greenstein and Nelson Polsby, eds. *Handbook of Political Science. Vol. 7. Strategies of Inquiry*. Reading, Mass.: Addison-Wesley.

Economist, The. (10/30/99).

Ekspert. (11/17/97, 2/16/98).

Elman, Colin. 1996a. "Horses for Courses: Why Not Neorealist Theories of Foreign Policy," *Security Studies* 6, 1: 7–53.

Elman, Colin. 1996b. "Cause, Effect, and Consistency: A Response to Kenneth Waltz," *Security Studies* 6, 1: 58–61.

Embassy of the United States, Kyiv. 1996. *International Management Insights*. (Lexis-Nexis Academic Universe).

Espejo, R. et al. 1996. *Organizational Transformation and Learning: A Cybernetic Approach to Management*. Chichester, U.K.: John Wiley & Sons.

Etheridge, Lloyd. 1985. *Can Governments Learn?: American Foreign Policy and Central American Revolutions*. New York: Pergamon Press.

European Bank for Reconstruction and Development (EBRD). 1995. *Transition Report 1995*. London: The Bank.

European Bank for Reconstruction and Development (EBRD). 1997. *Transition Report 1997*. London: The Bank.

European Bank for Reconstruction and Development (EBRD). 1998. *Transition Report 1998*. London: The Bank.

European Bank for Reconstruction and Development (EBRD). 1999. *Transition Report Update. April 1999*. London: The Bank.

Evans, George W. and Seppo Honkapohja. 2001. *Learning and Expectations in Macroeconomics*. Princeton, N.J.: Princeton University Press.

Evans, Peter B., Harold K. Jacobson, Robert D. Putnam, eds. 1993. *Double-edged Diplomacy: International Bargaining and Domestic Politics*. Berkeley, Calif.: University of California Press.

Farkas, Andrew. 1998. *State Learning and International Change*. Ann Arbor: University of Michigan Press.

Farnham, Barbara, ed. 1994. *Avoiding Losses / Taking Risks: Prospect Theory and International Conflict*. Ann Arbor: University of Michigan Press.

Fearon, James D. 1994. "Signaling Versus the Balance of Power and Interests: An Empirical Test of a Crisis Bargaining Model," *Journal of Conflict Resolution*. 38, 2: 236–269.

Fearon, James D. "Domestic Politics, Foreign Policy, and Theories of International Relations," *Annual Review of Political Science* 1: 289–313.

Federal Information Systems Corporation [Russia]. Various press-conference transcripts: 4/13/95, 9/25/95, 2/19/98, 3/5/98. (Lexis-Nexis Academic Universe).

Federal News Service [Russia]. Official Kremlin International News Broadcast: 7/19/00. (Lexis-Nexis Academic Universe).

Feigenbaum, Harvey, Jeffrey Henig, and Chris Hamnett. 1999. *Shrinking the State: The Political Underpinnings of Privatization*. Cambridge, U.K.: Cambridge University Press.

Financial Times, The. (8/30/95, 10/30/95, 11/4/95, 7/21/98).

Finnemore, Martha and Kathryn Sikkink. 1998. International Norm Dynamics and Political Change. *International Organization* 52, 4: 887–917.

Fokin, Vitold Pavlovich. Interview with author, Kyiv, Ukraine, November 18, 1997.

Frieden, Jeffry A. 1991. "Invested Interests: The Politics of National Economic Policies in a World of Global Finance." *International Organization* 45: 425–452.

Frieden, Jeffry A. 1999. "Actors and Preferences in International Relations," in David A. Lake and Robert Powell, eds. *Strategic Choice and International Relations*, 39–76. Princeton, N.J.: Princeton University Press.

Gaidar, Egor. 1996. *Dni porazhenii i pobed* [Days of Defeats and Victories]. Moscow, Russia: Vagrius.

Gallhofer, Irmtraud N. and William E. Saris. 1997. *Collective Choice Processes: A Qualitative and Quantitative Analysis of Foreign Policy Decision-Making*. Westport, Conn: Praeger.

Gardner, John W. [1965] 1993. "How to Prevent Organizational Dry Rot," in Michael T. Matterson and John M. Ivancevich, eds. *Management and Organizational Behavior Classics*. Fifth edition, 438–443. Homewood, Ill.: Irwin.

Garnett, Sherman. 1997. *Keystone in the Arch: Ukraine in the Emerging Security Environment of Central and Eastern Europe*. Washington, D.C.: Carnegie Endowment for International Peace.

Gartzke, Erik. 2000. "Preferences and the Democratic Peace." *International Studies Quarterly* 44, 2: 191–212.

Gaubatz, Kurt Taylor. 1991. "Election Cycles and War," *Journal of Conflict Resolution* 35, 2: 212–244.

Geddes, Barbara. 1990. "How the Cases You Choose Affect the Answers You Get: Selection Bias in Comparative Politics," *Political Analysis* 2: 131–150.

George, Alexander L. 1969. "The 'Operational Code': A Neglected Approach to the Study of Political Leaders and Decision Making," *International Studies Quarterly* 13: 2, 190–222.

George, Alexander and Timothy J. McKeown. 1985. "Case Studies and Theories of Organizational Decision Making," *Advances in Information Processing in Organizations* 2: 21–58.

George, Alexander L. and Richard Smoke. 1974. *Deterrence in American Foreign Policy: Theory and Practice*. New York: Columbia University Press.

Gerber, Alan and Donald Green. 1998. "Rational Learning and Partisan Attitudes," *American Journal of Political Science* 42, 3: 794–818.

Gerber, Alan and Donald Green. 1999. "Misperceptions about Perceptual Bias," *Annual Review of Political Science* 2: 189–210.

Geva, Nehemia and Alex Mintz, eds. 1997. *Decisionmakng on War and Peace: The Cognitive-Rational Debate*. Boulder, Colo.: Lynne Rienner Publishers.

Gitelman, Zvi. 1972. *The Diffusion of Innovation: From Eastern Europe to the Soviet Union*. Beverly Hills, CA: Sage Publications.

Glaser, Charles. 1994–1995. "Realists as Optimists: Cooperation as Self-Help," *International Security* 19, 3: 50–90.

Glaser, Charles. 1997. "The Security Dilemma Revisited," *World Politics* 50, 1: 171–201.

Gleitman, Henry. 1991. *Psychology*. Third edition. New York, N.Y.: W.W. Norton and Company.

Goldsmith, Benjamin E. 2001a. "Economic Liberalism and Security Preferences: A Comparative Case Study of Russia and Ukraine in the 1990s," *Demokratizatsiya: The Journal of Post-Soviet Democratization* 9, 3: 399–433.

Goldsmith, Benjamin E. 2001b. *Imitation and Transition in World Politics: Observational Learning and the Formation of Foreign Policy Preferences.* [Ph.D. dissertation, University of Michigan].

Goldsmith, Benjamin E. 2003. "Imitation in International Relations: Analogies, Vicarious Learning, and Foreign Policy," *International Interactions* 29, 3: 237–267.

Goldstein, Judith and Robert O. Keohane, eds. 1993. *Ideas and Foreign Policy: Beliefs, Institutions, and Political Change.* Ithaca, N.Y.: Cornell University Press.

Goskomstat. 1991a. *Narodnoe khoziaistvo SSSR v 1990g. Statisticheskii ezhegodnik.* [Economy of the USSR in 1990. Statistical Yearbook.] Moscow: "Finansy i statistika."

Goskomstat. 1991b. *Sotsial'noe razvitie SSSR 1989. Statisticheskii sbornik.* [Social Development of the USSR 1989. Statistical Collection.] Moscow "Finansy i statistika."

Goskomstat Rossii. 1997. *Rossiiskii statisticheskii ezhegodnik. Statisticheskii sbornik.* [Russian Statistical Yearbook. Statistical collection.] Moscow: [Goskomstat Rossii].

Gowa, Joanne. 1989. "Bipolarity, Multipolarity, and Free Trade," *American Political Science Review* 83, 4: 1245–1256.

Gowa, Joanne and Edward D. Mansfield. 1993. "Power Politics and International Trade," *American Political Science Review* 87, 2: 408–420.

Gray, Virginia. 1973a. "Rejoinder to 'Comment' by Jack L. Walker," *American Political Science Review* 67: 1192–1193.

Gray, Virginia. 1973b. "Innovation in the States: A Diffusion Study," *American Political Science Review* 67: 1174–1185.

Green, Donald P. and Ian Shapiro. 1994. *Pathologies of Rational Choice Theory: A Critique of Applications in Political Science.* New Haven: Yale University Press.

Grieco, Joseph M. 1988. "Anarchy and the Limits of Cooperation: A Realist Critique of the Newest Liberal Institutionalism," *International Organization* 42, 3: 485–507.

Grieco, Joseph, Robert Powell, and Duncan Snidal. 1993. "The Relative-Gains Problem for International Cooperation," *American Political Science Review* 87, 3: 729–743.

Griffiths, Franklyn. 1991. "Attempted Learning: Soviet Policy Toward the United States in the Brezhnev Era," in George W. Breslauer and Philip E. Tetlock, eds. *Learning in U.S. and Soviet Foreign Policy*, 630–683. Boulder, Colo.: Westview Press.

Gustafson, Thane. 1999. *Capitalism Russian Style.* Cambridge University Press.

Haas, Ernst B. 1990. *When Knowledge is Power: Three Models of Change in International Organizations.* Berkeley, Calif.: University of California Press.

Haas, Ernst B. 1991. "Collective Learning: Some Theoretical Speculations," in George W. Breslauer and Philip E. Tetlock, eds. *Learning in U.S. and Soviet Foreign Policy*, 62–99. Boulder, Colo.: Westview Press.

Haas, Ernst B. 1997. *Nationalism, Liberalism, and Progress: Volume 1, The Rise and Decline of Nationalism.* Ithaca, N.Y.: Cornell University Press.

Haggard, Stephan. 1990. *Pathways from the Periphery: The Politics of Growth in the Newly Industrializing Countries.* Ithaca, N.Y.: Cornell University Press.

Haggard, Stephen and Robert R. Kaufman. 1995. *The Political Economy of Democratic Transitions.* Princeton, N.J.: Princeton University Press

Hampton, David R. et al. 1987. *Organizational Behavior and the Practice of Management.* Fifth edition. [N.p.:] Harper Collins Publishers, Inc.

't Hart, Paul. 1990. *Groupthink in Government: A Study of Small Groups and Policy Failure*. Baltimore: The Johns Hopkins University Press.

Hemmer, Christopher. 1999. "Historical Analogies and the Definition of Interests: The Iranian Hostage Crisis and Ronald Reagan's Policy Toward the Hostages in Lebanon," *Political Psychology* 20, 2: 267–289.

Herek, Gregory M., Irving L. Janis, and Paul Huth. 1987. "Decision Making During International Crises: Is Quality of Process Related to Outcome?" *Journal of Conflict Resolution* 31, 2: 203–226.

Hermann, M. G., C. F. Hermann, and J. D. Hagan. 1987. "How Decision Units Shape Foreign Policy Behavior," in M. G. Hermann, C. W. Kegley, Jr., and J.N. Rosenau, eds. *New Directions in the Study of Foreign Policy*, 247–268. Boston, Mass.: Allen and Unwin.

Hershey, Marjorie Randon. 1984. *Running for Office: The Political Education of Campaigners*. Chathaam, N.J.: Chatham House Publishers.

Hershey, Marjorie Randon and Darrell M. West. 1984. "Senate Campaigners and the Pro-Life Challenge in 1980," *Micropolitics* 3, 4: 547–587.

Het'man, Vadym P. 1996. *Iak pryymalas konstytutsiia Ukrainy* [How the Constitution of Ukraine was Adopted]. Kyiv, Ukraine: RIA "IaNKO."

Het'man, Vadym Petrovych. Interview with author, Kyiv, Ukraine, November 3, 1997.

Hiaddey, Ronald H. 1992. *People, Polls, and Policy-Makers: American Public Opinion and National Security*. New York: Lexington Books.

Hilgard, Ernest R. and Gordon H. Bower. 1975. *Theories of Learning*. Fourth edition. Englewood Cliffs, N.J.: Prentice-Hall.

Hoberg, George. 1991. "Sleeping with an Elephant: The American Influence on Canadian Environmental Regulation," *Journal of Public Policy* 11,1: 107–132.

Holsti, Ole R. 1968. "Content Analysis," in G. Lindzay and E. Aronson, eds. *Handbook of Social Psychology*. Second edition, vol. 2. Reading, Mass.: Addison-Wesley.

Holsti, Ole R. 1969. *Content Analysis for the Social Sciences and Humanities*. Reading, Mass.: Addison-Wesley.

Holsti, Ole R. 1992. "Public Opinion and Foreign Policy: Challenges to the Almond-Lippman Consensus. Mershon Series: Research Programs and Debates," *International Studies Quarterly* 36: 439–466.

Holsti, Ole R. 1998. "A Widening Gap between the U.S. Military and Civilian Society?" *International Security* 23, 3.

Holsti, Ole R. and James N. Rosenau. 1993. "The Structure of Foreign Policy Beliefs among American Opinion Leaders—After the Cold War," *Millennium* 22, 2: 235–278.

Holsti, Ole R. and James N. Rosenau. 1996. "Liberals, Populists, Libertarians, and Conservatives: The Link Between Domestic and International Affairs," *International Political Science Review* 17, 1: 29–54.

Hook, Steven W. 1995. *National Interest and Foreign Aid*. Boulder, Col.: Lynne Rienner Publishers.

Horbulin, Volodymyr. 1996. "Nasha meta, nasha dolia" [Our Goal, Our Duty] *Polityka i Chas* [Politics and Time] 1: 3–8.

Huber, George P. 1996 [1991]. "Organizational Learning: The Contributing Processes and the Literatures," in Michael D. Cohen and Lee S. Sproull, eds. *Organizational Learning*, 124–162. Thousand Oaks, Calif.: Sage Publications.

Hurenko, S. I. 1991. *Polityka i Chas* [Politics and Time] 3: 3–12.

Huth, Paul K. 1996. *Standing Your Ground: Territorial Disputes and International Conflict*. Ann Arbor, University of Michigan Press.

Info-Prod Research (Middle East) Ltd. (Lexis-Nexis Academic Universe).

Interfax News Agency. *Interfax Russian News*. (Lexis-Nexis Academic Universe).

International Herald Tribune, The.

International Monetary Fund, et al. 1991. *A Study of the Soviet Economy*. vol. 2. Paris: [OECD].

ITAR-TASS. (Lexis-Nexis Academic Universe). (5/12/95, 12/13/95, 6/29/98).

Izvestiia. (4/19/91, 6/7/91, 11/26/91).

Izyumov, Alexei, Leonid Kosals, and Rozalina Ryvkina. 1995. "The Russian Military-Industrial Complex: The Shock of Independence," in Joseph Di Chiaro III, ed. *Conversion of the Defense Industry in Russia and Eastern Europe*. Report 3. 12–18. Bonn: Bonn International Center for Conversion.

Jacobson, Harold Karan and William Zimmerman, eds. 1969. *The Shaping of Foreign Policy*. New York: Atherton Press.

Jacoby, Wade. 2000. *Imitation and Politics: Redesigning Modern Germany*. Ithaca, N.Y.: Cornell University Press.

Jervis, Robert. 1976. *Perception and Misperception in International Politics*. Princeton, N.J.: Princeton University Press.

Jervis, Robert. 1988. "Realism, Game Theory, and Cooperation," *World Politics* 40, 3: 317–349.

Jervis, Robert. 1999. "Realism, Neoliberalism, and Cooperation: Understanding the Debate," *International Security* 24, 1: 42–63.

Jervis, R., R. N. Lebow, and J. G. Stein, eds. 1985. *Psychology and Deterrence*. Baltimore: Johns Hopkins University Press.

Journal of Commerce. (Lexis-Nexis Academic Universe).

Kaarbo, Juliet and Ryan K. Beasley. 1999. "A Practical Guide to the Comparative Case Study Method in Political Psychology," *Political Psychology* 20, 2: 369–391.

Kahneman, Daniel and Amos Tversky. 1979. "Prospect Theory," *Econometrica* 47: 263–291.

Kant, Immanuel. [1795] 1970. "Perpetual Peace: A Philosophical Sketch," in Hans Reiss, ed. *Kant: Political Writings*, 93–130. Cambridge: Cambridge University Press.

Katzenstein, Peter J. 1985. *Small States in World Markets: Industrial Policy in Europe*. Ithaca, N.Y.: Cornell University Press.

Keeney, Ralph L., Howard Raiffa, and Richard F. Meyer. 1975. *Decisions with Multiple Objectives: Preferences and Value Tradeoffs*. New York, N.Y.: John Wiley and Sons.

Keohane, Robert O. 1984. *After Hegemony*. Princeton: Princeton University Press.

Keohane, Robert O. and Joseph S. Nye. 1977. *Power and Interdependence: World Politics in Transition*. Boston: Little Brown.

Keohane, Robert and Joseph S. Nye. 1989. *Power and Interdependence: World Politics in Transition*. Second edition. New York: Harper.

Khong, Yuen Foong. 1992. *Analogies at War: Korea, Munich, Dien Bien Phu, and the Vietnam Decisions of 1965*. Princeton, N.J.: Princeton University Press.

Khto e khto v Ukraini [Who's Who in Ukraine]. 1997. Kyiv: K.I.S.

Kim, Woosang and Bruce Bueno de Mesquita. 1995. How Perceptions Influence the Risk of War. *International Studies Quarterly* 39, 1: 51–65.

Kimura, Masato and David A. Welch. 1998. Specifying "Interests": Japan's Claim to the Northern Territories and Its Implications for International Relations Theory. *International Studies Quarterly* 42, 2: 213–244.

King, Gary, James Honaker, Anne Joseph, and Kenneth Scheve. 2001. "Analyzing Incomplete Political Science Data: An Alternative Algorithm for Multiple Imputation," *American Political Science Review* 95: 49–69.

King, Gary, Robert O. Keohane and Sidney Verba. 1994. *Designing Social Inquiry: Scientific Inference in Qualitative Research*. Princeton, N.J.: Princeton University Press.

Kommersant-Daily. (4/12/96).

Kopstein, Jeffrey S. and David A. Reilly. 2000. Geographic Diffusion and the Transformation of the Postcommunist World. *World Politics* 53, 1: 1–37.

Kozyrev, Andrei. 1992. "Vystuplenie" [Speech.] *Mezhdunarodnaia zhizn* [International Affairs] 3–4, 91–98.

Krasner, Stephen D. 1985. *Structural Conflict: The Third World Against Global Liberalism*. Berkeley, Calif: University of California Press.

Krippendorff, Klaus. 1980. *Content Analysis: An Introduction to its Methodology*. Beverly Hills, Calif: Sage Publications.

Kto est Kto v Rossii. 1997 god [Who's Who in Russian. 1997]. 1997. Moscow: Olimp

Kto est kto v Rossii i byvshem SSSR [Who's Who in Russia and the Former USSR]. 1994. Moscow: Terra

Kuboniwa, Masaaki and Evgeny Gavrilenkov. 1997. *Development of Capitalism in Russia: The Second Challenge*. Tokyo: Maruzen Co., Ltd.

Kuchma, L. D. 1994. "Diemo poslidovno, u interesakh us'oho liudstva" [We Are Acting Responsibly, in the Interests of All Humanity] *Polityka i Chas* [Politics and Time] 12, 3–7.

Kuchma, L. D. 1996. "Nova arkhitektura bespeky v Evropi nemozhlyva bez Ukainy" [A New Architecture of Security in Europe is not Possible Without Ukraine] *Polityka i Chas* [Politics and Time] 7, 3–7.

Kuzio, Taras with Anthony Wilson. 1994. *Ukraine: Perestroika to Independence*. Basingstoke, U.K.: Macmillan.

Lairson, Thomas D. and David Skidmore. 1993. *International Political Economy: The Struggle for Power and Wealth*. Fort Worth, Tex.: Harcourt Brace College Publishers.

Lake, David A. and Robert Powell, eds. 1999. *Strategic Choice and International Relations*. Princeton, N.J.: Princeton University Press.

Lamborn, Alan C. 1997. "Theory and the Politics in World Politics," *International Studies Quarterly* 41: 187–214.

Larrabee, Stephen and Allen Lynch. 1994. *Russia, Ukraine and European Security: Implications for Western Policy*. Santa Monica, Calif: Rand.

Larsen, Stacey. 1997. *An Overview of Defense Conversion in Ukraine*. Paper 9. Bonn: Bonn International Center for Conversion.

Larson, Deborah Welch. 1985. *Origins of Containment: A Psychological Explanation*. Princeton, N.J.: Princeton University Press.

Larson, Deborah Welch. 1988. "Problems of Content Analysis in Foreign-Policy Research: Notes from the Study of the Origins of Cold War Belief Systems," *International Studies Quarterly* 32: 2, 241–255.

Lasswell, Harold D. 1950 [1936]. *Politics: Who Gets What, When, How*. New York: Peter Smith.

Lasswell, Harold D., Daniel Lerner, and C. Easton Rothwell. 1952. *The Comparative Study of Elites: An Introduction and Bibliography*. Stanford, Calif.: Stanford University Press.

Legvold, Robert. 1991. "Soviet Learning in the 1980s," in George W. Breslauer and Philip E. Tetlock, eds. *Learning in U.S. and Soviet Foreign Policy*, 684–732. Boulder, Colo.: Westview Press.

Leites, Nathan Constantin. 1951. *The Operational Code of the Politburo*. New York: McGraw-Hill.

Lepgold, Joseph and Alan C. Lamborn. 2001. "Locating Bridges: Connecting Research Agendas on Cognition and Strategic Choice," *International Studies Review* 3, 3: 3–29.

Letwin, Oliver. 1988. *Privatising the World: A Study of International Privatisation in Theory and Practice*. London: Cassell.

Levinthal, Daniel A. 1996 [1991]. "Organization Adaptation and Environmental SelectionZ: Iterrelated Processes of Change," in Michael D. Cohen and Lee S. Sproull, eds. *Organizational Learning*. Thousand Oaks, Calif.: Sage Publications, 195–202.

Levitt, Barbara and James G. March. 1996 [1988]. "Organizational Learning," in Michael D. Cohen and Lee S. Sproull, eds. *Organizational Learning*, 516–540. Thousand Oaks, Calif.: Sage Publications.

Levy, Jack S. 1994. "Learning and Foreign Policy: Sweeping a Conceptual Minefield," *International Organization* 48, 2: 279–312.

Liao, Tim F. 1994. *Interpreting Probability Models: Logit, Probit, and Other Generalized Linear Models*. Sage University Paper series on Quantitative Applications in the Social Sciences, 07–101. Thousand Oaks, Calif.: Sage Publications.

Long, J. Scott. 1997. *Regression Models for Categorical and Limited Dependent Variables*. Thousand Oaks, Calif.: Sage Publications.

Lukanov, Iuriy. 1996. *Tretiy Prezident: Politychnyy Portret Leon ida Kuchmy [The Third President: A Political Portrait of Leon id Kuchma]*. Kyiv: Tak; Spravy.

Lynch, Allen. 1987. *The Soviet Study of International Relations*. Cambridge, U.K.: Cambridge University Press.

Majone, Giandomenico. 1991. "Cross-National Sources of Regulatory Policymaking in Europe and the United States," *Journal of Public Policy* 11, 1: 79–106.

Mansfield, Edward D. 1994. *Power, Trade, and War*. Princeton: Princeton University Press.

Mansfield, Edward D., Helen V. Milner, and B. Peter Rosendorff. 2000. "Free Trade: Democracies, Autocracies, and International Trade. *American Political Science Review* 94, 2: 305–321.

March, James G., Lee S. Sproull, and Michael Tamuz. 1996 [1991]. "Learning From Samples of One or Fewer," in Michael D. Cohen and Lee S. Sproull, eds. *Organizational Learning*, 1–19. Thousand Oaks, Calif.: Sage Publications.

Markevych, Lubomyr. Interview with author, Kyiv, Ukraine, November 13, 1997.

Martin, Lisa and Beth A. Simmons. 1998. "Theories and Empirical Studies of International Relations," *International Organization* 52, 4: 729–757.

May, Ernest R. 1973. *"Lessons" of the Past: The Use and Misuse of History in American Foreign Policy*. New York: Oxford University Press.

Mazur, James E. 1994. *Learning and Behavior*. Third edition. Englewood Cliffs, N.J.: Prentice Hall.

McFaul, Michael and Tova Perlmutter, eds. 1995. *Privatization, Conversion, and Enterprise Reform in Russia*. Boulder, Colo: Westview Press.

Meindl, J. et al. 1996. *Cognition Within and Between Organizations*. Thousand Oaks, Calif.: Sage Publications.

Midlarsky, Manus I. 1978. Analyzing Diffusion and Contagion Effects: The Urban Disorders of the 1960s. *American Political Science Review* 72, 3: 996–1008.

Milner, Helen V. 1997. *Interests, Institutions, and Information: Domestic Politics and International Relations.* Princeton, N.J.: Princeton University Press.

Mingst, Karen. 1999. *Essentials of International Relations.* New York: W.W. Norton and Company.

Mining Journal, The. (Lexis-Nexis Academic Universe).

Ministerstvo Statystyky Ukrainy [Ministry of Statistics of Ukraine]. 1993. *Naselennia Ukrainy 1992. Demohrafichnyy shchorichnyk.* [The Population of Ukraine, 1992. Demographic yearbook.] Kyiv: "Tekhnika."

Modelski, George. 1990. "Is World Politics Evolutionary Learning?" *International Organization* 44, 1: 2–24.

Moravcsik, Andrew. 1997. "Taking Preference Seriously: A Liberal Theory of International Politics," *International Organization* 51, 4: 513–553.

Morgenthau, Hans J. 1967. *Politics Among Nations: The Struggle for Power and Peace.* Fourth edition. New York: Alfred A. Knopf.

Morgenthau, Hans J. and Kenneth W. Thompson. 1985. *Politics Among Nations: The Struggle for Power and Peace.* Sixth edition. New York: Alfred A. Knopf.

Moroz, O. O. 1995. "Vidstoiuvaty interesy Ukrainy" [To Defend the Interests of Ukraine] *Polytika i Chas* [Politics and Time]. 1: 3–6.

Morrow, James D. 1988. "Social Choice and System Structure in World Politics," *World Politics* 41, 1: 75–97.

Morrow, James. 1994. *Game Theory for Political Scientists.* Princeton: Princeton University Press.

Morrow, James. 1997. "A Rational Choice Approach to International Conflict," in Nehemia Geva and Alex Mintz, eds. *Decisionmakng on War and Peace: The Cognitive-Rational Debate,* 11–31. Boulder, Colo.: Lynne Rienner Publishers.

Moscow Times, The.

Mozgovoi, O. N. 1997. "O deiatel'nosti gosudarstvennoi komissii Ukrainy po tsennym bumagam i fondovomu rynku," *Gosudarstvennyi informatsionnyi biulleten o privatizatsii.* 1:35–36.

Nahaylo, Bohdan and Victor Swoboda. 1989. *Soviet Disunion: A History of the Nationalities Problem in the USSR.* New York, N.Y.: The Free Press.

Nezavisimaia gazeta. (Lexis-Nexis Academic Universe).

Nye, Joseph S., Jr. 1987. Nuclear Learning and U.S.-Soviet Security Regimes. *International Organization* 41, 3: 371–402.

Pavlenko, Sergei. 1996. "Against State Ownership," *The Moscow Times* 2/28/96.

P'iatnyts'kyy, Valeriy Teziyovych. Interview with author, Kyiv, Ukraine, April 18, 1997.

Pipes, Richard. 1968. *The Formation of the Soviet Union: Communism and Nationalism, 1917–1923.* Cambridge, Mass.: Harvard University Press.

Poel, Dale H. 1976. Diffusion of Legislation Among the Canadian Provinces: A Statistical Analysis, *Canadian Journal of Political Science,* IX, 4: 605–626.

Pollins, Brian. 1994. "Canons and Capital: The Use of Coercive Diplomacy by Major Powers in the Twentieth Century," in Frank W. Wayman and Paul F. Diehl, eds. *Reconstructing Realpolitik,* 29–54. Ann Arbor, Mich.: University of Michigan Press.

Pomfret, Richard. 1991. *International Trade: An Introduction to Theory and Policy.* Cambridge, Mass.: Basil Blackwell.

Powell, Robert. 1991. "Absolute and Relative Gains in International Relations Theory," *American Political Science Review* 85, 4: 1303–1320.

Powell, Robert. 1993. "Guns, Butter, and Anarchy," *American Political Science Review* 87, 1: 115–132.

Pratt, John W., Howard Raiffa, and Robert Schlaifer. 1995. *Introduction to Statistical Decision Theory*. Cambridge Mass.: MIT Press.

Radio Free Europe / Radio Liberty (RFE/RL). *RFE/RL Newsline*.

Ray, James Lee, 1989. "The Abolition of Slavery and the End of International War," *International Organization* 43, 3: 405–439.

Ray, James Lee. 2000. "Democracy: On the Level(s), Does Democracy Correlate with Peace?", in John A. Vasquez, ed. *What Do We Know About War?*, 299–316. Lanham, Mar.: Rowman and Littlefield.

Raymond, Gregory A. 2000. "International Norms: Normative Orders and Peace," in John A. Vasquez, ed. *What Do We Know About War?*, 281–297. Lanham: Rowman and Littlefield.

Razumkov, Oleksandr Vasil'ovych. Interview with author, Kyiv, Ukraine, April 15, 1997.

Reischauer, Edwin O. 1974. *Japan: The story of a nation*. Revised edition. New York: Alfred A. Knopf.

Reiter, Dan. 1996. *Crucible of Beliefs: Learning, Alliances, and World Wars*. Ithaca, N.Y: Cornell University Press.

Reiter, Dan and Curtis Meek. 1999. "Determinants of Military Strategy, 1903–1994: A Quantitative Empirical Test." *International Studies Quarterly* 43, 2: 363–387.

Remington, Thomas F. 1999. *Politics in Russia*. New York, N.Y.: Longman.

Resende-Santos, Joao. 1996. Anarchy and the Emulation of Military Systems: Military Organization and Technology in South America, 1870–1930. *Security Studies* 5, 3 : 193–260.

Richerson, Peter J. and Robert Boyd. 2000. *"Climate, Culture, and the Evolution of Cognition,"* in Cecilia Heyes and Ludwig Huber, eds. *The Evolution of Cognition*, 329–346. Cambridge, Mass.: MIT University Press.

Rigby, Thomas Henry. 1990. *Political Elites in the USSR: Central Leaders and Local Cadres From Lenin to Gorbachev*. Hants, U.K.: Edward Elgar.

Riker, William H. and Peter C. Ordeshook. 1973. *An Introduction to Positive Political Theory*. Englewood Cliffs, N.J.: Prentice-Hall.

Roberts Clark, William. 1998. "Agents and Structure: Two Views of Institutions," *International Studies Quarterly* 42, 2: 245–270.

Robinson, Daniel N. 1976. *An Intellectual History of Psychology*. New York, N.Y.: Macmillan Publishing Co.

Rogers, Everett M. 1995. *Diffusion of Innovations*. Fourth edition. New York, N.Y.: The Free Press.

Rogowski, Ronald. 1999. "Institutions as Constraints on Strategic Choice," in David A. Lake and Robert Powell, eds. *Strategic Choice and International Relations*, 115–136. Princeton, N.J.: Princeton University Press.

Rosati, Jerel A. 1998. "The Politics of U.S. Foreign Policy Revisited," in Jerel A. Rosati, ed. *Readings in the Politics of United States Foreign Policy*, 588–605. Fort Worth, Tex.: Harcourt Brace College Publishers.

Rose, Richard. 1991a. "Introduction: Lesson-Drawing across Nations," *Journal of Public Policy* 11, 1: 1–2.

Rose, Richard. 1991b. "What is Lesson-Drawing?" *Journal of Public Policy* 11, 1: 3–30.

Rosecrance, Richard. 1986. *The Rise of the Trading State: Commerce and Conquest in the Modern World*. New York, N.Y.: Basic Books.

Rosenau, James N. 1966. "Pre-theories and Theories of Foreign Policy," in R. Barry Farrell, ed. *Approaches to Comparative and International Politics*, 27–92. Evanston, Ill.: Northwestern University Press.

Rosenthal, Ted L. and Barry J. Zimmerman. 1978. *Social Learning and Cognition*. New York: Academic Press.

Rossiia i sovremennyi mir.

Rousseau, David L., Christopher Gelpi, Dan Reiter, and Paul K. Huth. 1996. "Assessing the Dyadic Nature of the Democratic Peace, 1918–1988." *American Political Science Review* 90, 3: 512–533.

Rowen, Henry S., Charles Wolf, Jr., and Jeanne Zlotnick, eds. 1994. *Defense Conversion, Economic Reform, and the Outlook for the Russian and Ukrainian Economies*. New York: St. Martin's Press.

Ruggie, John Gerard. 1997. "The Past as Prologue?: Interests, Identity, and American Foreign Policy," *International Security* 21, 4: 89–125.

Russett, Bruce. 1993. *Grasping the Democratic Peace: Principles for a Post-Cold War World*. Princeton, N.J.: Princeton University Press.

Russett, Bruce and John Oneal. 2001. *Triangulating Peace: Democracy, interdependence, and International Organizations*. New York: W.W. Norton and Company.

Russett, Bruce, Harvey Starr, and David Kinsella. 2000. *World Politics: The Menu for Choice*. Sixth edition. Boston, Mass.: Bedford/St. Martin's.

Russia and Commonwealth Business Law Report. 10/16/92. (Lexis-Nexis Academic Universe.)

Rybkin, Ivan. 1997. "Rossii segodnia prezhde vsego ugrozhaet vnutrennie opasnosti . . . " [Russia today is threatened by internal dangers first of all . . .], *Mezhdunarodnaia zhizn* [International Affairs] 5: 18–27.

Schuman, Howard and Jacquelin Scott. 1989. "Generationa and Collective Memories," *American Sociological Review* 54: 359–381.

Scott, William A. 1955. Reliability of Content Analysis: The Case of Nominal Scale Coding. *Public Opinion Quarterly* 19, 3: 321–325.

Scott, William G. 1993 [1961]. "Organization Theory: An Overview and an Appraisal," in Michael T. Matterson and John M. Ivancevich, eds. 1993. *Management and Organizational Behavior Classics. Fifth edition*, 137–158. Homewood, Ill.: Irwin.

Segodnia. (12/22/95).

Shapiro, Gilbert. 1977. "The Future of Coders: Human Judgments in a World of Sophisticated Software," in Carl W. Roberts, ed. *Text Analysis for the Social Sciences: Methods for Drawing Statistical Inferences from Texts and Transcripts*, 225–238. Mahwah, N.J.: Lawrence Erlbaum Associates.

Shapiro, Robert Y. and Benjamin I. Page. 1988. "Foreign Policy and the Rational Public," *Journal of Conflict Resolution* 32, 2 (June): 211–247.

Shen, Raphael. 1996. *Ukraine's Economic Reform: Obstacles, Errors, Lessons*. Westport, Conn.: Praeger.

Shleifer, Andrei and Robert W. Vishny. 1998. *The Grabbing Hand: Government Pathologies and Their Cures*. Cambridge, Mass.: Harvard University Press.

Shpek, Roman Vasyl'ovych. Interview with author, Kyiv, Ukraine, November 28, 1997.

Shvydanenko, H. A. 1993. *Pryvatyzatsiia v Ukraini: 500 pytan, 500 vidpovidey* [Privatization in Ukraine: 500 questions, 500 answers]. Kyiv: Libra.

Simmons, Beth. 1994. *Who Adjusts?: Domestic Sources of Foreign Economic Policy*. Princeton: Princeton University Press.

Simmons, Beth. 2000. "International Law and State Behavior: Commitment and Compliance in International Monetary Affairs," *American Political Science Review* 94, 4: 819–835.

Simon, Herbert A. 1996 [1991]. "Bounded Rationality and Organizatonal Learning," in Michael D. Cohen and Lee S. Sproull, eds. 1996. *Organizational Learning*, 175–187. Thousand Oaks: Sage Publications.

Sitkin, Sim B. 1996 [n.d.]. "Learning Through Failure: The Strategy of Small Losses," in Michael D. Cohen and Lee S. Sproull, eds. *Organizational Learning*, 541–577. Thousand Oaks: Sage Publications.

Siverson, Randolph M. and Harvey Starr. 1990. "Opportunity, Willingness, and the Diffusion of War," *American Political Science Review* 84, 1: 47–67.

Skokov, Iurii. 1995. "Vneshnepoliticheskie vzglady partii: Kongress russkikh obshchin [The Foreign Policy Views of Parties: Congress of Russian Communities]," *Mezhdunarodnaia zhizn* [International Affairs] 11–12: 12–14.

Smith, Mark. 1993. *Pax Russica : Russia's Monroe Doctrine*. London: Royal United Services Institute for Defence Studies.

Smith, Steve. 1986. "Theories of Foreign Policy: An Historical Overview," *Review of International Studies* 12: 13–29.

Snidal, Duncan. 1991a. "Relative Gains and the Pattern of International Cooperation," *American Political Science Review* 85: 701–726.

Snidal, Duncan. 1991b. "International Cooperation among Relative Gains Maximizers," *International Studies Quarterly* 35: 387–342.

Snyder, Jack. 1991. *Myths of Empire: Domestic Politics and International Ambition*. Ithaca, N.Y.: Cornell University Press.

Solchanyk, Roman. 1998. "Ukraine, Russia, and the CIS," in Lubomyr A. Hajda, ed. *Ukraine in the World: Studies in the International Relations and Security Structure of a Newly Independent State*, 19–43. Cambridge, Mass.: Ukrainian Research Institute, Harvard University.

Spiegel, Steven L. 1991. "Learning in U.S. Foreign Policy: The case of the Middle East," in George W. Breslauer and Philip E. Tetlock, eds. *Learning in U.S. and Soviet Foreign Policy*, 264–301. Boulder, Colo.: Westview Press.

Starr, Harvey and Benjamin Most. 1991. "Democratic Dominoes: Diffusion Approaches to the Spread of Democracy in the International System," *Journal of Conflict Resolution* 35, 2: 356–381.

Stein, Janet Gross. 1996. "Deterrence and Learning in an Enduring Rivalry: Egypt and Israel, 1948–73," *Security Studies* 6, 1: 104–152.

Steinbruner, John D. 1974. *The Cybernetic Theory of Decision: New Dimensions of Political Analysis*. Princeton: Princeton University Press.

Stewart, Abigail J. and Joseph M. Healy, Jr. 1989. "Linking Individual Development and Social Changes," *American Psychologist* 44, 1: 30–42.

Strang, David. 1991. "Global Patterns of Decolonization, 1500–1987," *International Studies Quarterly* 35, 4: 429–454.

Stroev, Egor. 1997. "Ves vopros dlia Rossii . . . " [The whole question for Russia . . .] *Mezhdunarodnaia Zhizn* [International Affairs] 1: 3–10.

Subtelny, Orest. 1990. *Ukraine: A History*. Toronto, Can.: University of Toronto Press.

Tetlock, Philip. 1991. "Learning in U.S. and Soviet Foreign Policy: In Search of an Elusive Concept," in George W. Breslauer and Philip E. Tetlock, eds. *Learning in U.S. and Soviet Foreign Policy*, 20–61. Boulder, Colo.: Westview Press.

Thornhill, John. 1996, "Russia set to Intervene More in Industry," *The Financial Times* 11/29/96, 3.

Transparency International. 1999. *Corruption Perception Index.* Accessed at www.gwdg.de/~uwvw/histor.htm, March 5, 2000.

Tullock, Gordon. 1992. "Games and Preference," *Rationality and Society* 4 1 (January): 24–32.

UNIAN News Agency. (Lexis-Nexis Academic Universe).

United Nations Conference on Trade and Development (UNCTAD). 1995. *World Investment Report 1995.* Geneva: United Nations.

United Nations Conference on Trade and Development (UNCTAD). 1999. *World Investment Report 1999.* Geneva: United Nations.

United Nations Conference on Trade and Development (UNCTAD). 2000. *World Investment Report 2000.* Geneva: United Nations.

Van Oudenaren, John. 2000. *Uniting Europe: European Integration and the Post-Cold War World.* Lanham, Mass.: Rowman and Littlefield.

Walker, Jack L. 1969. "The Diffusion of Policy Innovations Among the American States," *American Political Science Review* 63, 3: 880–899.

Walker, Jack L. 1973. "Comment: Problems in Research on the Diffusion of Policy Innovations," *American Political Science Review* 67, 4: 1186–1191.

Wallander, Celeste A., ed. 1996. *The Sources of Russian Foreign Policy after the Cold War.* Boulder, Colo.: Westview Press.

Waltz, Kenneth N. 1979. *Theory of International Politics.* New York: McGraw-Hill.

Waltz, Kenneth N. 1996. "International Politics is Not Foreign Policy," *Security Studies* 6, 1: 7–53.

Waschuk, Roman A. Interview with author, Kyiv, Ukraine, November 10, 1997.

Washington Post, The.

Weber, Robert Philip. 1990. *Basic Content Analysis.* Second edition. Newbury Park: Sage Publications.

Wedel, Janine R. 1998. *Collision and Collusion: The Strange Case of Western Aid to Eastern Europe, 1989–1998.* New York: St. Martin's Press.

Weisberg, Sanford. 1985. *Applied Linear Regression.* Second edition. New York: John Wiley and Sons.

Wendt, Alexander. 1992. "Anarchy is What States Make of it: The Social Construction of Power-Politics," *International Organization* 46, 2: 391–425.

West LB Country Profile: Ukraine. 1999. Quest Economics Database. Janet Matthews Information Services. (Lexis-Nexis Academic Universe).

White, Brian. 1989. "Analysing Foreign Policy: Problems and Approaches," in Michael Clarke and Brian White, eds. *Understanding Foreign Policy: The Foreign Policy Systems Approach*, 1–26. Hants, England: Edward Elgar.

Wittkopf, Eugene R. 1990. *Faces of Internationalism: Public Opinion and American Foreign Policy.* Durham, N.C.: Duke University Press.

Wittkopf, Eugene R. 1996. "What the Public Really Thinks About Foreign Policy," *Washington Quarterly* 19, 2: 91–106.

Wittkopf, Eugene R. and James M. McCormick, eds. 1999. *The Domestic Sources of American Foreign Policy: Insights and Evidence.* Third edition. Boulder, Colo.: Rowman and Littlefield Publishers.

Wolfers, Arnold. 1962. *Discord and Collaboration: Essays on International Politics.* Baltimore: Johns Hopkins Press.

World Bank, The. 2001. *World Development Indicators 2001.* Available from www.worldbank.org/data/wdi2001/index.htm. Accessed July 25, 2001.

Wyrwicka, Wanda. 1996. *Imitation in Human and Animal Behavior.* New Brunswick, N.J.: Transaction Publishers.

Xinhua News Agency 11/23/97. (Lexis-Nexis Academic Universe.)

Zimmerman, William. 1969. *Soviet Perspectives on International Relations: 1956–1967.* Princeton, N.J.: Princeton University Press.

Zimmerman, William. 1973. "Issue Area and Foreign Policy Process," *American Political Science Review* 67, 4: 1204–1212.

Zimmerman, William. 1987. *Open Borders: Nonalignment and the Politics of Evolution in Yugoslavia.* Princeton, N.J.: Princeton University Press.

Zimmerman, William. 1994. "Markets, Democracy and Russian Foreign Policy," *Post-Soviet Affairs* 10, 1: 103–127.

Zimmerman, William and Robert Axelrod. 1981. "The 'Lessons' of Vietnam and Soviet Foreign Policy," *World Politics* 34, 1: 1–24.

Zisk, Kimberly Marten. 1997. *Weapons, Culture, and Self-Interest: Soviet Defense Managers in the New Russia.* New York, N.Y.: Columbia University Press.

Zlenko, A. 1992. "Novi realii zovnishn'oi politiky" [New Realities of Today's Politics] *Polityka i Chas* [Politics and Time] 1: 3–8.

Zurn, Michael. 1997. "Assessing State Preferences and Explaining Institutional Choice: The Case of Intra-German Trade," *International Studies Quarterly* 41: 295–320.

INDEX

Abkhazia, 109
absolute gains, 40, 41, 42, 43, 124, 143n6
Argentina, 104, 109, 112
Asia, 5, 58, 59
  see also individual countries
Association of Southeast Asian Nations (ASEAN), 43
Athens, 7
autarky, 67, 68, 98, 100, 107, 124
Aven, Petr, 89

Ball, George, 4, 113
Beliaev, Sergei, 91
Black Sea, 99
Bolsheviks, 64, 65, 109
Bondar, Oleksandr, 86
Braverman, Aleksandr, 94
Brazil, 112
Britain, 6, 79
  see also United Kingdom
Bulgak, Vladimir, 93
Bunich, Pavel, 94
Burkov, Sergei, 92

Canada, 14, 58, 102
  Managing Asymmetrical Relationships (MAR) program, 13
Chernobyl Atomic Power Station, 101
Chernomyrdin, Viktor, 48, 66, 80, 105
Chile, 78, 112
China, *see* People's Republic of China (PRC)
Chornovil, V'iacheslav, 64, 121, 129
Chubais, Anatolii, 66, 80
Civic Union (Russia), 90
Cold War, 22, 29, 100
colonialism, 119
Commonwealth of Independent States (CIS), 12, 101, 144n10

Communism, 6
  in Russia, 98
  in Ukraine, 64
  see also Bolsheviks
complex interdependence, 43, 118
Council on Security and Cooperation in Europe (CSCE), 53
  see also Helsinki Accords, Organization for Security and Cooperation in Europe (OSCE)
Czech Republic, 59, 82
Czechoslovakia, 67, 88, 89

democracy, 6, 53, 106, 116, 125, 127
demonstration effects, 3
diffusion, 3
Dornbush, Rudiger, 104
Dubinin, Iurii, 52, 53, 54, 55, 143n7, 144n9
Duma, *see* Russia, State Duma

Efimov, Vitalii, 92
Estonia, 82, 109
Europe, 7, 12, 43, 53, 54, 55, 58, 59, 67, 88, 94, 100, 104, 108, 112, 117, 119, 144n10
  see also individual countries
European Union (EU), 7, 12, 43, 53, 54, 55, 58, 59, 67, 88, 94, 100, 104, 108, 112

financial-industrial groups (FIGs), 83, 84
Finland, 79
Fokin, Vitold, 80, 101, 121
foreign aid, 59, 114, 153
  see also technical aid
formative events, 3, 7, 9, 11, 15, 33, 38, 68, 70, 71, 73, 76, 100, 102, 107, 112, 113, 118